Ordinary People As Monks and Mystics:
Lifestyles for Self-Discovery

Do What You Love, the Money Will Follow:
Discovering Your Right Livelihood

Elegant Choices, Healing Choices:
Finding Grace and Wholeness in Everything We Choose

LIVING HAPPILY EVER AFTER

Creating Trust, Luck, and Joy

Marsha Sinetar

VILLARD BOOKS   NEW YORK   1990

Library of Congress Cataloging-in-Publication Data

Sinetar, Marsha.
Living happily ever after : creating trust, luck,
and joy / Marsha Sinetar.
p.   cm.
Includes bibliographical references.
ISBN 0-394-58391-4
1. Happiness.   2. Adaptability (Psychology)   I. Title.
BF575.H27S56
158—dc20   89-22410

*Grateful acknowledgment is made to the following
for permission to reprint previously published material:*

Academic Press Limited: an excerpt from "Vision Without
Sight" by A. W. Lampl and G. W. Oliver from *Journal of Analytical
Psychology.* Volume 30 (1985). Reprinted by permission
of Academic Press Limited. New Directions Publishing
Corporation: an excerpt from *The Way of Chuang Tzu* by
Thomas Merton. Copyright © 1965 by the Abbey of Gethsemane.
Reprinted by permission of New Directions Publishing
Corporation. Van Nostrand Reinhold: an adaptation
of "Being Values" from *Toward a Psychology of Being*
by Abraham Maslow (D. Van Nostrand, 1968 edition).
Adapted by permission of Van Nostrand Reinhold.
Viking Penguin, Inc.: an excerpt from "Wail,"
in *The Portable Dorothy Parker.* Copyright 1926, renewed
© 1954 by Dorothy Parker. Reprinted by permission
of Viking Penguin, a division of Penguin Books USA, Inc.

Manufactured in the United States of America

2   4   6   8   9   7   5   3

FIRST EDITION

Book design by Carole Lowenstein

This book is dedicated to my mother with love.

The folk tale is the primer
of the picture-language of the soul.

—JOSEPH CAMPBELL

Preface

Many people contributed their time and talents to this book. My thanks to Jill Hannum, who helped me in the earliest editing stages. My friend Lyn Delliquadre provided her insights and suggestions after the manuscript was completed. I am indebted to Pam Bacci for her word processing and proofing skills and for her steady attention to detail during the nearly three years this book was under way. There were countless revisions; I lost track. The professional care with which Pam treats every aspect of manuscript preparation deserves special mention. My thanks too to Mary Tyner for her fine research help, and to Linda Allen, my agent, for her unwavering faith in this project. I have great respect and special appreciation for Diane Reverand, executive editor and vice president of Villard Books, whose meticulous editorial notes greatly improved the manuscript. Finally, I would like to acknowledge those friends, colleagues and readers who took time to talk and write to me about the multiple issues of creative adaptation. They told me about their own family and friends and about themselves, and these examples of resourcefulness and courage stimulated and enriched my work during these years of writing.

Contents

LIVING
HAPPILY
EVER
AFTER

Introduction

Broadly speaking, and in most cases, the fairy tale is a
dramatic projection in symbolic images of
the life of the psyche.
—W. H. AUDEN

All children, all adults, probably every one of us somewhere
deep within yearns to "live happily ever after." This, in part,
explains the charm and attraction that fairy tales have for humanity. They promise happy endings. While children are permitted, at least for a short time, to dream of happy endings, we
adults are not granted this luxury. We are taught, as soon as we
can grasp the lesson, to be "realistic." We are urged to believe
we live in a world where luck, trust and even happiness are
things only fools or children expect.

In this book, I explore a different notion: that happiness exists
on a far more grand, profound level than fairy tales ever prom-
ised; that glad endings are indeed possible; and that almost all
problems have solutions, if only in the way we see them in our
minds. I am not speaking about superficial, plastic happiness
based on the denial of our dark side, negative feelings or life's
rich mysteries. If anything, I suggest exactly the opposite: that
happiness in adulthood requires full, courageous engagement
with all of these elements—that life becomes full and fulfilling to
the extent we surrender wholly to its radical, incomprehensible
call.

I also say unequivocally that whether or not our life story is
conventionally "happy," or our endings glad, or our problems

solved, we approach something akin to joy—happiness's far richer cousin—by giving our all to problems that beset us, whatever their outcome. In other words, happiness, better yet sustainable joy, is gained to the degree we handle whatever life gives us to master. Sometimes this means we must control events, and sometimes this means we let go of control, renunciating, accepting what is in good faith and simple, uncomplicated dignity. Those who are able to resolve this paradox without requiring a rule for every specific situation are on their way to lasting well-being, and I will describe some of the factors that make this resolution possible.

If as adults we still yearn for fairy-tale happiness, all gingerbread sweetness and light, we'll probably be disappointed. This is because adult realities about creating luck, trust and true joy differ from those of children. To me that seems the point of growing up: emotional maturity means grappling with reality and assuming the responsibility for our own choices within the context of a real world. This assumption generally consists of a slow birth of understanding, perhaps an even slower integration of our higher nature and faculties into daily, ordinary life. This book is about the *adult process of maturation,* although for the most part I use the lessons of the fairy tale and the crisis or problematic situation as a means of discussion.

Our adult yearnings, sufferings, most fearsome trials and deepest hurts can help us *if* we use these to face our demons. Facing what we fear involves both mental and emotional skill-building and includes the development of what I term a *creative adaptive response.* Throughout this book I suggest that a significant component of adult happiness flows from living out our self-transcendence—an act that means we go beyond what we know into the unknown. And this requires faith.

There is no tidy correlation between the fairy tale "Hansel and Gretel" and our own life journey. Yet each of us shares something in common with the children in this story, if only that we too want safety, love and security and can empathize with the brave brother-sister team from the depths of some primitive, interior understanding. Considered through the filter of higher mythology, "Hansel and Gretel" serves us as a heroic legend, not simply as a children's bedtime story.

In *The Uses of Enchantment,* child psychologist Bruno Bettelheim suggests that the story of Hansel and Gretel "gives body to anxieties and learning tasks of the young child." Among these is the rigorous coming to terms with reality that each child must discover when he or she faces—then masters—fear, feelings of abandonment, regressions and cravings for reassurance and permanent comfort. If we do not master the realities of life as children, we will certainly be forced to when we are adults. If we do not control these realities as adults, we will miss our opportunity to develop fully as human beings. This is in part what it must mean to fail at life.

Scholars Louis and Bryna Untermeyer, who included Hansel and Gretel in the "Heroes and Heroines" section of their marvelous *Household Tales,* and Andrew Lang have pointed to the similarities between the plot, incidents and characters of this Grimm Brothers' tale and the ancient mythologies of primitive cultures. The Jason myth, for example, with its pre-Greek origins and elemental ideas, can be traced to what Lang calls "savage communities" the world over. Its motifs are those of "Hansel and Gretel": the flight from danger; a testing by and escape from trouble; humans aided by animals (and/or supernatural beings); the series of hair-raising adventures in which people learn about themselves, develop self-knowledge and inner strength; finally, a victorious ending, which assures us that the heroes lived "happily ever after."

I too find these elements both ancient and quite modern. Such essential trials and learning tasks follow us all into contemporary life. To illustrate this, I have often juxtaposed Hansel and Gretel's ordeal against that of our own present-day need to face and master rapid change. It is our mastery of skills and self that helps us live happily ever after in the true and deepest sense of the phrase. Despite not knowing "how" to do so, we must continually meet and conquer novelty, change and surprise. When we trust our abilities in this domain, we can rest easy in all others. I call this innovative solution-finding *creative adaptation,* which is more than merely adopting conventional routes of response that are dictated, or expected, by others. Those who live happily ever after become creative adaptors who resourcefully and realistically master novel circumstances, much as the heroes and heroines of myths and fairy tales overcome their hard tasks.

Creative adaptors also expect the world, at least in part, to adapt itself to them. This expectation fuels their vitality and perhaps, in the long run, fuels their problem-solving power as well. Some invisible, hard-to-define x factor lets them live happily ever after while others, in similar situations, cannot cope. For instance, two men I know suffered strokes not long ago. One is still recovering in the hospital and is seriously depressed. Yet from what I am told, his stroke was not as debilitating as the other, more stubborn and willful man's. The second man left the hospital prematurely, against his doctor's advice, and is recuperating in fine fashion at home—a circumstance his neurologist calls "a miracle." The miracle may rest in this man's approach to the problem, as well as in the constellation of skills and attitudes he and his family used to meet the demands of the moment. Surely his is no less a miracle than Hansel and Gretel's escape from the wicked witch, for each found a way out of a tangible dilemma. Finding a way out, especially when we think there isn't one, is a miracle and seems, at least to me, God's answer to our life's prayer.

I am convinced that individuals who flourish in the face of change (perhaps because of it) activate some form of creative adaptation. Their stories are inspiring, and usually their lives have happy endings even though—as all lives must—they eventually end. Those who flounder probably have not developed this rich inner resource and are left vulnerable and defenseless. In the chapters that follow, I attempt to show why people who flourish are no less heroes and heroines than Hansel and Gretel. For the most part, the cases I cite are of people who are growing in personal power. This power sustains them and lifts their spirits even in the darkest times.

Whenever we develop and use our inner resources to rejuvenate, revitalize and develop our life and strength—in other words, when we *creatively* adapt to circumstances—we stir some heroic quality in ourselves, however full of shortcomings we may be in other respects. That stirring, in turn, brings optimism and hope. Then too, like Hansel and Gretel (like any hero), we emerge larger as persons from our ordeal. While we learn many of these abilities in childhood, we can also develop them later in life. Although we do not customarily think that adults need to grow and learn, in fact they do. The healthiest, happiest people keep growing and learning all their lives.

Children believe that happiness comes by virtue of magic potions and spells cast by fairy godmothers. They do not see themselves as actors in the process. But adults learn that more often than not, true joy is gained by active personal effort, courage and incredible resourcefulness—in other words by creative adaptation. Creative adaptation is more or less unrelated to age, gender, material circumstances, good character or education. Almost anyone can develop his or her own creative adaptive response mechanisms and thus awaken the hero or heroine within. Therefore, we have much to feel optimistic about, and possibly much to learn.

Joseph Campbell's book *The Hero with a Thousand Faces* assigns three stages to "the adventure of the hero." The first is *departure*, in which the hero or heroine is called to adventure. The second is *initiation*, in which a difficulty or danger is met and dealt with. The final stage is *return*—the hero or heroine overcomes the problem, finds a way out and gains the wherewithal to live happily ever after. With the theme of creative adaptation in mind, I have divided this book into three analogous parts, each of which can be related to Hansel and Gretel's ordeal as well as to our own contemporary, adult need to be creatively resourceful. My book is not about myth. It is about building the skills that help us deal effectively with reality. I speak of reality as the seen and unseen world, as encompassing both natural and supernatural elements. By "supernatural" I mean those facets of experience that logic, our five senses and mind alone cannot comprehend.

In Part One, I suggest that the creative adaptive solution to being "called to adventure" involves developing trust or faith that we have what it takes to make it through. In this section I give an overview of three key synergistic sets of traits or skills that make up our creative adaptive response: 1) positive self-valuation; 2) learning resourcefulness; and 3) growth toward autonomy. Each trait or skill mutually depends on and cooperatively works with others in the total set of skills. I try to show how these skills help us maneuver through and eventually escape the trials of our "adventure."

Hansel and Gretel, for example, are forced out of their home by an inhospitable stepmother and a weak father. They find themselves in a dark forest—lost, hungry and alone. Here are two little homeless children, from a dysfunctional family, tossed out into the wilds of life without support or nurture. What could be more modern? Real-life people today can also feel—can also *be*—very much lost and alone in their struggles. Every day we read about vast numbers of adults undergoing therapy, addiction counseling or hospitalization because of their dysfunctional pasts. Then, too, there are sudden catastrophes that can strike any of us, impersonal trials that don't care what kind of parents we've had or what century we inhabit. In Part One, we meet a man who must flee his home when it and everything in it go up in flames. His creative adaptive response to this departure from his normal life stimulates our discussion of the three basic skills which must be strengthened in order to respond successfully to change in our own life. We also meet a woman *learning* to master the same three basics after leaving an eleven-year marriage in which she was physically and mentally abused. Like Hansel and Gretel, the people in Part One have set out to make it through the dark woods of their lives to safety. They hone their creative adaptive skills during their journey.

In Part Two, I present each key skills cluster in more detail, paying attention to the way in which the human mind can tap into its own creative resources and potential. Our creative resources are, without debate, *the* inner tools with which we achieve initiation into life and meet problems head-on. Then too, there is a dimension to the use of our creative powers that involves cultivating *all* our innate "intelligences," not just our logical processes. Just as Hansel and Gretel overcame tribulation by relying on unusual aids—in this case animals or supernatural forces in addition to their own intelligence—we too can access* both natural and supernatural elements. To do this, we must be open to that within us which is "archaic." Jung termed this domain the collective unconscious and taught that it has great influence over our creative process. Others—theologians, for example—might convincingly argue that the domain of the supernatural belongs exclusively to God. I agree. Thus, throughout this book, I emphasize faith, belief, and what is known as the metanoic process, also known as a conversion experience or transformation. Some people prefer to view this matter differently, in purely secular terms.

---

* Understandably, many people object to computer terms to describe human thought processes. But our mind is like a computer. Mind created computers, based on its own experience and self-observation. Words such as "imprint," "access," "program" and even "hardware" and "software" legitimately describe human behavior because computers mirror the minds that create them.

Whatever language or imagery we favor, it seems certain that there are those who live happier lives than others. I try in these pages to describe the *process* by which most happy people live, whether consciously or unconsciously.

I suggest that by developing *all* our innate powers, our various intelligences, we stack the deck in our favor in a way no one yet fully understands, gain our own good fortune and are numbered among the world's "lucky." Silvano Arieti's research, upon which I have relied for much of my own treatment of the creative process, suggests that a "magic synthesis" is helpful to creativity, and that this synthesis merges both conscious and nonconscious worlds to produce sought-after solutions. Part Two is my attempt to assemble the aggregates of these two worlds, as well as to discuss the requisite skills for their merger.

Part Three focuses on what it takes to live happily ever after, and explores the "return" phase of every hero or heroine's journey. I compare this phase to our own creation of satisfying life roles in which we learn how to serve ourselves as well as others. We return home, as it were, by becoming autonomous, by ceasing to put our faith solely in external, worldly powers as agents of rescue or validation and by cultivating our faith and intrinsic capabilities. By learning to live truthfully in tune with our own visions, by living out our personal realities in daily life in a way that serves us *and* others, we begin to feel as if we *deserve* to live happily ever after.

When we return from vanquishing the wicked forces in our lives we return with newfound treasure. Sometimes this is material gain: Hansel and Gretel found pearls and gems in the witch's cabin, but we might gain worldly success or interpersonal wealth. Certainly enhanced creative adaptive skills are real, if intangible, treasures too. These let us design our lives so that we can honor our natural and quite healthy urge to be our best selves. The greatest treasure is that we "come home"— return—to our truest selves, recover our essential core self, and from its lush resources and reserves express our highest potential. From *this* return we serve our own lives and those of others. The return to this home brings joy.

This book is meant as a support and an encouragement for those who are or inevitably will be living through diverse, ambiguous or novel times. The late twentieth and the twenty-first centuries will introduce global shifts; some of these have already begun. Humankind lacks a practical personal blueprint for action. Today's problems seem more turbulent than those faced by our ancestors. The impact of changing demographics, technology, workplace management, family structures, economic or environmental catastrophes (droughts, pollution, nuclear accidents or war, etc.) and other so-called megatrends will leave many people scrambling to find secure footing on what may seem to be an unstable, shifting ground of being. I list these several trends to make a single point: a happy life—however we personally define happiness—depends on creative adaptation. Creative adaptation is no longer a luxury limited to those few, well-educated or innovative persons who read books by articulate, farsighted futurists. As futurist Alvin Toffler predicted, creative adaptive skill is increasingly a global necessity.

If we hope to grow toward an elevated, enlightened existence, then our success as persons and as a species must be secured: individual development is required if we would have an enlightened human community. For this reason, the skills I describe have social as well as personal implications; the way we individually respond to change has social consequences as well.

I have written this book with two specific purposes. First, I wish to present a unified, conceptual framework about how people creatively change, adapt and grow—how they creatively *use* themselves and use crisis or change as a life teacher. I have provided a broad picture of creative adaptive skills, so that almost any reader can easily understand what these skills are and design his or her own self-development programs.

I treat both crisis and change as challenges and allies, as means of enriching and enlarging life and giving it more meaning. I interpret the word *change* to mean *any* external or internal event or stimulus that asks us to adapt, adjust or alter our way of being and our life. I use the terms "creative adaptive," "adaptive skills" and "renewal skills" interchangeably. Then too, I treat some aspects of the discussion in a very general way, as is the case, for example, with the phrase "life crisis," which can be interpreted in several different ways. A life crisis is usually defined as a significant event that is acute, short-term and intense, demanding our immediate response. Some researchers speak of a life crisis as a role transition. They focus on the way people must adjust their self-images, self-worth, values, beliefs or behaviors while undergoing a crisis. Others, calling a life crisis a "stressor," focus on how the event forces people to regain their equilibrium. They may even study how it affects physical health.

In order to deal exclusively with the synergistic cluster of adaptive skills, I have ignored these fine interpretative distinctions and used the terms "life crisis," "change," "crisis," "trauma" and "transition" to refer to single and similar phenomena—events that demand we alter or shift our usual way of thinking, acting, living or being in order to get on with life. This book is thus written for the reader who simply wants to feel better emotionally, function more effectively and experience more personal or work competency despite problems *and* despite living in a world of rampant change. While I have used primarily case examples of people who change with the help of therapy, it is certainly possible to alter oneself and one's life for the better without this tool. The last chapter explores an ancient self-help method. How much help we need in overcoming our limits or problems, to whom we turn for help, how intense our reliance on a guide or helper: these are all very personal decisions, outside the scope of the book.

My second purpose in writing this book is to give readers encouraging, concrete, consistent images—positive role models or prototypes—of what it might take to develop their own creative adaptive skills. As an educator with long, practical teaching experience, I know that people learn best by "seeing" an answer mentally, having it click into their minds and neural systems as real. When we experience "Aha! Now I know what the solution is!" we realize an answer in a way that sparks true understanding. We can then leverage this understanding in many ways. One way is to apply an insight to other, seemingly unrelated problems. This is not to say we do not learn from our errors, but that positive images of our goals or of solutions create thought and behavioral pathways for achieving them.

We learn to ride a bike, for instance, by watching others ride bikes, and by focusing on our own successful bike-riding experiences. Even when we fall, and learn from that, we regain our balance by remembering how it feels to *keep* our balance—not by musing about what it felt like to fall or by mentally replaying the way we hit the ground. In other words, we develop a bike-riding consciousness, not a bike-falling consciousness. The positive mental model (and our actual experience) of riding helps our learning in a substantive way so that we rarely forget how to ride and can maneuver through other instances when we need balance. Similarly, readers might use this book to build a creative adaptive consciousness.

I've tried to present my personal interviews to help readers envision what competent, creative behaviors are all about and thus—mentally and actually—plot their own self-improvement course. The first and second purposes of the book are woven together to produce a concrete image of what it takes to flourish through change. This concrete image is a composite picture that flows directly out of my conceptual discussion about adaptive skills. Hansel and Gretel and the true-to-life case stories show us how; my narrative shows why creative adaptation works and, more important, why this response—perhaps more than any other external aid—has the potential to let us move beyond ourselves, beyond our trials, to experience real happiness.

We can change from experiencing ourselves as persons with hopeless problems to knowing ourselves as persons with tremendous creative power. We can learn to *use* each seemingly insurmountable problem to express more of who we are at our finest. We are reborn, renewed, as a result of our active, resourceful engagement with a challenge. Through this engagement we experience being "at home" in the world. This is the first part of the "living happily ever after" equation. The second part is this: once at home in the world, we realize we are fully equipped to be a positive, productive, hospitable force in it. This realization and our subsequent actions make for a glad heart.

PART ONE
Creating Trust

NCE upon a time there dwelt on the outskirts of a large forest a poor woodcutter with his wife and two children; the boy was called Hansel, and the girl Gretel. He had always little enough to live on, and once, when there was a great famine in the land, he couldn't even provide them with daily bread.

One night, as he was tossing about in his bed, full of cares and worry, he sighed and said to his wife, "What's to become of us? How are we to feed our poor children, when we have nothing more for ourselves?"

"I'll tell you what, husband," answered the woman. "Early tomorrow morning we'll take the children out into the thickest part of the wood. There we shall light a fire for them and give them each a piece of bread. Then we'll go on to our work and leave them alone. They won't be able to find their way home, and we shall thus be rid of them."

... "But I can t help feeling sorry for the poor children," added the husband.

The children too had not been able to sleep for hunger and had heard what their stepmother had said. ...

Gretel wept bitterly. "Now all is over with us."

"No, no, Gretel," said Hansel, "don't worry. I'll find a way out, no fear."

1

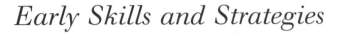

Early Skills and Strategies

Sometimes, when a field of corn has been beaten down
by a storm, we find a small spot, sheltered by hedges or
bushes, in which a few ears still stand upright. . . .
Perhaps they will last all winter, perhaps they may
even be seed for the future.
—Jacob and Wilhelm Grimm

And when the old people had fallen asleep, [Hansel
went outside]. . . . The moon was shining clearly, and
the white pebbles . . . glittered like bits of silver.
Hansel bent down and filled his pocket. . . . Then he
went back and said to Gretel, "Be comforted, my dear
little sister, and go back to sleep," and he
lay down in bed again.
—The Brothers Grimm, "Hansel and Gretel"

A friend of mine, whom I will call Peter, is a mathematician
turned mutual-fund manager. His home was both his castle and
his electronic cottage. Computer storage banks held years of
market-trend analysis and probability graphs. One night a bad
storm caused a major short in the electrical system. Peter had
only enough time to get himself and his son out of the house
before it burned to the ground. A decade of research and every
possession went up in smoke. Later he said:

I went into a state of shock. I was left with nothing except the
clothes on my back and some things that neighbors brought to
me. But soon—within a matter of days, really—I felt strangely
free.

It was as if my possessions and all that equipment and all those charts and graphs had weighed me down. I didn't own *them;* they had begun to own *me.* I was keeping myself busy supporting all that stuff. Since then I've felt freer than I've felt in years—to create and think and grow, as a person and in my work. As a result of that fire, I've started a lot of new directions—directions I'd never have been able to take without that initial loss, gigantic as it was.

Peter's story is an initial example of how a life surprise—even a tragic one—can be handled healthfully, ingeniously. His positive interpretation of the event and his manner of handling himself in the fire's aftermath, illustrate what I call the *creative adaptive response.*

Effectiveness Depends on Creativity and Adaptation

"Hansel and Gretel" is a simple tale of realism and practical advice, not necessarily one of great psychological mystery. It teaches us that daily life requires us to meet our challenges creatively. Both happy and sad events in life demand creative responses. Both have the power to undermine our sense of balance and our ability to act effectively. Both force us to take on different roles, think and behave in untried patterns. Our effectiveness depends to a larger degree than we might imagine on creativity, adaptive skill and sheer commonsense practicality.

A skill is the ability to use knowledge effectively. Adult problem-solving includes a complex of skills, each supporting the other: *thinking skills* (how we assess, conceptualize or plan what to do about a matter), *performance skills* (how well we execute our plan and evaluate what we have done, for example) and even *emotional skill*—how we feel about ourselves as learners, our attitudes about problems will affect the way we use knowledge to solve problems.

The person who *believes* he or she can figure out how to do a thing has more skill to use information than someone who fears problems just can't be solved. Helplessness is learned, as is powerfulness. When we face problems, our emotions are translated into attitudes, thus becoming assets or liabilities. We use our emotions to help us apply our knowledge or to keep us stuck. Hansel and Gretel used fear constructively: they channeled their emotions into productive actions. Their story instructs us that what works in the long run is learning to use our minds strategically to solve our problems.

Problem-Solving Skill Is a Key

One person can have more textbook knowledge or greater formal education than another. But whoever uses his knowledge more effectively in solving problems will have greater problem-solving skill. If a person's attitude is negative when facing a predicament, if he doesn't wish to be bothered with the situation, if it intimidates him, if he characteristically backs away from problems, it matters little how much knowledge he has. Negative attitudes are likely to result in maladaptive responses rather than creatively adaptive ones. Attitudes determine how a person uses his knowledge to solve problems.

Peter's creative response to the fire was possible for various reasons. He had survived a painful divorce several years earlier, and his self-esteem had been enhanced when he saw himself behave responsibly and fairly in that situation. Earlier still in his life he had been a successful football player, and I speculate that certain key athletic abilities (e.g., discipline, dealing with setbacks) led to his growing into a competent adult. As a mathematician, Peter is able to think in abstract, far-reaching and creative terms, and this also gives him a strategic mental advantage: he is intellectually equipped and trained to rethink and reinterpret data conceptually. This conceptualizing ability provides another clue to dealing with change productively. With Peter's personal combination of inner attitudes and mental skills, he has taught himself to be powerfully *able*. He now automatically turns tragedy into opportunity.

The creative adaptive response is not, however, something everyone cultivates, although everyone has similar capabilities. Many people undermine their own creativity—and their own happiness—by overplanning or by being negative. They thwart their ability to meet new experiences effectively. In fact, they may actively *fight* a change—resist it at every turn. Often their greatest battle is with themselves; they resist their own growth and personal development. This, as we shall see, limits their ability to be creative and also deprives them of joy.

"Every wall is a door," Emerson reputedly said. But some people cannot imagine a way out; to them a wall is a wall—just a solid obstacle that blocks their way. Be assured: Imagination is a key to creative adaptation. Those who cannot "see" or play with possibilities in their minds may shun responsibility when facing a transition. They lean on others to do their thinking for them. Or they blame their friends, families or fate for unpleasant events. They may have a morbid self-hatred that kills their joy and hope and turns against others too. Or they adopt passive, helpless responses, even physical limitations, that prevent them from making fruitful choices and actions. They may get more pleasure out of complaining than out of mastering their situation. Since optimism is absolutely essential when dealing with new realities, their pessimistic outlook is the death knell of cultivating change skills.

Of course, occasionally each of us needs to lean on someone else. During times of trouble there is even a poignant sweetness to admitting our weaknesses; this bonds us to others. We are human and need one another. The natural give-and-take of strength and affection that develops in crisis situations between people who trust each other makes friendship special and fulfilling. Hansel and Gretel demonstrate this throughout the tale.

Themes of cooperation, loving devotion and mutual dependency that run through Hansel and Gretel's ordeal are continually emphasized. The two plan together and think of one another; yet—and this too is a powerful thread—each child's mind also works well independently. Hansel creates a way to return home. Later Gretel ingeniously disposes of the witch. Each child takes a turn reassuring the other, being strong, remaining hopeful. They each learn that independent thinking frees them of constricting limitations and fears.

Our ability to change and adapt successfully to life's pressures and problems lies within us, not with a strong other. Our inner resources help us confront outer circumstances in a uniquely competent way. Our creative adaptive response comes from developing this inner set of resources, and this development stirs in us a state of being in which fear—although experienced—is not debilitating. At least we are able to act.

Creative Adaptive Responses Enlarge
Our Usefulness

Some people never quite develop their inner resources. To them, even the small and quite ordinary negative events of life are seen as nightmares. A woman I know, a secretary in a fast-changing business, has excellent skills. She is personable when she wants to be and could manage an entire department, not to mention function smoothly in her present job. But she is unhappy with her job. She is apathetic and lethargic, and sits at her desk all day eating candy bars, gaining weight and doing as little work as possible. Her manager, trying to be helpful, actually doing harm, demands little and looks the other way. As a result, her life is on hold. Her inertia and lack of active involvement in either imagining or seeking work she prefers (or in doing the work she is being paid to do), her overeating and evasions are uncreative, maladaptive responses. She avoids taking responsibility for her job and her life, hurting herself in the long run. Even though her passivity gives her relief (rest from a job she dislikes) in the short run, overall she keeps herself behind a subjective brick wall. In her mind and heart, she is stuck.

If we were to examine the history of many psychiatric patients, we would find they have dealt with their major life problems in similar but more extremely maladaptive ways. They function poorly under pressure; they emerge from each problematic situation less able to deal with the next. Instead of using their wits to escape frustrating or conflicted circumstance, they collapse in on themselves, become helpless or in other ways demonstrate their inability to deal with reality. In his wonderful book *Creativity*, Silvano Arieti writes that while some people may be original or spontaneous—as many psychiatric patients indeed are—they cannot be considered creative if they do nothing useful with their originality. Their inventive mental images, ideas and divergent feelings come to naught:

The qualities of uniqueness, originality, and divergence are frequently recognized in the thinking of mentally ill persons, especially schizophrenics. These patients use unusual expressions in their speech; they give uncommon answers to common questions, and their behavior appears bizarre. However, their unusualness is very often associated with a quality of bizarreness and is almost always a far cry from creativity. (Arieti, 1976, p. 8)

Creativity, according to Arieti, is thus not simply originality or "unlimited freedom." It imposes disciplines, structure, restrictions on us in the service of bringing into being something of larger usefulness in terms of human experience. As we explore the various aspects of creative adaptation, we must keep this in mind. Creative people, specifically those who are growing toward autonomy, enjoy freedom but are practical too. These people contribute to themselves and to life. By this I mean that the creative process requires a boundless consciousness, perhaps even depends on certain personal freedoms. In no way do I suggest that creativity is an unrestrained or anarchistic state. As we develop the creative adaptive response we develop discipline and self-control. Then too, each truly creative act establishes, to use Arieti's phrase, "an additional bond" between ourselves and the world. Our response enlarges our life. More important, the life experience of others is enhanced or dignified because of and through our contribution, our creative products or our life itself. It is critical that we think of creativity not as the trait of a lucky few, but instead as a fundamental quality of our own widest awareness or boundless consciousness.

I will develop the concept of "boundless consciousness" throughout this book. For now we can think of it as a mind hospitable to its own unconscious forces and images. Hansel and Gretel, for example, may have possessed a boundless consciousness—or at least they symbolized the kind of open mind that has practical problem-solving value. Early in their abandonment, a small white bird leads them to a gingerbread house. It turns out to be an unfriendly house, but at least they do not starve to death. Later, a white duck helps them get back home. The children's natural rapport with these creatures would seem to indicate that many signs, resources and states of mind can help us if we stay open and innocent. Birds and small animals often are dream symbols of our inner self, the living self that would communicate with us, that seeks expression through us. When we have a boundless consciousness, we use the images and processes of our nonconscious awareness to deal with life's demands.

Each of us has the choice to interpret a life event in a way that either builds our strength and self-respect or undermines it.

In an effort to build a model of adaptive effectiveness, one researcher (Caplan, 1964) defined seven characteristics of people with effective coping behaviors in many different life changes and crises. According to Caplan, such people

· assertively explore the reality issues they face and maintain an energetic, active search for information that will help solve the problem;
· freely express positive and negative feelings and tolerate their own frustration;
· are active in invoking help from others, asking for assistance and support when they need it;
· break problems down into manageable bits and then work through them one at a time;
· are continually aware of their own fatigue level, and monitor their anxiety (or tendency toward disorganization) by pacing themselves;
· are flexible and willing to change, and demonstrate active mastery of their feelings wherever possible, while accepting the inevitable when they must;
· trust themselves and others and have an undergirding optimism about themselves and their future. (This final trait is, like the others, evidence that their self-esteem is high.)

A Synergy of Skills Is at Work

My own work in volatile, radically changing organizations and my research into the life-styles, values and choices of actualizing, gifted adults (Sinetar, 1986) leads me to believe that a *synergistic complex* of skills is used by effective creative adaptors. Three of the major skills are discussed throughout this book: *positive self-valuation, resourceful learning* and *drive toward au-*

tonomy. I call these "skills" because attitudes, ideas and abilities are tools, quite plastic and malleable. They can be encouraged, developed, strengthened, altered, enhanced and put to use to benefit life. The strength of these skills governs the extent to which we dignify our lives.

These skills nurture both happiness and creative problem-solving: positive self-valuation, learning resourcefulness, and the growth toward autonomy. These three fully intertwined clusters are mutually supportive, and synergistic (see Figure 1). I call these "clusters" because within each skill area are embodied groupings of many traits, all necessary to activate the skill in us. Each cluster overlaps the others. As any one skill area develops, all become strengthened; the strength of each determines the

FIGURE 1

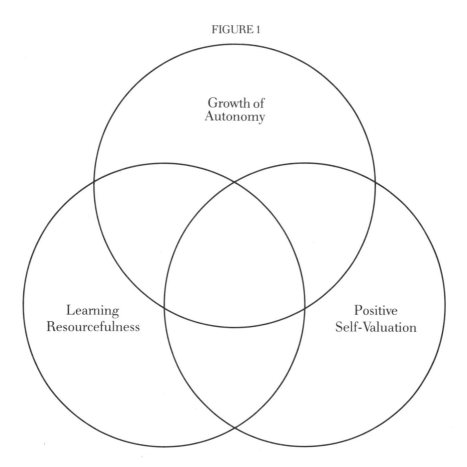

Growth of
Autonomy

Learning
Resourcefulness

Positive
Self-Valuation

strength of the whole. The more we develop each of these skills, the greater our chances of dealing creatively with challenge while also maintaining a healthy, positive outlook on life. Not surprisingly, this development is linked substantively to our perception that, despite difficulty, life is "worth it." Before examining each skill set in greater detail to see how it affords us thinking flexibility and generally a more productive approach to life's demands, let us look at how the lack of these same skills can affect happiness.

The best problem-solvers demonstrate an inherent drive to develop these often latent, but incredibly useful inner capacities. When developed, these capacities—such as learning to do something for ourselves that others had always done for us or that we felt we couldn't possibly do alone—enlarge us as individuals. Think of a newly divorced woman who doesn't know if she can support herself. By mastering emotional or economic self-sufficiency problems, the woman emerges a more capable, complete person than before her divorce. She answers at least one question affirmatively: "Can I make it on my own?" Her yes answer is accompanied by an expanded self-view as well as by her ability to make life choices based on that transformed self-conception.

By contrast, when we cannot depend on ourselves we are deprived of strength. The how-to approach or the quick-fix method of problem solving so popular in today's self-help literature and in most organizational training programs can be counterproductive. We are hurt when we lean too heavily on any expert or authority figure about how to get there. Leaning on another person's formula for problem solving undermines *our* self-trust, thought processes or learning initiatives and thwarts our autonomy. *We enhance our own creative problem-solving skills and self-esteem by figuring out independently how to do things that are difficult.* It is precisely the wish for easy answers that undermines personal renewal and creative adaptation. And it is precisely the lonely task of working out solutions (even if we make mistakes, have setbacks or go more slowly than we would wish) that strengthens our overall self-respect and vitality. A solitary trial-and-error approach stimulates our brains, engages us fully in a matter. It holds our attention, energizes us and develops creative adaptive strengths for future use. As we learn to trust our own minds to solve our life problems, and take small risks to learn new ways of dealing with ambiguity, we emerge expanded as thinkers and persons.

Negative Experiences Can Help Us Grow

People who have never failed at anything, whose childhood paths were overly protected, who have managed somehow to avoid major setbacks can lack confidence when facing trouble in later life. The strongest example of how effective early-life adaptive skills are formed is found among children whom researcher Maya Pines termed "resilient." Of children who have had horrible early-life experiences—such as growing up with abusive or mentally ill parents—Pines found that about fifteen percent fit the "invulnerable" category. They not only survived their traumas but thrived in spite of all odds to become adults with strong autonomy, self-reliance, adaptability and interpersonal skills. Clearly these children developed their creative adaptive responses to change and hardship at an early age (Pines, 1980, 1984).

This small minority of effective youngsters share several characteristics:

· They know how to attract and use adult support.
· They actively strive to master their environment.
· They have a sense of personal power, even volunteering to help others whom they believe to be even needier than they.
· They develop a high degree of autonomy early in life.
· They are actively involved in projects of interest and do well in most of the things they try.

Pines quotes Dr. Norman Garmezy, a professor of psychology who specializes in resilient children: "They work well, play well, love well and expect well, despite deprivation" (Pines, 1984, p. 37).

The inner frame of reference of many outwardly secure or otherwise independent persons speaks to this fact: independent people tend to trust their own problem-solving skills *because* they have been tested and have passed the test of dealing with change or adversity.

Conflict, problems, sudden change—these hold the seeds of a special tension which, when dealt with properly, helps us stretch beyond ourselves as we are and as we grow into something more. The psychiatrist A. Reza Arasteh has suggested (1965, p. 61) that intense discomfort provides a shock "which then instigates existential awareness." Arasteh's work on what he terms "final integration in adults" is laden with quotations from the fully-enlightened thirteenth-century poet Rumi, who also espoused the value of discord to inner growth and happiness:

> All your anxiety is because of your desire for harmony.
> Seek disharmony; then you will gain peace.

In just this spirit, I too view change or personal crisis as a shock to growth. Certainly change spurs mastery over life if approached creatively, for example, if interpreted as sport or challenge. My point of view developed early in life, no doubt because of the disharmonies in my own life.

My father was an entrepreneur. I remember him as urbane, intellectual and restless, eager for the stimulation of travel and competition. His life seemed more meaningful, certainly more exciting, when he was traveling, creating businesses, making deals.

I knew both of my parents as kind, sensitive, extremely honest and well-intentioned. But early, perhaps as young as four or five, I also knew there was something seriously disorganized about our life.

By the time I reached the fourth grade, I'd attended about thirteen different schools, primarily British or parochial schools in the Far East and Malaysia. Typically, my parents would first travel by themselves to a new country. I had a half-brother who lived in boarding schools for as long as I was growing up. Life must have been much harder for him than for me, although we never spoke of this. Only Christmas brought us all together. I too would remain in a boarding school while my mother set up a temporary home in the new country and my father determined business potentials there. Then, when they were ready, my parents sent for me. It was usually several months before I joined them; even then "home" for us was a hotel suite in some non-

English-speaking country. Generally, we remained there six months to a year.

In every country I was essentially on my own. When, for example, my parents went out at night for business dinners or social occasions I stayed by myself in our hotel suite, unattended. Room-service waiters or maids were there to answer my call if needed. This scenario was the norm for me from the age of six or seven. I don't recall this as a problem. Neither lonely nor wanting in any way, in fact I rather enjoyed my life.

Each trip was exciting. I loved getting freed from school and eagerly anticipated my travels. I discovered that fear and excitement were two sides of one coin, and I spent most of those years dealing perilously in that currency. Fortunately, I liked adventure. The dark and oily back streets of foreign cities were fascinating to explore. I loved the smell and taste of exotic foods, and—even more—loved wandering about and talking at leisure with strange-looking, unknown but apparently friendly people. Left on my own, I had my ways of having fun.

By comparison any school was dull, grim and unattractive. The airless odor of musty halls, the same in every school, said it all. Intellectually a wasteland, school seemed just a boring, barren place one had to go to sit down for a while.

Despite the fun of frequent travels, overall it was not an easy time. My parents found the moves difficult on their relationship. I in turn felt their strain. Oddly enough, when left to my own supervision (especially when unencumbered by the dictates of school) I was happy.

When I was thirteen, my father suffered a massive heart attack. He had brought us to the United States the previous year and was trying—quite unsuccessfully, it seemed to me—to set up a permanent home and business in California. One May afternoon, I came home from school with friends to find an ambulance parked in front of our apartment. The ambulance attendants brought a stretcher past me, and the unidentifiable someone on it whispered to me, "Don't worry. I'll be all right." That voice lied. Within forty-eight hours my father died, and with his death our small, exotic family system expired too.

From then on, largely through my own intuitive planning and

manipulations, I was on my own. A distant cousin—to whom I shall always be grateful—helped me return to yet another boarding school. My mother was too distraught to argue about this, and I was strong in my desire to stay put. I felt confident that by myself I would be fine, but I felt no such assurance if I had to continue traveling. My father, more than my mother, had been our family's stabilizing influence, and now that he was gone, I preferred to take care of myself.

As much as I hated living in boarding school (and now I am speaking of a deep, sustained loathing), it was preferable to flitting about the world. When my father died, I welcomed the structure and discipline of school. Apparently an already well-formed adult in me knew what the child needed. But with boarding school came new turmoil: I was introverted and private, so there were endless confrontations with boisterous, aggressive children—all of which I lost, of course. This humiliating plight lasted until I gradually found my interpersonal footing, learned to escape social intrusion and even began to like a growing number of my classmates. This enjoyment amazed me. With experience, my bumbling social skills improved. Eventually I saw that I could use my wits to get along. The stronger, bigger children and bullies no longer intimidated me. But that was not until I was older and had endured several tormented years.

Looking back, I see I concocted an expedient self-protective ploy: by cultivating the friendship of both the honor students *and* the dishonorable ones, I got along with almost everyone. This was an unconscious strategy. I discovered I was using this tactic *long* after it had stood me in good stead and long after I came to like both groups of people. For right or wrong, befriending my peers was my way out of that particular problem. I had to learn a competent way of relating to people or would continue to be victimized.

By this story I am not suggesting that we must overcome an insecure childhood in order to develop creative adaptive skills as an adult. I am saying that the sooner we know ourselves as capable problem-solvers, the better. However we gain that knowledge, self-trust is one key to adult problem-solving skill, as well as a critical component of positive self-valuation.

Some people obtain self-trust through childhood stability. Their happy or secure lives allow them the solid base from which to explore and experiment with their worlds in important ways. Peter, whose home burned down, tells me his family life was secure and uneventful. Some gain self-trust, as I apparently did, by stabilizing themselves despite the instability of youth. They realize, in some deeply secret interior place, that their stability will come in time, and they know they must hold tight to a certain resolve that lets them endure during the storms of childhood.

A woman recently wrote to me about her abused childhood. Since she is obviously successful today in both her family and career life, I asked her how she retained her sanity and inner balance during those early years of misery. Her reply helps clarify how some children, maybe many, know their vulnerability yet learn to trust themselves anyway:

> I recognized that I could not respect my abusive, oppressive "parents." It was that very lack of respect for them that made me able to respect myself. Children who respect those who say they are no good are more likely to believe it. I never did.

The fact is that broad and essential creative adaptive competencies are learned in early childhood, as are significant attitudes about the self. These skills and self-opinions are derived from actual capabilities, from direct life experiences, as well as from our interpretation of ourselves and our life experiences. The exact experience or environment may be less significant than our unique perception of it. Peter, for example, has childhood memories of his mother proudly advertising his high IQ to anyone who would listen. My mother did much the same thing. Whether we were actually as gifted as our mothers believed seems less significant to adult development than the fact that through our own memories we developed faith in the power of our brains.

Such conviction contributes greatly to our creative adaptive success. Scripture teaches, "As ye believe, so be it unto you," and this sort of belief—a deep-seated conviction—forms at least a part of the knowledge that sustains and nurtures our ability to adapt creatively. Faith in one's own mind is the sine qua non of effective problem-solving and life management.

The "Act As If" Rule Works Too

In some adaptive responses, such as my childhood troubles with bullying classmates, trial and error may suffice to produce creative solutions. Yet often what we face can be so harsh, so untenable that a complete restructuring of reality offers the only possibility of escape. I am often asked in seminars, for instance, what one is to do if one lacks the positive childhood memories or experiences on which creative adult response is founded. The answer is deceptively simple: We must begin—right now, no matter what our circumstances—to act *as if* we have faith in our own brains and capabilities. This means taking action on that faith, not just holding positive thoughts. It also means we stop, as much as possible, acting helpless or depending on others for our "answers." This sounds harsh, but it works.

Over the years, I have observed the liberating power gained by those who learn to trust themselves. They stop undermining themselves. Given time, consistency and step-by-step prudence, if we think and act as if we are capable in low-risk areas, eventually we gain true capability to use in all areas. We enter a reality that we ourselves create by faithful adherence to an idea of self-worth and competence. This is not original: it has been reiterated in all the literature humankind has come to hold valuable. But this is often a strongly resisted idea. For many, the idea of being wholly responsible for their actions and relinquishing their dependence on others is unpalatable at best. At worst this idea is terrifying, and seems defiant, tempting fate. Unless we overcome this fear (and the rigid, punitive notions that hide behind it), we can never possess real power as effective human beings, power that was freely given us as a birthright, and that we do not have to "steal."

If we desire growth as creative adaptors, any number of experiential paths can lead us to success, if these help us gain autonomy, by teaching us competence and positive feelings about ourselves. Many popular mass movements for self-development may build skills, competencies or self-discipline. These may indeed heighten self-trust. But very few mass-growth programs reward autonomy. I have interviewed adults who quit major self-development schools of both Eastern and Western thought when they didn't find the liberation and personal powers they had been hoping for. Large-scale group movements probably do not cultivate independence—do not encourage adults to become autonomous thinkers who use their own minds to solve their own problems. Some guru or master usually is the ultimate word for this or that diet, habit, dress or life routine. Their wisdom and strength may help us for a time, but dependence on authority figures is simply less than humans the world over desire. The quite natural yearning of our species is to grow into whole, individuated persons who use their creative powers in their own inventive ways.

Creative Problem-Solving Through Metanoia

If one is burdened by a dysfunctional childhood or some other emotional handicap borne of adult trauma, then psychoanalysis or self-study or support groups led by gifted (or at the very least competent) counselors can help. The promise of working in this way is always that it is never too late to reinterpret our early experiences for the good. For positive reinterpretive acts to take hold of our consciousness, we must have a change of mind and heart so deep and substantive that it transforms our intellect's way of dealing with our past and our own selfhood. I refer to this fundamental transformation as *metanoia*, a word taken from the religious phenomenon of conversion. Joseph Chilton Pearce's writings seek to clarify this process:

> Metanoia is a specialized, intensified adult form of the same world-view development found shaping the mind of the infant. Formerly associated with religion, metanoia proves to be the way in which all genuine education takes place. . . . [It is] a seizure and a restructuring of the attending mind. This reshaping of the mind is the principal key to the reality function. (Pearce, 1971, p. 7)

While this full-blown conversion may seem extreme, the task elusive and out of reach to most of us, almost all of us have known or heard about people who achieved so substantive a change of mind and heart that they were then liberated from a problem: sickly children, who convince themselves they can gain health and then manage to do so; adults who despite lack of education or even illiteracy manage to school themselves; persons who suffer the loss of a family member and, although they at first think they cannot, go on to regain their ability to enjoy life again—these are all examples of the sort of total conversion, or metanoia, I describe in these pages. We can think of metanoia as a turning around, a deep mental shift perhaps, during which we change our allegiances and believe we can accomplish what before we held impossible.

The metanoic process—if we would be architects of our own—begins with our faith in the existence of the answers we seek. The three skills clusters mentioned earlier may need to be at least minimally in place for such faith to drive us. How, otherwise, could we hope to steer our own mind into such passionate conviction that what was once impossible becomes natural and easier. (And be assured, this is what the process entails.)

"Overbelief" is the term Marganita Laski coined to describe the intense belief we need to experience what we *wish* to see realized. The word means that we passionately believe in our wished-for goal, so much so that we are even convinced that supernatural powers will aid us if necessary. When Hansel and Gretel really escape their ordeal they are changed persons, not the same two children we met at the start of the story. The tale suggests supernatural, or at least unseen, supranormal, forces helped them throughout. For example, when they must cross a large body of water, a white duck helps them over it. This duck represents a mysterious living power, the kind we ourselves yearn for—and require—in those untenable circumstances when our own abilities seem insufficient to get us to safe harbor. When we lose a loved one or a job; when our health fails, overbelief and the metanoic process bring powers by which we find our way, although in forms unique to our life.

A bedridden woman wrote to me twice last year. First she wrote to say that her life seemed hopeless. She could not imagine a way to support herself given the limits of her physical state. Several months later, she wrote again, happily reporting the inception of her own at-home secretarial service. She would rely on a home computer as her primary partner. Somewhere between the first and second letter she must have experienced so substantial a change of mind that she gained the faith in herself necessary to take this bold step. This ordinary yet inspirational illustration conveys the latent power in conviction.

This case also shows that, whatever term we use—overbelief, metanoia, conversion—the revamping of individual belief happens in the quiet privacy of a person's mind. This conceptual overhaul is a beyond-words experience, truly the sound of one hand clapping. Self-disclosures about what happened or how such a thing occurs thus remain impossible to articulate. In Walt Whitman's words, "When I undertake to tell the best, I find I cannot. My tongue is ineffectual on its pivots. . . . I become a dumb man." Yet one thing is certain—the overbelief needed to effect a cure, increase self-esteem or take us to safe harbor during a crisis follows only intense conviction. The impossible becomes possible as we mentally leap, through faith, into the unknown, uncertain future, believing we will find our answers there.

Ancient mystics were able to fulfill the special relationship with God they sought, because they met certain requirements— undertook substantive psychological and emotional reeducation in the ways of a particular religious vocation. The mystic must first die to his egoistic self in order to be reborn to an enhanced self—one that experiences God personally. This same process, perhaps to a lesser extent, perhaps not, can be utilized by anyone who believes in her own creative adaptive power. The perceptual shaping process is identical whether one is a mystic, a scientist or an unemployed street person: to change our personal reality we must first build an intense conviction in the reality we seek.

This power is intrinsic to each of us, although we resist knowledge of this fact. With the development of our full humanity, our innate powers of consciousness grow as well. In order to develop these fully we must question old assumptions, the teaching of elders and society, and—more radical yet—renounce the rules of logic and inflexible, rational certainty by which we live. What I suggest is known and already practiced by every truly creative person (as well by every devoutly religious person who believes in miracles and divine power).

A questioning, regenerative mind, one that permits experimentation and learning, lies at the heart of the creative process itself. However, positive self-valuation, learning resourcefulness and the drive for personal autonomy seem also seeded in this heart. With these qualities in place, our chances for creative escape from almost any life circumstance become possible. We may know ourselves as fearful at every step of the way, but at least we believe in the existence of solutions. Then, like Hansel, we can confidently say, "Don't worry. I'll find a way out, no fear."

2

Mastering the Basics

The best way to predict the future is to invent it.
—ALAN KAY

[When the children awoke in the forest it was pitch
dark.] Gretel began to cry. "How are we ever to get out
of the wood?" she said. Hansel comforted her. "Wait
a bit," he said, "until the moon is up, and then we'll
find our way sure enough."
—THE BROTHERS GRIMM, "Hansel and Gretel"

Like Hansel and Gretel we develop our threshold for happiness
and even our problem-solving muscles early in life. The person
who during childhood knows himself to be energetic on his own
behalf will face setbacks in life in a healthier, more optimistic
way. Hansel's comment, "We'll find our way sure enough,"
depicts how this energy transmits itself into problem-solving skill
and attitudes. It also reveals why some people stay upbeat despite tremendous problems. On the other hand, those who are
passive victims or ineffectual problem-solvers when they are
young will likely be unhappy or lack vitality as adults, unless
they choose to change those behaviors.

Mastering the Basics: A Case Example

A woman I will call Lynette was an abused wife for more than
eleven years. As her story unfolds we see how positive self-

valuation, learning resourcefulness and growth toward autonomy are intimately linked.

During the early phases of her marriage, Lynette had unques-
tionably impoverished self-esteem. She was a dependent woman
with little faith in herself or her ability to separate herself from
a brutal husband. She could not imagine living happily ever
after. Thus she underwent two trials: her marriage itself and the
two-year transition period after leaving her marriage during
which she had to reconceptualize her life story. Lynette said that
she postponed leaving her marriage because she kept thinking
that things would get better and that if she just tried harder she
could avoid expressing the personal flaws that infuriated her husband. She felt she could thereby "fix" the whole relationship.

> I became addicted to hoping for change, when there was abso-
> lutely no indication that any change could or would occur. It was
> a hopeful but unhealthy belief and it obscured reality.

Lynette needed to overhaul her entire belief system. An important part of this task was to upgrade her self-esteem. She had
to learn to stand up for herself, to interpret events in her favor,
trust her own perceptions rather than those of others. By addressing these learning problems, she is also growing into her
own person:

> Over the past two years I've changed my awareness of being a
> victim to knowing that I'm in control of my life. I want to be good
> to myself first, then to my children. It had always been my hus-
> band first, then my children and finally myself. I was raised that
> way.

Before continuing to describe Lynette's retraining program, it
may help to dissect the three skills I call "the basics" in order to
understand their workings in Lynette's life—and ours.

POSITIVE SELF-VALUATION

High self-esteem and inner balance are both characteristics of
positive self-valuation. We might think of high self-esteem as an
optimistic, energized and positive "idea of self." This idea is

held in place by the actions of persons who believe they are likable, competent, worthwhile and powerful. By "powerful" I mean that a person feels capable deep within. Even when individuals with positive self-valuations do not know how to do something, even when they may know intellectually that they lack physical or material resources to solve their problems, they find a way through their dilemma. Hansel and later Gretel did exactly this when their instinct for survival took over, when logic would have failed them. By "powerful" I do not mean that those with high self-esteem feel superior to others or use their status or material resources to push others around. Rather, they trust their brains, competencies and intuitions in difficult situations.

Self-trust begets self-acceptance: people may know themselves to be imperfect, yet because self-trust is a supportive attitude, they can feel comfortable with themselves anyway, even feel *able* in ambiguous situations. Because of these feelings, they then adopt active, self-strengthening attitudes and behaviors, such as optimism, the ability to speak up for an unpopular (but perhaps personally meaningful) cause, the ability to take well-calculated risks or to experiment. Positive self-valuation plays an essential role in the creative adaptive process. It determines our aspirations and eventual achievements as well. On the simplest level, if we listen to the way people talk about interviewing for jobs (a difficult, awkward activity at best) we hear how their feelings about themselves might control life achievements. Those who feel inwardly confident maintain their inner balance during actual problem-solving. They are not completely thrown off by a tough question when interviewed; they do not get, as one man put it, inordinately "stressed out" while trying to figure out what to say or do. They function both during and after the interview. Although they may feel intimidated, frightened or nervous, they act as if they were able—fully prepared to go ahead with their next step. Their ability to control their minds and behaviors, their functional effectiveness in real-life situations are keys to their success: negative feelings do not dominate and rule their lives. Unlike Lynette, whose negativity and self-doubt rendered her helpless, those with high self-esteem move toward their needs and wants despite fear or self-doubts.

Regrettably, people with low self-esteem have exactly the opposite tendencies. Those with low self-esteem might prepare badly, if at all, for a job interview, not trusting themselves to know what to do if placed in a new situation. Believing himself unable to concentrate, one person fidgets, becomes distracted. Another arrives late. During the interview itself, if an interviewee feels she is displaying signs of nervousness, her inordinate self-involvement accelerates her self-consciousness, which in turn increases tension. Occasionally almost everyone has these experiences, but those with low self-opinions rarely have anything else.

While people with high self-regard maneuver smoothly around their stress (often by just admitting that they *are* scared and thereby neutralizing their stress or disarming criticism or harsh judgment), those who lack this adroitness are simply brittle. Living under constant duress and in an emotional environment of distress, they make matters worse. They may feel humiliated by apprehension that is really quite natural and then unconsciously punish themselves for what they perceive as a flaw. In sum, they fail to perform when it counts most. All of us who have blundered when challenged by the need to perform can easily empathize with this downward spiral of events. For those with negative self-valuation, this downward spiral becomes a life story. Even imagination works against those with low self-esteem, for they are mesmerized by what doesn't or "can't" exist. Sometimes just relearning that joy *is* possible or that good days can last is a major reality change.

Keeping Balance and Perspective

Inner balance is another key element of positive self-valuation. It can be described as the feelings, attitudes and competencies that allow us to remain inwardly poised, peaceful and integrated. Optimism, confidence—that feeling or sense that things will turn out well for us, even when they are a mess—all come under the umbrella of the term "inner balance." This sense of composure is so tightly woven into the fabric of self-trust / high self-esteem that it seems practical, for the purposes of this exploration, to discuss them as if they were one set of traits.

Homeostasis, as stress researchers call inner balance, is actually a term describing the steady, undisturbed internal environment of a living organism. Our internal environment must remain somewhat constant and stable despite changes or shocks to our system. When the demands of a situation or problem are too much for us, we experience varying degrees of inner chaos or disorder. As a rule, the more serious our problem, the more serious our internal disorder, and the less able we are to deal creatively with the external demand. In Lynette's case, because her self-trust was already at a low ebb when she was first married, her ability to see her way clearly out of the chaos of her life was impaired. Had her early life been more stable, had she been better loved as a child, Lynette would not have stayed around to be hit a second time by her husband. Once would have been enough for her to have known exactly what to do.

Say we receive bad news and are thrown into the doldrums. We lose our sense of "all-rightness." We feel at sea for a while. Such experiences happen to everyone, and this description of inner balance is not meant to imply that certain people avoid stress completely. But if we have inner balance and self-trust, we quickly rebound. In every area of life, those who trust themselves deal more effectively with life stresses than do those who feel unworthy or inept or who know themselves as unreliable.

In terms of individual problem-solving, inner balance (physiological steadiness or homeostasis) is likelier to be achieved by those with the greatest capability for adjustment. The confident individual who feels secure enough to reorganize herself in whatever way she must achieves inner balance most quickly. Take, for instance, two people who are divorcing. The one who most substantively reorganizes his or her life (not just paying lip service to what must be done, but taking the steps and time to repair interior wounds; not merely staying at home and watching TV, but initiating a meaningful social life) will achieve ease sooner in the new circumstances than the one who just slides along hoping to "feel better," as if by magic. Time does heal emotional wounds, but our attitudes and actions can help time along.

Taking Changes in Stride

The more tense and rigid we are, the more likely we have a brittle response style: we crack under small pressures. The employee who gets perturbed when his coffee-break time is changed is too easily thrown off balance. His lack of flexibility may be a lack of positive self-valuation. Sometimes, of course, a brittle response is just an indulgence, a bad habit or a sign that something else is troubling us. Low self-esteem, however, does undermine our ability to deal with ambiguity, pressure or lack of structured guidelines. On the other hand, positive self-valuation produces the ability to concentrate on present tasks or issues despite uncertainty, or to take change in our stride. Persons I counsel during times of company mergers who believe in their own capability and worth feel on solid footing, despite company fluctuations. They feel, and actually are, able to focus on their jobs. Suzanne Kobasa's study of AT&T executives during that company's restructuring found that the hardiest people were those who interpreted those changes as a challenge, were committed to their jobs and felt, overall, in control of life (Maddi and Kobasa, 1984).

People with positive self-valuation often find change stimulating—at worst, disappointing or inconvenient. But when faced with the need to change, they generally feel in control, competent and at least subjectively protected. This is not to say such persons are impervious to bouts of anxiety or confusion, only that they don't feel someone else must protect them from either their feelings or their circumstances. Instead, they know they are capable of mustering whatever skills or composites of help (new technical knowledge, actual physical protection, financial or material aid) in addressing their needs. As Hansel says with eager self-assurance, "I'll find a way out. No fear."

Learning Resourcefulness

Learning seems an additive process, relying on multiple, distinctive skills, intelligences and attitudes. Each and every skill within the learning complex helps us control our daily performance and life needs. Moreover, it is a life stance, characterized by openness to knowledge, self-questioning and flexibility even to the point of changing one's mind. The best learners may not be the most consistent people. Learning also stimulates us. Through our minds and brains we create worlds within worlds. Learning requires a capacity to take risks, to experiment, to tolerate ambiguity, to let go of what has been learned in order to gain new information and understanding. It is impossible, for example, to be a creative learner—by this I mean to do more than simply memorize facts or obey directions—without being comfortable with open-ended, unanswerable questions. This means we maintain inner balance while teetering on the edge of not-knowing. Effective learners therefore can both be inconsistent—because they have to remain flexible—and greatly enjoy not-knowing. Their natural curiosity heightens the pleasure of searching for knowledge; their quest for answers is as exciting to them as a suspenseful mystery drama is to others.

The artist whose goal is to create a novel form of expression can easily experiment for years, all the while remaining centered and highly focused. Even though it may be years before the artist finds out if her sought-after form holds possibilities, her inner stability remains constant. Part of the delight of artistic expression is just this ambiguity: the uncertain, challenging climb up the mountain, rather than the safe or routine arrival, excites.

Entrepreneurs—artists of a different sort—put money, time and intense emotional energy into their ventures before knowing whether their investment will pay off. Those who cannot sustain not-knowing never discover much. Learning resourcefulness depends on experimentation.

According to Silvano Arieti, the creative process can be thought of as the way a human uses what is "already existing and available and changes it in unpredictable ways" (Arieti, 1976). The creative process lets us transcend our usual thinking mode in dealing with our environment or ourselves. Some have defined creativity as bringing into existence something new, something that has never appeared before, be it idea, invention or way of relating to the world. Creativity is the life blood and essence of problem solving. It is the common denominator that links together any number of other human attributes, the thread that runs through life or work competencies and everyday resourcefulness.

Plato described true artists as persons who give birth to some new reality. For him, true artists dealt with being itself. In this exact sense, our own creative process is activated when we try to bring ourselves into being in a new way. Lynette, for instance, began thinking like an artist as soon as she began imagining herself free—as soon as she started "playing" with new personal realities. Her improved life was an offshoot and outcome of her interior artistry.

Delight in Organizing Chaos

Creative people organize chaos. They impose simpler, more refined understandings on complex patterns. They "see" (i.e., perceive the world, data, social trends, technological laws, legal structures etc.) in comprehensive, ordering ways. Scientists who locate coherent patterns and principles in nature, whether these relate to sub-particle physics or planetary systems or the way birds migrate, seem no different to me than financial analysts or economists who spot new waves of data in stock trends or in the numbers they analyze. To accomplish this organized "seeing," they must love freedom and chaos. Anyone whose mind works in this way understands what artist Ben Shahn meant when he said, "I love *Chaos:* it is the mysterious, the unknown road. It is the ever-unexpected, the way out: it is freedom, it is man's only hope. It is the poetic element in a dull and orderly world."

To love freedom and chaos so, our minds must work in a particularly orchestrative way. Creative minds move beyond problems, beyond data. Such minds continually play with data and with possibilities, until—from some primitive wellsprings of consciousness—new patterns, answers and insights are composed. All human minds have inherent creative capability, even though they differ in their level of creative power and in the degree of usefulness of the things they bring into being. There is a decided difference, for instance, between a Dante or a Shakespeare and a sometime poet who struggles to produce simple verse. Nevertheless, it is the process that is significant to those of us who would create adaptive solutions for our life. To initiate this process in our lives we may want to think about how we, as individuals, prefer to learn, imagine and think, or ask ourselves how we learn when we are in our "best form."

Some people are visual: their optic systems are incredibly well developed, sensitive to color, pattern, light or texture. Others are auditory: they learn best—and enjoy themselves most—while listening to tapes or lectures. Still others are kinesthetic: they use their bodies to create, as well as to learn, and have well-developed nervous and coordination systems that promote wonderful discoveries. While these differences define the fashion in which they most effectively use their minds to gain knowledge and reinterpret data or experience, all creativity is but another side of learning itself. Anyone can learn and create whose imagination can be taught to play with life's real demands.

Whatever our learning style and our own peculiar creative inclinations, as we develop our creativity we improve our chances of imagining how to live effectively. Creativity and learning are two sides of a single coin. As we learn, we take in new information and understanding. When we are resourceful learners, we are able to use the knowledge in novel ways that help us master our world, our problems and the progressively complex situations in which we find ourselves. As in the case of the artist whose work grows ever more pure and truthful along a certain line of effort, at its best, learning (life experience, the process of study, thinking, leveraging knowledge) permeates our entire being and life with wisdom and capability. The more resourceful we are, the better learners we will be and the more capable of change we will become.

Resourcefulness undergirds the entire problem-solving process. Improvisation, play, experimentation are at work in us when solving problems. Hansel's first attempt to find a way home provides us with a classic view of successful improvisation. Hansel, realizing his fate, waits silently in bed, feigning sleep. After his parents fall asleep, he gets his chance. He slips outside and gathers pebbles which lie in front of the house glittering "like bits of silver" in the moonlight. He puts these in his pocket and returns to bed. Heart pounding, he tries to rest. The next day he drops the pebbles along the path as signs toward home. Hansel lies when his father asks him what he is doing: "Oh, Father," says Hansel, "I am looking back at my white kitten, which is sitting on the roof waving me a farewell." At the heart of Hansel's improvisation is his keen desire to reach a goal, a goal he has pictured in his mind as central to his and Gretel's survival. This picturing process, his intense desire to fulfill a goal, his risk taking and ongoing experimentation are all keys to successful improvisation.

The Sunday mechanic who improvises while tinkering with his car may or may not know something about the machine he is trying to fix. Still, he plays with possibilities as he works: he may lack wire and substitute a hairpin. He sees what he wants to do—on a very practical level he is creating. At some level of his being, he must first feel free to play—must feel capable of imagining and imaging a solution before he attempts to use the hairpin.

This is the precise experimental stance we need when facing any problem: we imagine and image our end goal. We play with possibilities. We experiment. Perhaps we take risks. We tenaciously persevere without giving up hope. Such attitudes are easier with self-trust than without.

Letting Go as a Learning Tool

There is enormous value to being able to "let go." By this I mean the art and action of discarding old, outworn ideas or habits. The most resourceful learners seem to let go easily.

Suppose that Hansel, early in the tale, had believed, "We are doomed." He might have cried himself to sleep instead of tiptoeing outside to find pebbles in the moonlight. His belief—or lack of belief—would have thwarted his mind's ability to come up with solutions. So too in our case: our feelings, and subsequent choices, are held in place by our belief systems, and yet— as this and subsequent chapters will show—beliefs and feelings can be changed. *On our own, or with professional help, we can change our minds.* People do this every day—no matter what their age or circumstances.

In order to alter our subjective world or our self-view, we must let go of our original thought, "I am unable to do this or that." Instead of self-destructively victimizing ourselves with our own persistent hold on old ways of approaching something, we must detach from our point of view in order to evaluate its efficacy. To detach means to let go.

People who behave helplessly have belief systems that say they "cannot do." They have put this idea into firm place early in life. As we will presently see, and as other texts have described, all beliefs are self-creations. We create and learn what to believe from infancy, from our interactions with people and environment. This enculturation process is necessary for human survival. In adulthood—or even earlier—some begin to realize that these beliefs can be changed. Altering our self-view means to choose to believe the best about ourselves in spite of the evidence against us. This requires faith and perseverance. Whether we choose to believe in God, or in the Republican party, or in the idea that a woman's place is at home, or that a man must support his family is less significant to our discussion than the fact that we ourselves have chosen these beliefs. Consciously it can help us to accept the additional notion that we ourselves can alter our beliefs. To detach ourselves in this way is also part of learning resourcefulness. To let go in this way is to unlearn what we have learned all too well.

To unlearn unproductive beliefs, we must supplant them with more helpful ones. Unfortunately, almost no one wants to do the hard work this entails. Our contemporary trend toward instant, quick-fix approaches ensures that we maintain ourselves as dependent, rather than independent, learners who lean eternally on the world's experts, authority figures, the media, our parents, teachers and others for our ideas. Letting go is critical to creative adaptation because resourcefulness or solving problems while entrenched in outmoded opinions and behaviors is impossible.

The woman who believes her place is at home, but who nonetheless yearns for greater intellectual stimulation, may finally realize that one option is to return to school. Another option might be to go to work. She is not free to create or choose either option, not free to commit herself to college, to work or to her conception of what will make her "happy," unless she unlearns the central idea: that her place is at home and it is "wrong" to leave it. For this woman, thinking, reading, talking about both old and new ideas, mentally experimenting with new ones, making slight adjustments in her old way of seeing and doing things (for instance, letting her family make dinner one night a week) will get easier as she becomes an independent thinker—that is, as she puts energy and drive into gaining objectivity about her ideas and beliefs. Independence is not gained overnight, so she will have to give this program time.

Letting go of outworn ideas becomes more feasible when we are sustained by positive self-feelings and a memory of having been successful learners in the past. The mind encodes behavior. If we have seen and felt ourselves meet other challenges, as discussed in chapter 1, then we have at least a semblance of faith in our ability to grapple with new challenges and master these. Keeping an open mind about our situation and remaining flexible and optimistic in the face of unpleasant or frightening news are part of this learning composite, even though, on the face of it, we may not be used to thinking of "learning" in this manner. Learning resourcefulness involves opening our thinking to a place in us that is *beyond* conscious awareness. It is from this "place" or state that creative adaptation emerges.

The person who restructures his self-view along the lines of a resourceful learner, will, of necessity, be one who abandons the old way of seeing himself as "helpless." Resourcefulness begets power. Hansel does not dwell on the failure of the bread-crumb trail, but energetically initiates new ways to get out of the forest using his own instincts. Gretel, first dependent on her brother, learns to be self-reliant while Hansel is trapped in the witch's cage; eventually she frees herself and her brother. Throughout the tale both children demonstrate hardy perseverance and stubborn tenacity. The fairy tale instructs us that age and gender matter less than learning skills: if we are old enough to learn, we can teach ourselves how to use our mistakes and survive almost any ordeal.

Helplessness is learned. Mastery is learned. Letting go is learned too. However, this matter of "unlearning" is often perplexingly hard. In our culture, where we place high value on fixity, on controlling destiny and on having and accumulating things, some may think letting go a dangerous notion. They live rooted in the idea that things bring security. Others just find that letting go is work. One woman said, while learning to become more optimistic, "I don't know what I'm going to do when I'm not depressed anymore. I've gotten so used to the blues, these feelings are like my friend. I'm *used* to feeling down. I've nothing to replace these emotions with, so it's hard to be more cheerful." This reminds me of Dorothy Parker's line: "All my pretty hates are dead,/And what have I left?"

As we let go of outmoded habits we release much pent-up energy. People who have given up an addictive habit know what this is like. A client who had lost many pounds (simply by letting go of bingeing on junk food while watching television at night) said that he had so much extra time he didn't know what to do with it. He realized he had to retrain himself in order to be more productive; only as he released himself from bondage to the other habits did new ones emerge. As he altered his evening binge habits, a whole battery of attitudes and behaviors changed too. He felt better about himself. He noticed aspects of his home and life that required attention. His garden received more focus and time, his garage got a long-needed cleaning out. In the process, he came to know himself in a completely revised way— as a man with energy, a taste for order, an inclination to use time productively. In this vein, substituting new for old by assigning ourselves positive tasks while trying to change our mind and habits allows us to let go of the negative.

Resourceful learning includes the knack of gathering and processing information. It requires high levels of motivation— mental fuel—for following through on problem-solving demands. Certainly it involves a host of higher-order thinking skills. As we become capable, resourceful learners, we also grow more self-sufficient and autonomous. Nothing has more value for our creative adaptive ability than embracing freedom, ambiguity, the lack of structure. Fortunately, autonomous people exhibit a need, not only a liking, for freedom. This need is a hallmark of human health. After Lynette started imagining a better life for herself, she needed to act on the possibility of this notion; her need was another sign she was growing into fuller human functioning.

Growth Toward Autonomy

Positive self-valuation and resourceful learning (unlearning and the adaptive use of new knowledge) are but two keys for those who hope to create options in their lives. A third essential is the ability and willingness to grow into self-sufficient, independent persons. To grow into ourselves as persons, being—to use Kierkegaard's apt phrase—"that self which we truly are," is what I mean by "growth toward autonomy."

Autonomy implies self-reliance and self-sufficiency. The self-sufficient person thinks and handles himself independently, developing beliefs and a choice pattern that enable him to live out the self he truly is: his best self. By contrast, those who shrink from autonomy also shrink from taking responsibility for their lives, preferring to lean on the thinking or directives of others as a means of knowing what to do. This pitiful tendency spirals us downward into an ever-widening abyss where eventually we are lost to ourselves.

Independence is a critical psychosocial tool for growth *and* creative functioning. Many skills combine for creative problem-solving: a search for information; the free, robust expression of feelings (both positive and negative); the skill of breaking down problems into manageable bits (so that each bit can be handled separately, one at a time, thereby gaining mastery over the whole); the ability to sustain hopeful, practical faith in our intended outcomes—these skills *and* steps can be accomplished only by those who are growing toward autonomy.

Nor are these persons easily dissuaded from their own perceptions or likely to accept the opinions of authority figures (parents, spouses, professional "experts" such as lawyers and doctors) simply because the authority has spoken. Individuals with high self-esteem know how to keep their own point of view and/or emotions intact while dealing with significant others and do this using a range of responses. By contrast, those who lack positive self-valuation can easily be swayed or manipulated by others.

The correlation between a positive self-view and a healthy, independent stance toward authority figures is significant. We cannot achieve inner balance or become more capable problem-solvers when we don't pay attention to what we feel inwardly, when we discount our own perceptions or pay excessive homage to experts or anyone else's point of view. During times of rapid change or difficulty we help ourselves by staying in control of our emotions and actions. It is significant that Hansel does not bow to his intended fate simply because his parents have dictated it. His survival takes precedence over obedience to parental will. Gretel too defies authority when she tricks the witch.

However, we must not think that following parental or expert advice automatically means we are passive victims with low self-esteem. A friend who overcame lymphoma said she did everything she could to prevent future occurrences by following her doctor's orders to the letter. She also leaned on family support and steeled herself emotionally for whatever might happen. Another person, who overcame the same disease, said he believed he could prevent future recurrences by controlling his diet. His doctor had no advice to give him on that subject, so he turned to a macrobiotic community and followed its teachings as best he could despite a heavy travel and work schedule. He believes he helped save his own life by taking responsibility for what he ate. He also accepted traditional medical care. These examples illustrate how different people adopt diverse behaviors to stay in control of themselves during a crisis. Though their actions differ, they remain in charge of themselves even when relying on the help and expertise of others. By selecting some preferred, believed-in and helpful solution themselves, they increase their sense of control despite a painful struggle for survival. By actively attempting to master the situation, through whatever means seem most appropriate, they stay fully involved. They are energized and expressive throughout their ordeal. Behind their active involvement with problems, behind all desire to stay in control, at the center of their being lies the firm conviction that their efforts and they themselves can make a difference in their lives.

What Can Be Done Now to Improve What Already Exists?

The independent person has the strength and integrity to see things as they are—instead of as someone else wishes him or her to see it. The autonomous person feels strong enough to question authority or experts or the "way it has always been done." Gaining autonomy may be a lifelong process for the most part, yet those with the independence of mind to improvise (e.g., to use a hairpin in place of a wire) demonstrate how much that characteristic helps when problem solving is at stake. Only when free to question the rulebook, the prescribed way of seeing and doing things, can we truly solve problems in our lives. This is not to suggest improvisation for everything, only that we should gain enough skill to improvise if required.

In situations of personal trauma, the theme of independence runs through the comments of those who feel they have mastered the situation. However people gain mastery over trauma, it is always accompanied by feelings of increased independence with respect to the illness or circumstance.

Successful creative adaptors ask:

- What can I do now to manage the situation?
- How can I handle myself so that I will be more effective, victorious, overcoming?
- Who is doing—who has done—what I need to do? What behaviors and attitudes do they embody?
- When have I felt powerful, in charge, in control?
- How did I feel then?

These sorts of questions and all the ancillary insights their answers bring equip us with greater autonomy. With insight we gain the advantage of identifying what we need, value, want or must do. Autonomous people initiate action from a starting point of self-sufficiency *or* they grow toward self-sufficiency while learning to triumph over their dilemma.

The tale of Hansel and Gretel is replete with elements of viciousness. The parents abandon their children in a forest. The witch poses a cannibalistic threat. The children themselves are forced into violent response: Gretel tricks the witch to enter the hot oven that is meant to cook Hansel and herself. Again this is not so much psychological as simple realism: our own experience tells us life is not always peaceful and pretty. Using common sense, we realize, as Hansel and Gretel and ancient storytellers apparently did, that to create or be victorious, we must sometimes destroy, tear down or let go. When we graduate from school, relocate, change jobs or change our minds we have to release former friends, communities or ideas. A thread that runs through this book, and probably through all our lives, is that in order to survive we often must do things that are difficult, risky, uncomfortable. Autonomous persons most effectively manage such actions. It is ironic that while *triumph, mastery* and *victorious* are warlike words, the creative adaptive response, however destructive it seems in the short term, is ultimately a peaceful, faith-filled, transcendent response, motivated by a will to live and a love of self and other.

Improving Our Self-Treatment

Lynette's learning process shows us she has a long, slow way to go. Lynette knows she has to learn how to rely on her own intuition, her own sense of what is real. Over the years her husband convinced her that only his perception of the world (i.e., of their relationship, their marriage, her, etc.) was valid. Nowhere in Lynette's conscious mind did a reality exist that was based on her own direct experience or feelings. She was only dimly aware, for example, that she contributed to her own storehouse of sufferings. Similarly, within any of us the circuitry of perception can get twisted, distorted, disorganized so that proper functioning of our critical faculties is impaired. When we distrust our own ways of interpreting reality we render ourselves impotent. Lynette let her husband tell her how to comprehend life. This was one of the ways she treated herself badly: she gave him too much power over her mind. Since he was demeaning her (and since he himself was unstable), she had chosen a faulty guide as a conduit for her key input on reality. If we contrast Lynette's response to what we hope is our own healthier one, we see how dangerous it is to accept anyone else's interpretation of events in place of our own thinking. This is not to suggest that we avoid objective counsel but that we hold ourselves responsible for the final discernments, perceptions, decision making and so on. Although most of us know we must learn to retain independent, objective judgment, many of us forfeit our independence all the time in lesser ways. The sooner we recognize our dependencies, the better.

Tracking Lynette's progress, we see that increased learning skill enables her to develop positive self-feelings:

> This has been a slow and painful transition for me. I've been used to someone else doing my thinking for me—even though I'd never have admitted it. My husband was so dominant, what he said went —even when it went against me. I have had to learn I wasn't helpless then, am not now, and there is always a choice between being happy and being miserable. I was the one who made the choice.

Lynette grows healthy because she is willing to learn the hardest lesson: she had had a role in her own suffering.*

---

* I do not wish to leave readers with the impression that the abuser's *responsibility* for abuse is in any way avoided or diminished by the argument that people bring on their own victimization. However, within the context and discussion of learning theory, neither can we skirt the obvious, that some are quicker to say no to intolerable situations than others. The question remains: Why is this so?

One of the hardest things I've had to swallow is that I played just as much a part in the bad stuff as my husband did. My awareness about this grew gradually. My psychiatrist recommended that I attend a six-week self-esteem course with a group of other women.

We have been given three tapes to take away, to play again and again, reinforcing the new ideas. We also have index cards to read and reread. I'm having to let go of my old beliefs in order to learn that: *I create my own happenings. I cannot do better by trying harder. I have to be willing to accept a new way of thinking if I want my life to work. I cannot change my habits or awareness by just wanting to—I must be ready, emotionally, before the change will take.*

Readiness to learn, as any primary school teacher knows, is related to self-esteem. Researchers into school success (and by this I also mean "learning success") have found that several factors can be barriers to adult learning (Clabby and Belz, 1985). These are:

· ambivalence about success;
· fear of risk-taking;
· overdependence on authority figures;
· tension;
· intrusive memories of past poor learning experiences;
· psychological defense of oneself against the new learning.

None of these barriers involves IQ! All relate to positive self-valuation, degree of autonomy and overall openness to learning, or learning resourcefulness.

Believing in Ourselves as Learners and as Valuable Persons

Clabby and Belz's study revealed that functionally illiterate adults learned to read when there was trust within the group, and when each learner accepted himself or herself as a learner— as someone who had potential for learning. The students were taught to notice what they did to promote or defeat their own learning, or what they did to gain, reject or distort information. This objective observation is essential to our own increased learning skills: we may unconsciously thwart ourselves by backing away from the very skills we need, or by holding negative attitudes about ourselves. If we do not *believe* we can improve our self-opinion, we are unlikely to.

Like these adult students, Lynette had to learn to view herself objectively in order to see that she caused her own problems. She too grew to know herself as a learner, saw with time that she could improve her self-view and her response to abuse, and increase her self-trust. She began to notice that much of the time she defeated herself. One of Lynette's hardest lessons was to know herself as a positive, productive and competent person. This knowledge is the foundation of high self-esteem, yet often the most difficult for many to accept—that they are capable and valuable as persons. Early training, our own collusion with that training—by which we give away our power, give others authority over us, imbue others with rights and wisdom they probably do not have—makes it almost impossible in adulthood to accept the good in what we do. We will easily attribute positive traits to others, but deny ourselves recognition for the exact same traits.

> I cannot accept a compliment to this day. It's even hard to me to see for myself that I've done something worthwhile in this growth process. My psychiatrist tells me that a lot of significant changes have occurred in me, but this part of my growth—the ability to see myself as capable, deserving, independent—is the slowest of all.

I suggest that this is Lynette's slowest learning area because this is the idea hub that holds her old belief system in place. Her early belief was: "I am not worthwhile, I *can't* do things that rate compliments, I am not valuable." Learning to believe in new ideas, especially when these change our self-view, requires substantive reeducation.

Self-Directed Restructuring of Self-Beliefs

In the previous chapter, I discussed metanoia as a fundamental transformation of mind and heart that allows us to perceive the world and ourselves in a revised way. This radical transmutation of perception is involved in all self-change, wherein the individuals restructure themselves, their universe, their entire value system and perceptual field.*

Lynette's story serves as a concrete example of how the metanoic process begins. The individual herself must be author and text of the procedure of change. She must immerse herself in thinking and behaving acts that sustain and reinforce the new belief system. Lynette was intelligent enough to select a psychiatrist who got to the crux of the matter. Have no doubt: Whom we select as guide along the way is a critical choice. All doctors, all lawyers, all teachers, all gurus are not equally gifted—not all have our best interests at heart. Lynette had to become fully engrossed with her own intensive, continual, mind-and-belief-altering program in which she herself could experience the building process of her new ideas. She structures her own conversion, re-creates herself, is the designer and architect of her own re-created self-and-world view.

Such transformation is a long process.† The faster we wish to go, the more completely we must submerge ourselves in a revised way of thinking, acting and self-feedback that radically alters our world view and our fundamental view about ourselves. We can alter our belief systems if they don't work productively for our lives. At minimum, we may find it helpful to become more aware of what we do believe about ourselves and the world. In this book I return frequently to this theme in order to reinforce the idea and possibility of a self-directed transformation process. As observed in an earlier footnote on cults and other "mind-bending" groups, the methodology always involves the individual actively, but not always in the role of author of his or

---

* I am speaking, throughout, of the self-initiated metanoic process, although cults, politicos, advertisers and other mind-benders use these same techniques. Here too, autonomous persons decide to whom, and to what ideas, they will give loyalty.

† As in St. Paul's conversion, instantaneous personal transformations and miraculous, spontaneous healings do occur. These seem a grace. No one can say with certainty how miracles occur. No one has yet described the exact process by which they happen, or how they might be reproduced. Moreover, for those of us who feel it somehow impolite to trespass into this domain, that—for instance—this might be God's special territory, Thomas Merton's comment that everything is ours because everything is His seems sound. "It seems everyone is more or less obsessed with this great illusion of ownership and possession. What is strictly mine? He is mine. And what is His? I am His. But when this becomes clear, there is no place left . . . for anything resembling Prometheus" (Merton, 1961, p. 37).

her own change project. To my knowledge, there are only a handful of people researching self-directed metanoia, while it is altogether too common to hear of "experts" and other would-be guides who would change us, for a price.

The metanoic process demands we reinforce only a single idea (at most a select few). Lynette's remarks prove that she participates in a support program that repeats the same few ideas, behind which sits a single idea of positive self-worth. In a way, we cut a "groove" (like that on a record) to make an imprint in our mind. This groove or impression then helps us return mentally to the new, exact and most helpful way of thinking needed for our best adaptive response. For example, now, whenever Lynette finds herself with an abusive person, she must automatically return to the place and idea within herself where she knows she is worthwhile, where no one can convince her otherwise. This "simple" idea underpins her well-being as a human. Yet constructing the new belief and putting the idea to work are not easy—practice, repetition, perseverance are required, as Lynette's comments indicate.

Lynette's early survival strategies involved positioning herself as an inadequate person. Perhaps once, as a child, she thus gained the love, care or attention she needed from the adults around her. As children, without some attention—negative or positive— we cannot survive. For adults, getting emotional satisfaction through negative attention is a killer strategy. Lynette's change involves altering her central beliefs and reconfiguring herself— *in her own mind*—as adequate, competent and worthwhile. That is why this learning process can take so long: learning means undoing the old, building the new, then developing faith in the truth of what is built. Lynette's early strategies also included distrust of self. She let others determine her "reality." As a youngster, she put more faith in what other, dominant persons said about her and about reality than she did in her own feelings or discernments. This is another unfamiliar but healthy idea (i.e., "I can trust myself, my feelings, perceptions, etc.") that she must construct in her mind before her creative adaptive response style becomes fully productive. When Lynette receives a valid compliment, she must automatically respond internally: "Yes, it's true—I do this well. What a competent person I am in these matters." At present, she has trouble remembering that she does anything well, so she is learning to structure or create a fresh memory-groove, in order to hold a new primary idea of self. Who else can build up this idea or think it for her? Lynette knows what idea of self she wants to live by, and what idea she wants to be rid of:

> I don't give myself credit. I still have lots of trouble with that and with what people think. Maybe I'm wrong, but at least now I don't automatically assume that I'm bad. I've started dating lately, but here too, I've found myself slipping into my old ways.
>
> I got involved with someone new. He even proposed to me. At first I was so happy. I thought all my problems were solved. Then I realized I still believed a man should "rescue" me.

Lynette must also be a quick and sturdy learner, because her automatic desire and tendency (based on early strategies) will be to relate herself to another strong, seemingly all-powerful and rescuing person. In fact, she proves herself to be in charge of her change process, thinking first of her own inner feelings when making decisions about a new man in her life. This is revolutionary, the first time she consults herself, asks herself how *she* feels about things. Her remarks teach us how the metanoic process works:

> I'd never been in touch with my intuition before. Lately, I'm starting to notice that it's there—this is a growth in autonomy for me. I am growing into my own person. I am changing at the core and this change will have a lifelong impact on me for the better.

Summary

I am glad to report that Lynette's story has a happy ending. She, like Hansel and Gretel, has responded over time in a way that enables her to live "happily ever after." Today she is becoming a writer and has already had several poems published. She is often asked to speak at community events (people in her community know of her victorious reeducation program), and she acts as a role model, encouraging others who are trying to find their way. Recently she wrote me a letter saying that she no longer wants to be known as a "former abused wife" but as an artist. Lynette demonstrates that positive feelings, learning re-sourcefulness, and growth toward autonomy are key aggregates of the creative adaptive response. Her story helps us trace the steady, slow process of self-directed change, showing us why each of us must take control of our own circumstances and change-projects, whatever these may be.

This is not to suggest that guides, teachers or support persons are unnecessary to our growth—far from it. If we are to build positive self-feelings, become resourceful learners and grow into autonomous persons, we must utilize others as resources and helpers—not as infallible gods or superhuman rescuers. We must also design our change so that we are enhanced, as indi-viduals with greater problem-solving skill, when we emerge on the other side of our dilemma.

Autonomy, self-valuation and ability to learn resourcefully are woven tightly into what amounts to creative skills; these three clusters of abilities work together to enable us to meet life's demands ingeniously. Without autonomy we cannot think in-dependently or hear internal cues; we are deaf to our own inte-rior voice and deepest wishes and give greater weight to the opinions of others than to our own. The advice of doctors, man-agers, parents or friends then sways us from our best directions. Advice is akin to information: if we place too much significance on what others tell us without doing our own thinking, reading or reflecting, we deprive ourselves of objective research. The autonomous person is capable of creative, critical thinking be-cause he or she less readily submits to convention or suppresses conscience and conscious choice.

Without the skill of resourceful learning, we cannot experi-ment in novel or traumatic situations, where we don't know our way. Yet experimentation—especially, but not only, the mental imaging that precedes novel action—is part and parcel of overall judgment, decision making and choice. Our skill as experiment-ers enables us also to neutralize excessive fear and anxiety. When we are active, doing something on behalf of our needs, we are less likely to feel anxious. If we remember having been suc-cessful in the past when we didn't know what to do, we can recall how moving, if only cautiously, into untried areas can generally minimize inordinate fear. At the same time, risk taking in the area of concern has been practiced and is better understood, so there we have a built-in governor preventing too impulsive, self-defeating reactions. Our own trial-and-error acts teach us how to overcome.

Finally, positive self-opinion lies at the heart of our ability to detach ourselves from negative or changing situations and examine them objectively. By detaching ourselves emotionally from circumstance, by feeling in our deepest self that we can manage regardless of outcome, we make it possible to stay in control of worries, of the unknown, of our future. There are no guarantees of a safe or happy future, of course, just as life offers no real insurance policies. But our faith and subsequent resourcefulness give us a fighting chance for positive outcomes.

Lynette may not always succeed. Hansel and Gretel could easily have been eaten up by the witch. And we ourselves may fail at what we try. But what alternative do we have but to try to solve our problems creatively? By mastering the basics we do everything in our power to live faithfully in line with the promise of our being.

PART TWO
Creating "Luck"

ND when the full moon had risen he took his sister by the hand and followed the pebbles, which shone like newly coined silver pieces, showing them the path. They walked all through the night, and at daybreak reached their father's house again. They knocked at the door, and when the woman opened it she exclaimed, "You naughty children, what a time you've slept in the wood! We thought you were never going to come back."

But the father rejoiced, for his conscience had reproached him for leaving his children behind by themselves.

Not long afterward there was again a great famine in the land, and the children heard their stepmother address their father thus in bed one night: "Everything is eaten up once more. We have only half a loaf in the house, and when that's done all is over with us. The children must be gotten rid of. We'll lead them deeper into the wood this time, so that they won't be able to find their way out again."

3

Beyond Thinking

Luck is just another name for God.
—HINDU SAYING

They wandered about the whole night and the next
day, from morning until evening, but they could not
find a path out of the wood. They were very hungry,
too, for they had nothing to eat but a few berries they
found growing on some bushes. . . . On the third
morning, they set about their wandering again.
—THE BROTHERS GRIMM, "Hansel and Gretel"

Hansel and Gretel learn, and teach us, about survival. To survive, they must learn from their mistakes. After his successful innovation with pebbles to mark the way home, Hansel tries using bread crumbs and fails. The two children later follow a little bird to a gingerbread house and stuff themselves full of sweets, thus falling prey to their own hunger and the witch's seduction.* In time, perhaps only after she and Hansel escape,

---

* Bruno Bettelheim interprets the children's actions as unrestrained and greedy, and says they are "fooled by the pleasures of oral satisfaction." These regressions rob them of problem-solving power. This seems harsh. Hansel and Gretel have fasted for three days. They are little children. We feel sorry for them. But Bettelheim has a point: this tale was transmitted from what Andrew Lang termed the "savage stage of man." Primitive life *was* harsh. Contemporary life is harsh as well—be it in the suburban or urban wilds. These tales were, in the main, lessons in survival. What seems stern and unforgiving at first blush makes sense when we are in the throes of an adult crisis or a childhood one: we must stay alert, try as much as we humanly can to retain our strength and independence and heighten our problem-solving ability. Relying too much on comfort, safety, the loving kindness of others can keep us stuck.

Gretel may learn that crying about problems doesn't help her find a way out of them but that active, instinctive behavior may well save their lives. In a similar way, our creative adaptation requires that we become willing students of what works and what doesn't.

To live effectively in a world of constant change requires either that we learn new things (such as technical skill or information, a revised way of working or relating to others, a reconstructed view of the world) or that we apply what we already know in productive ways. Creative adaptation also demands that we combine various learning and unlearning strategies as well as blend different mental processes. These abilities have relatively little to do with what we normally think of as intelligence.

Many people who function creatively in everyday life are naturally adept at higher-order thinking. They gather, process and synthesize information rapidly and effectively. Some, if not most, are quite unaware of their capabilities. They are skilled in their initial assessment of a task or problem as well as in the actual doing of it, even if they are poorly educated or untrained.

One study found that relatively "unskilled" milk-processing workers, after experience on the job, had highly developed problem-solving abilities. They were utilizing more efficient mental strategies to manipulate milk products or dairy units than the formal algorithms taught in mathematics classes. The knowledge they relied on was not something they had learned in school, but was gained through their real-life experience and then applied to new problems. Each of us relies on such knowledge, called tacit intelligence, in order to live well (Sternberg, 1985).

At times it is natural for each of us to experience difficulty when faced with incoming data, new ideas or responsibilities, or change. We may become easily confused or thrown off balance if it all comes at us too rapidly or if the problems are significant to our well-being. We may not sort out the initial data in an orderly or correct fashion. Perhaps we never really learned to manage our time or our minds, or to set priorities. We might be poor information-gatherers, failing to locate the key points of an issue, leaning too heavily on minor irrelevant issues, seeing all points as having equal importance. Or we could actually be inadequate thinkers, unaware of just how to develop and use our mind's subtlest functions properly.

High IQ Does Not Guarantee Creative Life Success

Some of us think we cannot improve these deficits or that we can think and learn effectively only if we have high intelligence. We think that the higher our IQ scores the better our marks will be in school, or the more successful our life. This is not entirely accurate, although no one can deny that many of the world's greatest contributors had, and do have, gifted intellects and that the majority of well-schooled persons are able to earn respectable incomes. However, something more than a gifted intellect or monetary success is probably at work in true personal success.

Each of us has no doubt noticed the surprising lack of any real correspondence between academic success and job or life success. Just think of the old joke about the Ph.D. bookworm who cannot tie his shoes without help. Bright students, on their school's honor rolls, often end up as merely average, bland adults with unimpressive creativity quotients. On the other hand, we must all know at least one "late bloomer" who awoke to her potential and from then on was an inspired performer.

Intelligence as we traditionally consider it and life success are only loosely connected. For one thing, intelligence is not fixed. Recent research indicates that this is an outdated, perhaps even a discardable idea. While I do not suggest that a seriously impaired learner can be taught to become a neurosurgeon, I do believe that almost anyone with normal mental functions can learn to think, learn and use his mind more creatively. Becoming practically resourceful and self-sufficient may have more to do with appreciating our mental processes and using them properly than it does with anything else.

Developing Higher-Order Thinking Skills Often Means Transcending "Logic"

Yale professor Robert J. Sternberg shines perhaps the brightest, most prolific and optimistic light on this subject to date. His writings suggest that intelligence consists of multiple-component processes—both analytic and performance processes—as well as mental strategies for combining these. Sternberg uses the term "higher-order processes" to describe complex sorting, analytical and planning skills. Recognizing and defining a problem, deciding what mental mechanism to use to solve it and ordering (organizing, making data coherent) thinking strategies are all higher-order mental skills. Our effectiveness in the early planning stages of problem solving, for example, depends to a great extent on how we have learned to structure the major issues of that problem. That learning itself depends on understanding how we think and how our mind functions.

Sternberg and others believe that instruction and development, can be helpful: we can be taught to use our minds more effectively. To put it another way, intelligence, and certainly analytic or creative skill, can be developed.

Jerome Bruner, in his book *In Search of Mind*, writes that the mind is active and creative, that it is capable of moving "beyond the information given" (Bruner, 1985). Other intelligence researchers suggest that just as we have a "sixth sense," a super-awareness about people or things around us, in terms of intelligence we may have a seventh sense: we can be, and often are, aware of our own mental processes, and we can develop the capacity to reflect on how we learn and how we solve problems (Nisbit and Shucksmith, 1984). The term "mental energy" has been used by researchers to describe the motivational components of intelligence, namely the volition, the will, the intelligent person has to translate his or her mind's products into usable actions that benefit life itself. Some people have more mental energy than others to apply to problem solving.

Each of these ideas defines intelligence as the ability to learn or profit from experience (Sternberg, 1981) and to transcend factual data, information and problems, to comprehend and adapt successfully to real-world circumstances. Resourceful learning provides us with more powerful tools than just the ability to regurgitate what authority figures have taught us. Learning requires that we use our minds as intricate levers to enlarge our life explorations, to build new understandings and knowledge, much as engineers use machinery to construct physical structures.

Varieties of Intelligence

Sternberg believes various subsets of intelligence have practical implications for everyday problem-solving. Componential intelligence may make us bright on IQ tests, and thus acceptable to school or work authorities who use the results of these test scores to predict our academic or job success. But componential intelligence is only one form of intelligence, basically that which serves our analytical needs, those intelligence functions now popularly called "left-brain," linear or logical thinking. Componential intelligence relates to the way we gather, sort and process information in common-logic fashion. While useful and necessary, this is by no means the only intelligence function of the mind, and it is certainly not the sole sponsor of creative ideas. Another subset, already noted, tacit intelligence, involves that understanding which is not taught in school or even openly expressed. Sternberg contrasts the knowledge that can be tested by exams we can study for, with the knowledge we must use to make a career judgment. He concludes: "Much tacit knowledge is probably disorganized, informal and relatively inaccessible, making it potentially ill-suited for direct instruction" (Sternberg, 1985, p. 439). Another form of intelligence is experiential, the mental ability to link past and present experience, to combine these understandings into useful insights for our current or future needs. Another, contextual intelligence, helps us interact with the environment, in order to read the context of a situation correctly.

Since problems are usually solved at the level of their context, people with strong contextual intelligence are often called "street-wise" or "street-smart." They are fine improvisers, they think well on their feet and are quick studies in new situations. They may or may not have high componential IQs, but they are excellent manipulators of people and their environment. In my observation and experience, top management influencers in almost every organization, regardless of type, and young street-gang leaders in almost every urban ghetto possess in common strong contextual intelligence. Although they have almost nothing in common in terms of socioeconomic backgrounds, education or daily experience, they share a way of sizing up and solving problems. Regardless of age or background, these individuals are finely tuned into their environment and themselves; they discern what needs to be done and generally figure out without being told how to do it. I suggest they solve problems and think primarily at the transcendent level of their minds, thus merging conscious and nonconscious processes although they might not realize it. This merger richly profits them.

Hansel and Gretel never attended school. For all we know, their componential intelligence may have been only average. As we have seen, each made mistakes. Hansel could have dropped bits of cloth instead of crumbs. But just as surely these children were using all their intelligences to escape the witch and get home. Their eventual triumph resulted as much from their concerted efforts as it did from the "luck" of the supernatural, although this tale, like other classics, certainly suggests that a mix of human effort and the supernatural is involved in life success.

The "Irrational" Has Its Own Intelligence

Those people who develop and use various types of intelligence, who tune into more than just obvious sources of self- and environmental input, who are able to move beyond merely rational thought are very often called lucky.

Silvano Arieti proposes the term "tertiary process" for the special blend of mental mechanisms we use when we create useful, real-life solutions. Traditionally, the creative process has been confined to that primitive "irrational" mental domain that fell under the general heading of what Freud called "primary processes." These involved the unconscious, best known to most of us through dreams, the symbols of art and myth, the strange, even eerie world of psychosis. Secondary processes, the mind's rational operations, include componential intelligence and common-logic mechanisms. The tertiary process, Arieti suggests, is where the two processes (primary and secondary, irrational and rational) meet, blend and produce creative insight:

> Instead of rejecting the primitive (or whatever is archaic, obsolete or off the beaten path), the creative mind integrates it with normal logical processes in what seems a "magic" synthesis from which the new, the unexpected, and the desirable emerge. (Arieti, 1976, p. 13)

Creativity demands that we be receptive to our irrational processes—not in order to become irrational, but rather to utilize hidden answers, insights, directions, hunches, intuitions in the service of our life's needs. Arieti describes the combination of objective detachment and passionate immersion in a subject, a seemingly contradictory mental attitude that may allow that special "magic" synthesis. Creative minds quite effortlessly and naturally function in this contradictory way. Toying with problems so that one sees the mind's play objectively, while being lost in its playful daydream, is precisely the thinking mode that eventually produces insight and answer.

Yet so many adults fear and resist having a friendly, easy relationship with their primitive mental processes. They deprive themselves of their most life-supporting resource. On the other hand, artists, entrepreneurs, craftspersons of all kinds enter a state we might liken to the tertiary process. This is an ancient understanding: there is nothing new here whatsoever, save for the helpful description Arieti provides.

Enculturation: How We Learn to Fear Freedom and Chaos

If we have minds capable of such power, if we can so easily use our mind's tertiary process, if we all have the completely natural capacity to transcend problems and receive or construct solutions imaginatively, why do so many of us have so many problems? For one thing, we fear, perhaps even hate, our own chaos and freedom. Related to this, rooted in it, is the reality of our having been taught not to think rather than to think creatively. We have been encouraged to depend on others to do our thinking for us and have been rewarded for it. Hansel and Gretel may have had the advantage in escaping their predicament precisely because they were still children and had not learned fully to censor their creative thoughts. While as children we too may have had a wonderful zest for learning, wonder and invention, and may have enjoyed our true selves (our feelings, inclinations, talents, our aspirations), only a few of us retain such vitality and excitement in adulthood. Parental coaching, school systems, graduate schools, government and private institutions (any bureaucracy that keeps individual creativity and innovation under control) push us away from independent thinking. We are systematically taught to depend on others for our solutions. We are even taught to hate ourselves for the disobedient wish that we could create our lives as we need and want. This schooling away from self is a natural part of the enculturation process of every society. Enculturation is the way in which the young of all societies are brought into the perceptual framework and value system of their particular worlds.

The socialization process starts at birth. If we examine our own school days, for example, when our learning skills were shaped (thwarted or honed to perfection), we can no doubt remember ourselves being rewarded for the speed and competence with which we learned to appreciate others' expertise. Instead of being acknowledged for the alacrity with which we used our minds, or for our distinctiveness, or for the dreamy states of mind that brought forth unusual answers, we were usually shown (by example, coaching, coaxing and coercion) how to look to and even lean on our teacher as information giver and source of knowledge. In most societies only the very young, the ancient, and the fools, artists or poets are permitted perceptual license. Most of us learn to understand this, then bend ourselves accommodatingly, at least outwardly, so that we "get along." Hansel and Gretel are told, initially, that they are bad for staying away from home. Yet their stepmother cunningly leads them deeper into the woods to be again rid of them. The children know they must get home. They act against her plot, as they eventually act out against the authority of the witch. But most children, needing the love and approval and the warmth of belonging, choose to comply with authority rather than assert themselves. In time, compliance is their preferred modus operandi; similarly, in time, some adults grow to love their own self-enslaving tendencies.

Many teachers prefer students with high IQs but low creativity. Students who are obedient, cooperative, self-controlled are easier to teach and have in class. Interestingly enough, these teachers have strong parental support for their preferences. Perhaps most parents of bright, solidly productive but highly conforming children value conformity. The by now well-known research of Victor Goertzel and Mildred Goertzel stressed that conforming adults had mothers, conformists themselves, who wanted their children to be compliant, "acceptable" and, eventually, professionally successful. Not surprisingly, even highly intelligent youngsters from these homes grow up to be flat, unimaginative, often overcontrolled, appallingly unoriginal adults (Goertzel and Goertzel, 1962).

I have taught graduate-level classes in which adult students became outraged if they had to dig in the library for answers to open-ended questions. I have addressed audiences of executives who also get easily confused and visibly disturbed when directions for group activity are not linear, precisely worded and highly directive. In the corporate environment, business executives exhibit similar dependencies when placed in student roles. Workshops and management training programs tend to be instructor dominated and lecture oriented. Even when these are full of simulated exercises, participants are dissatisfied with discussion groups that do not end on a note of certainty, that do not give them *the* answers to problems.

This is old news. Most of us know and accept this from our personal experience. Yet what we may not realize is how costly this dependency training is in terms of human creative power. When we use other people's thinking for every conceivable life issue, when we don't make waves or exist on our own terms and in our own unique way, we fail to build the skills that can save us when life presents us with tough problems. When other people's thinking and answers cannot rescue us, we are usually too far gone—dependent, passive, mentally weak, unimaginative—to figure out on our own what we want to or must do.

This situation alarms me. Everywhere I look, but especially in the corporate environment where I spend much of my time (an environment that *says* it wants to become more globally competitive, creative, innovative), I see courses designed to teach people how to do mind-numbingly simple things.* Seminars exist (and they are well attended, and costly) that tell employees how to plan their work, how to present speeches, play corporate politics, get a

---

* Although in the early eighties the best companies trimmed their training staffs in an attempt to reduce both budget and middle management employees, and although today increasing numbers of companies are moving from "telling" courses to simulations and modeling, the U.S. has a long way to go. American organizations of one hundred or more employees spent 39.6 billion dollars in 1988 in training and outside educational services. This is 6.2 billion dollars over 1987 expenditure. But American consumers still prefer Japanese-made products to their U.S. counterparts. Lack of innovation or initiative, the quality of products, and judgment are still national business concerns. Polls indicate that worker satisfaction with jobs would increase if opportunities for autonomy, creativity and responsibility were provided. I do not suggest cutting back on corporate education programs, but rather that we reexamine the process of programs and upgrade the teaching of thinking skills and general learning resourcefulness in schools, industry and community education programs.

job, leave a job, dress, write a business letter and so on. These courses teach memorization and conformity, not higher-order problem-solving. Many of them subject participants to lectures that are merely lists of commonsense rules that any adult with average intelligence could (and should) easily figure out alone. As a matter of fact, I believe training for severely learning-disabled students uses teaching methods similar to those used in the business world! For instance, recently I read that students with Down's syndrome learn best by a slow, methodical, step-by-step how-to procedure, in which teachers re-explain and model simple directions in heavily supervised practice sessions. This sounds suspiciously like a business training course to me.

The cheerless fact is that middle management is not expected to exercise resourcefulness; nor is anyone else—at work, in school or in personal life. That seems part of our national problem. Many employers are dismayed when I speak of this. Those who agree immediately want a course to teach their employees how to be more creative! They are vexed when I suggest they begin evaluating employees on the *quality* of their judgment calls, and their alarm heightens when I recommend that a healthy start for such evaluation is at the senior management level. This is not a facetious suggestion. Our mind is exquisitely able and meant to construct systems of knowledge—new information, accommodations, blendings and fusions of data and understanding, practical adaptations of old skills. We can create information as well as construct our adaptation to both old and new knowledge—but not if we have been schooled away from our own creative power. If we are acknowledged and then rewarded for teaching ourselves to solve problems—business problems, for instance—then we can, and will, rise to the occasion.*

Evaluating Our Judgments

The power struggle between the individual and society is by now outdated, completely worn out. The world's current change rate

---

* When I taught English, I required middle school students to analyze poems, short stories and even song lyrics, largely without my help. Once a beautiful, auburn-haired pre-teenager complained bitterly that one of Robert Frost's poems was "much too hard"—as if I were an idiot to think she could discern its hidden meanings. I insisted. She triumphed. Then for the rest of the day she beamed with pleasure, her self-esteem bolstered to a new high. Discovering our competence serves us all our lives.

has accelerated so aggressively that unless individuals world-wide are empowered with personal change skills (i.e., creative adaptive powers) and unless bureaucracies loosen their stranglehold on innovative processes, society may not survive. The problems that our world must solve depend on individuation and creative autonomy for each of us.

We can all evaluate ourselves on the quality of our judgments and other higher-order thinking skills. Countless lists of thinking skills are available. I find psychologist Harry Levinson's leadership traits among the best for evaluating these skills. He suggests (Levinson, 1980) that would-be leaders analyze their judgments on the basis of the following dimensions, which we can use to assess our own everyday problem-solving skills:

· *Abstracting capabilities:* How well do we conceptualize, organize or integrate information into a coherent frame of reference?
· *Tolerance for ambiguity:* How well do we manage ourselves in confusing or chaotic times? Artists, entrepreneurs and other creative persons, for example, are known to enjoy organizing chaos.
· *Practical intelligence:* How well do we manage in our day-to-day life as problem-solvers? We all know of people with advanced degrees and supremely well-developed abstracting skills who have no common sense.
· *Judgment:* How good is our judgment? Do we know when to ask for help and can we avoid the trap of shooting ourselves in the foot with the advice others give us? Do we know when to act and when to wait until times are right for action? An old saying has it that we should not teach people specifically how to do a thing, but rather should help them know what results they want and then let them figure out how to get those results on their own.

A Case Study: Gaining Clarity, Improving Performance

Personal salvation lies in our taking greater, not less, responsibility for what we know and do and how we do it. We must build problem-solving skills—for experimentation and for monitoring our errors so that we learn from each mistake—and move forward instead of drowning in a sea of self-blame and defeat. Steven,* a young executive I counseled, learned to build these very skills.

Initially, Steven's manager thought the young man had a "time management" or a "lack of preparation" problem. This was only superficially correct. The longer Steven and I talked, the more his weaknesses seemed to be in the initial skills he used when he met a problem. He received and processed information poorly at the start. His own urgency to complete an assignment seemed to get in his way. Using Sternberg's vocabulary, I outlined two different problem-solving skills in an attempt to help him sort and process information more effectively.

1. *Conceptualizing:* Steven needed to "stand back," examine the problem strategically, gain perspective and ask himself several clarifying questions:

· What is the big picture here?
· What are the priorities in this assignment?
· Are there any special urgencies or critical issues here?
· Where can I get more information that will help me understand the larger picture more accurately and broadly?
· What mental processes will I use and what actions can I take to approach this problem, to begin to understand it, to solve it?
· Have I ever encountered anything like this before? How did I solve it?

People who abstract easily see the micro in the context of the macro. Before jumping in to act on a matter, we too must step back and conceptualize a problem into a coherent image or larger contextual frame of reference. In truth, effective conceptualizing encompasses planning. Effective conceptualizing

---

* "Steven" is a composite character. He represents countless aspiring executives who search everywhere but their own hearts for ways to be effective. Their approach to relatively simple problems seems unnecessarily convoluted and confused. Years of apple-polishing for authority figures—teachers, professors and managers—decades of memorizing expected answers or company procedural handbooks or this year's success formula from this year's favored MBA program erodes what common sense they inherited at birth. This seems why, to paraphrase Groucho Marx, American corporate intelligence is becoming a contradiction in terms.

means we view everything from an "endpoint"; we envision ourselves taking concrete steps to solve the matter and see the essential qualities of the problem within its more global setting. We see the end in the beginning when we "see" correctly.

I am not suggesting that we skip quickly over the planning stages, although many people are instantaneous, intuitive planners. But planning time and mode differ for each individual. An essential task all along the way is for us to familiarize ourselves with our mind's unique process of planning, while acquiring information and conceptualizing skill in order to build on strengths and correct weaknesses.

2. *Organizing:* This skill requires that Steven create a step-by-step plan and execute the various tasks undergirding the goal to be achieved, without contaminating either plan or action with excess emotion.

Steven cared too much. His emotional stake in a matter cluttered his mind—rendered him useless as an organizer. His intense feelings subverted his mind's smooth functioning. He jumped into the deep end of his assignments before knowing what was there, before discovering the shape, depth or breadth of the problem. He outlined a plan, even initiated a flurry of action, before considering the sagacity of his overall plan or the consequences of the actions themselves. His mind was occupied with a host of tangential, largely irrelevant details that made problem solving messy and inordinately complicated. While some err by making complex subjects too simple, Steven's liability was doing the opposite, seeing molehills where mountains still existed. Worst of all, he gave his manager an incoherent set of recommendations that had little to do with the contextual heart of the problem.

He needed to teach himself to slow down, and to ask organizing questions:

· What exactly do I have here?
· Where do I want to go with my actions, and how does that destination relate to where I find myself now?
· Whom else might I talk to about this?
· What else might I read as a source of information to help me get feedback on my own biases and my perspective?

More than do anything special to the problem, these kinds of questions organize and settle the person who is asking. They give him a critical distance from the problem. It is certainly possible that learning disabilities exist when someone cannot abstract, see the big picture, learn from experience or comprehend cause and effect. However, such was not Steven's problem. Steven needed to establish an orderly inner focus as the prerequisite to the clear thinking he wanted. Because his initial thought process was driven primarily by his impulsive, hyperactive nature and his desire to please authority figures, his mind fled from its own source of answers. In his haste to solve a problem, his mind attached itself to externals. Rather than attempt to glimpse the whole pattern, he focused on any bright fragment of the puzzle that happened to catch his attention. Clarity comes from spotting patterns within the patterns that one sees *within* the whole.

People who score high on tests that measure reasoning ability take ample time for global planning. Only when they fully understand the larger problem do they initiate action. However, sometimes their analysis is quite unconscious and instantaneous, as often seems to be the case with highly creative people. But even people who are called geniuses in their field take time to immerse themselves in the study of a problem. Their full immersion incubates insight, gives rise to intuition and to workable, if not always successful or brilliant, solutions.

It does not, incidentally, necessarily follow that such immersion makes one adept at implementing the solutions. Sometimes people who are expert in the initial conceptualizing stage or who are excellent planners are poor executors during the performance stage. It is not that they don't know what to do, but they may lack thoroughness when dealing with the steps of the solution. Perhaps Hansel was similarly impatient to see his ideas for a solution in operation when he threw bread crumbs on the ground. He hoped the crumbs would help him find his way back home, but he didn't think matters through carefully enough to realize that the birds might gobble up his signposts. Clearly, Hansel had the intelligence to plan effectively, but he was rushed and anxious. Too often, the details of bringing an answer to life may seem trivial, tiring or boring, and so they are easily overlooked.

I have noticed this tendency in various disguises. For example, when creative, gifted technical professionals are promoted into management jobs, their thinking mode and impatience can get them into trouble. As managers they must take time to interact with people. Their real love, however, may be technical or abstract, conceptual thinking. Their favored task will then get their best working attention, while they rush through other tasks that are to them uninteresting. As a result, they may be perceived as insensitive, inadequate managers. In much the same way, our thinking habits may be lopsided, rushed or not fully developed. Some creative minds are nagged by a raging self-doubt. Others require more structure and discipline to be effective. Still others are too time-bound or perfectionistic and must continually battle self-imposed structure. Whatever the case, it is each person's job to learn his or her own thinking strengths and plan a way to improve thinking weaknesses.

A Personal Development Plan

Because everyone's thought patterns are unique, each needs his own rule(s). To develop into resourceful learners and good problem-solvers, we must identify what thinking skills we need to improve. We may want to become better planners. We might need stronger conceptualizing abilities or desire greater intuitive power. Perhaps we wish for enhanced follow-through skills. All of these are learned skills.

To pinpoint the type of development we must undertake, to map out a plan, requires self-assessment and perhaps even assessment by diagnosticians.* Even in developing a self-help plan, creative adaptors will have the edge, since they tend to use what is offered by way of resources effectively. Those who want more specific guidance may be stumped. A sort of catch-22 results. People who are fine information-gatherers and -processors pull relevant data into an organized, usable whole. They discard the rest. Those with learning problems may not get past the recognition that something is wrong. Fortunately, more and more college campuses offer courses in higher-order thinking skills, and for those in doubt this seems a likely place to start digging for ways to improve personal thought processes.

---

* While I have listed various questions we can ask ourselves, these are hardly sufficient for those with severe thinking or learning handicaps, whatever these might be. Those who want more information about building thinking skills may refer to the bibliography at the back of the book.

Creative adaptors have other, related, learning skills as well: they gather information from various sources, are broad synthesizers of a wide assortment of disciplines, readings and conversation. They expertly sort out, store and retrieve information. When asked how they've managed to arrive at this expertise, they rarely know. The ability is interwoven with their thinking skills. It is interesting that learning researchers usually categorize the skill of information gathering separately, even though gathering information is needed all the way along the problem-solving line. We build our storehouse of knowledge and our understanding of entire subjects with information; then we use information as we act; and finally, to evaluate our performance or project possible consequences, we may need to gather more information.

Characteristics of Effective Improvisers*

As noted, one of the many forms of intelligence involves a sort of "street sense" that permeates all stages of learning. Street sense allows us to think and act independently and spontaneously, without undue intellectualizing or analysis. With this sense we don't need to be told specifically how to do things. We have a broad, intuitive comprehension that allows us to plan, take action, gather information so quickly that it all seems one process. In reality, many mental processes occur sequentially, if not simultaneously. A senior executive officer I know thinks out what to do while apparently acting on those same thought processes. He seems to possess two forward gears, operating at the same time, synergistically: one gear, or mental function, is working full-speed on what to do; it conceptualizes and evaluates the consequences of each option. The other function gives the command to do the right thing in the right way. In contrast, most people think first, then—needing differing amounts of time to reflect—act (if they act at all). The executive I mentioned thinks/acts—all in one "motion." To onlookers there is almost no time lapse between his thought and his action. This is one form of street sense, as I mean it, and I liken the workings of my

* For a refreshingly clear article on the cerebral side of the creative process, see Kaha, 1983.

client's mind to the workings of the mind/body of a fine dancer. The fluid master dancer becomes the dance. He need not think about how to do each step. He exhibits skill. Improvisations are instantaneous—the novel step seems as effortlessly taken as the practiced step. In like fashion, a highly developed, disciplined mind promotes right answers and right action: *the mind becomes the right answer/action.*

Like professional athletes, naturally gifted yet disciplined in their sport, minds such as this simply flow—spontaneously and gracefully self-correcting when necessary, without interruption or blocks from an overactive, judgmental or anxious intellect. The great basketball player Larry Bird is often quoted as having said of another basketball great: "That's not Michael Jordan on the court, that's God on the court—disguised as Michael Jordan." Creative improvisers think and behave this way: everything they do looks easy, artful; their answers "flow." We all have similar minds—potentially graceful, potent, powerful. Moreover, almost everyone can develop mental flow, in varying degrees, by diligent effort, by disciplining and managing the attention. I believe the practice of managing attention eventually merges thought and action so that spontaneous, fluid creative effectiveness occurs in both realms, thinking and acting.

The Use of Role Models

To grow as an independent, resourceful thinker, it also helps if we fix our minds and observational powers on the most effective role models we can find. This is the way complex human behaviors are learned: not in the main by trial and error, but by data and language transmission and by continual observation (Bandura, 1971). Moreover, it is insufficient simply to place ourselves in the company of skilled models (i.e., of persons who can do what we hope to learn), as many popular interpreters of modeling theory suggest. Numerous variables affect our learning, such as our knowing what relevant cues to study, how much we admire and like the models, and our own previous successes with similar complex observational projects (Bandura, 1969; 1971). Still, it is not impossible to draft a program of this sort for ourselves. By using positive role models (which then become mental images and blueprints for our eventual action plan), we help ourselves develop the very skills we are observing. Sometimes having a consistent role model and mentor helps, as in the case of an athlete who takes direction from more expert peers or from a coach. Sometimes a combination of role models helps us.

Because I had no previous business experience when I first started my business practice ten years ago, I found it useful to study the decision-making styles of entrepreneurs I admired. I did this from a distance, not knowing many entrepreneurs personally at the time. Unconsciously, I created aggregates of "best case" examples—people I'd seen and heard on television or radio or read about in magazines. I simply imagined how people I admired would handle themselves in certain situations. I "played" with scenarios of my own invention and used my memory of these composites to help me plan a strategy for my business practice.

By watching others do something well (or by thinking about our own past successes, in which case we act as our own role models), we teach our subjective self—brain, nervous system, emotional self—how to get what we objectively want or need. As we train our observational powers and memory, we saturate our consciousness with coded images of what it takes to do whatever we need to do. These codes may be words, gestures or sequences of tasks; these help us duplicate the performance in question. Instead of dwelling on what we don't have, cannot do, are not, we can more profitably become absorbed with having, doing or even being what we want. "Don't dream it, *be* it" was a slogan I heard frequently around the time I started experimenting with this principle.

Being anything requires intense thought and skillful action. We also have to feel our way into new roles. Such thought, feeling and action are optimized by observing those who already are what we want to be; who already do what we want to do, and then trying to experience in vivid sensory terms what it would feel like to be such a person or do a particular thing. Children learn to speak and walk precisely in this manner: they observe, mimic, feelingly comprehend and in time become skillful speakers and walkers in their own right.

This simple, natural technique also generates numerous ideas about what to do next. It is not that any one observation specifically reveals an exact next step, but that our imagination is somehow accelerated, our inventiveness activated as we dwell on a desirable behavior or watch someone behaving in an optimal fashion. This is an adult form of play—one way we, as adults, transform goals into accomplishment. Such play is our re-creational task. By studying and feelingly comprehending someone else or imagining a desired outcome in order to learn how to do or have what we wish, we allow our mind's free-associative abilities to turn things into what they now are not. Playfully, we imagine the unimaginable. Best of all, through these rich envisioning processes we can see ourselves doing what we believe we cannot do. In this way we change our beliefs. In time we are able to meet each moment's demand with increased effectiveness, and quite possibly with increased luck too.

4

Managing Attention, Absorbing Wisdom

The heart has its reasons which reason knows
nothing of.
—BLAISE PASCAL

At midday they saw a beautiful little snow-white bird
sitting on a branch, which sang so sweetly that they
stopped still to listen to it. And when its song was
finished it flapped its wings and flew on in front of
them. They followed it to a little house, on the roof of
which it perched.
—THE BROTHERS GRIMM, "Hansel and Gretel"

A regulated attention and a disciplined mind are helpful allies
when we undergo a major change, crisis or personal growth
project. By contrast, Hansel and Gretel's distraction with the
luscious house cost them dearly. In overcoming an obstacle our
first step may be simply to quiet our minds so that we are not
distracted by worries about things we can do nothing about. As
we learn and practice this art of managing our own attention, we
come to appreciate better what William James meant when he
wrote that we make sense out of chaos, feeling and information,
much as a sculptor selectively expands, or limits, marble with his
tools. The sculptor chooses, in a very specific way, to extricate
one image from among the many different forms hidden in that
stone. In just this way, James wrote, the mind is "at every stage
a theatre of simultaneous possibilities." This means we must,
and certainly can, select one thing over another, suppress, in-
hibit and reinforce "the agency of attention." To create solutions

it helps to get our minds off the problem and think instead about—imagine—the thing we want, as if it existed now.

We can liken our problem to a chunk of marble—dense, immense, immovable. Our attention is a tool with which, we manipulate the marble—selectively expand or limit it—in order to pull out one image from all the possible forms. A focused attention thus creates new sets of attitudes and beliefs and brings to light unexpectedly useful answers, especially if we attend to insights and interior revelations. In time, a disciplined attention also becomes skilled in seeing patterns of meaning and information in the very chaos it watches.

Gregory Bateson addressed the critical role such patterns play in our search for meaning in ourselves and life. He studied both verbal and nonverbal realms of life: art, poetry, nature, linguistics, behavior. In all these he found, and instructed others how to find, patterns, repetition, redundancy and predictability in order to understand life, the universe and the mind itself. Bateson saw all these as orderly and organized—as systemic, living systems. In one remarkable passage in his book *Steps to an Ecology of Mind*, he suggests that information about the unconscious is encoded in outer cultural forms, in art or music, for example, and that the patterns and redundancies of these codes are there so that we can learn the important psychic information housed within us.

In this same vein, Bateson believed the Freudian theory of the unconscious was "upside down." Instead of regarding our conscious life and reason as normal, and our unconscious as mysterious and ever in need of proof or validation (i.e., arguing that this realm does in fact exist; looking to dreams or slips of the tongue, for instance, to ensure ourselves it is really there; etc.), we would do better to think of *all* consciousness as mysterious, not just the nonconscious. Furthermore, our nonconscious is "continually active, all-embracing" and completely necessary (Bateson, 1972, p. 136).

Bateson cites Isadora Duncan's comment, "If I could tell you what it meant, there would be no point to dancing it," and speculates refreshingly that all art is a particular type of message that is diminished, even falsified, by words because it is a message "about the interface between conscious and unconscious." Furthermore, he reminds us that skill in art, in fact all skill, has as its message much that is unconscious, that cannot be communicated verbally. If you have ever visited a museum or art gallery and wondered why you became uneasy when other viewers of the exhibit tried to express verbally what they thought about the works, it may be that their words actually did intrude upon or falsify the message the art conveyed. There are numerous jokes and cartoons about posturing, overintellectualizing art critics who gather around some work and discuss it as if they understood it logically. The ineffable, mysterious message in a piece of art makes it larger, more satiated with information than words can ever transmit. We cannot glibly critique a work of art, because mere verbalizing always lacks something; words are not all-embracing, unlike the codes and messages in the work itself.

In "Love and Joy About Letters," an essay on the alphabet as an art form, artist Ben Shahn quotes at length the great mystic Rabbi Abulafia. Abulafia taught that the alphabets of different cultures held the deepest metaphysical mysteries of life. He believed that one could achieve "the ultimate, ineffable abstraction of union with God" if one were to practice letter writing with devoted, sustained focus. Quoting Abulafia, Shahn describes how instruction was given to the ancient student of letter writing. The student was to clean himself and his clothes thoroughly. If possible, he was to wear only white garments as a symbol of light for mind and heart. If he was practicing his lettering at night, he was to light many candles until the room in which he worked was brightly illumined. He should, in sum, position himself in every way—attitude, physical posture and intent—to serve God. In other words, the lettering session became a meditation, a devoted work session, to be done with absolute mindful attention:

> Now begin to combine a few or many letters, to permute and to combine them until the heart be warm. Then be mindful of their movements, and of what thou canst bring forth by moving them. . . . And when thou seest that by combinations of letters thou canst grasp new things which, by human tradition or by thyself thou wouldst not be able to know, when thou art thus prepared to receive the influx of divine power which flows into thee, then turn all thy true thought to imagine the Name. (Morse, 1972, p. 163)

This "divine power," this grasping of "new things which, by human tradition or by thyself" cannot be known, and Abulafia's final promise that the letterer would understand other things not previously knowable is the mind penetrating its deepest mystery for its own purposes. Perhaps this is how through human effort we meet with and gain rapport with the supernatural. Any activity we do with fixed attention while simultaneously keeping our awareness alert and detached can, eventually and over time, bring us the "new things" which by human tradition cannot be known. Prayer, meditation, devoted absorption—over-belief—are all such activities. These produce knowledge that holds the answers we seek for our life's questions.

To use art, dance, sculpture, poetry, dreams, meditation or various physical disciplines like running or yoga to work through a problem is to gain access to far more information than if one were merely to "think rationally" about the thing. Bateson believed we could appreciate the entire circuitry of the mind by reading the patterns in art forms, from the repetitions and redundancies we found there. To try to comprehend the mind without these is to distort our knowledge of the mind's systematic and integrated nature.*

Opening to the Nonconscious

We worry too much about solving our problems logically, on the level of those problems. Eli Siegel, whose artful book *Self and World* I just discovered, makes this salient comment: "Happiness is the feeling that the self is at one with reality as a whole. The feeling that the will of the self is at one with reality makes for dynamic tranquility. This is what each self must have as its purpose" (Siegel, 1981, p. 165). In precisely this spirit, I maintain that our thinking is at its finest when our mind arrives at a "dynamic tranquility" as a result of having resolved the contradictions of a problem. This resolution is, I believe, most perfectly

---

* Hansel and Gretel's adventure gives added weight to the idea that our unconscious sends us friendly, helpful messages. Images of white birds throughout the tale show us that, if only in the long run, triumph is possible if we pay attention. Then too, the children's highest development and their ability to return home come only after they traverse a large body of water. Water too symbolizes the unconscious. The tale of Hansel and Gretel cannot be understood without reference to these images from the nonconscious, "irrational" aspects of life. By these elements they are greatly aided, as are we.

achieved through the right use of our mind's powers. Dynamic tranquility is a special resolution, attained only when our mind travels beyond what it knows, transcends itself, observes itself with passionately absorbed detachment. Here problems get solved in a big, creatively useful way. Here we find ourselves able to carry out Rabbi Abulafia's instructions: "Render [these matters] whole, and in all their detail."

We must concern ourselves more with becoming whole-seers, with coming to friendly terms with our dynamic tranquility. This is primarily a mental stance, an exercise whose goal is to cultivate an open, transparent relationship between conscious and unconscious. In this way our conscious mind continually receives input, images, fleeting bits or fragments of ideas from its nonconscious, subterranean spouse.

When I am with my most creative friends, our minds play in this arena—the interface of logic and illogic—perhaps without our even knowing it. This is hard to describe, but sometimes the play even joins our minds so that we think of ideas simultaneously. Parents and children who are "on the same wavelength" do this automatically, as do numerous husbands and wives. The point here is not that synchronicity exists—our common experience already tells us that it does—but that there is a realm that is beyond mind as we know it, beyond the neat and tidy systems of our world, beyond that organ which we know as our brain, beyond our logic and rational understanding. Many artists, inventors, composers and writers report that in their finest hours of creation, they simply become vehicles, tap into another dimension of knowing, that this superior knowledge flows through them. Bach reputedly said, "I write the notes as I hear them—it is God who makes the music." Kenneth Atchity, a writer and producer with keen good sense about the creative process, instructs would-be writers to get in touch with their own dreams and visions about what they hope to write. Atchity believes that all writing begins with a dream or an image of what the writer wants to say, and that this dream can occur during sleep, in daydreams, even as a "vivid hallucination that fills in the image of what you must write so precisely that all you finally have to do is transcribe what you see when you close your eyes" (Atchity, 1986, p. 18).

Whether we get ideas from nature, from each other, from

supernatural sources or from our dreams, daydreams or vivid hallucinations seems less significant for creative problem-solving than is our opening ourselves up to the broadest possible tributary of inspiration.

When we use only our rational mind, we are left more or less stupid, uneasy, distracted, unfriendly—in an adversarial stance toward the situation we hope to handle. Anytime we try to solve problems using only a portion of our mind, and a fraction of that portion at that, we can grow uneasy, even frightened. This must be because we are not paying attention to the right or full spectrum of clues. We have multiple intelligences at our disposal, each designed with its own purpose, each aiding the other aspects of our intelligence to help us maneuver through or interpret reality.

We may emerge less comfortable, rather than more confident, after attending certain formal classes in "life instruction" (e.g., how to find a job, how to start a business) because these subjects are often taught in too linear or logical a fashion. This method denies us the opportunity to blend in our own subjective wisdoms with the facts presented. Many of my clients admit feeling scared or inept after attending national career fairs or placement sessions. They hear much valuable information at these sessions, but it is often presented in an impersonal, statistical way or in halls crowded full of competitive, even frenzied, people. A friend who is now a nationally known host for a syndicated radio show was taught by his communications professor in radio school that only one person in his whole graduating class would ever get a well-paying job in the industry. Many students became so upset by that statistic, felt so hopeless and defeated, that they didn't even try to find work in their chosen fields. They accepted their professor's grim logic and his data as a prophecy and, without challenge or faith, resigned themselves to less desirable work.

The mind aided by its nonconscious processes is calmed, corrected and directed by the codes and imprinted skills or understanding of the human race. These inner messages are embedded in the mind's intricate circuitry. These inner clues also hold knowledge, collective awareness and primitive, ancestral species learning that order and organize us so that we feel able to do what must be done. Aided in this way, we gain actual skill to do a thing even though we may not know how we have gained it or why we feel comforted.

Thomas Merton, in his book *The New Man*, suggests that the very grace that permits our nonconscious to flood us with answers and guidance flees from a confused, disordered and overly passionate mind, obsessed with its own emotions. But, Merton reminds us, grace also flees from our tyrannical superego, whose inflexible rigidity as well as "infinitely jealous resourcefulness guards its throne" against insights or what some might call the divine or supernatural sensibilities and directives of the unseen, illogical universe.

Toward a "Higher" Consciousness

More than a decade ago, economist Ernst F. Schumacher wrote that one of the "indispensable conditions of understanding" was to realize that we live in a world of higher and lower. By "higher," he meant not a place up or down on a rigid, spatial ladder, but rather a deep, superior insight, more complexly able to absorb or comprehend the totality of some lesser, lower, thing. "Higher consciousness," then, refers to the elevation of our awareness to include comprehension of more than what was known before. Such comprehension makes us more skillful, insightful, capable. Need I say this achievement influences our solutions, behaviors and life outcomes in like fashion?

In his beautiful book *A Guide for the Perplexed*, Schumacher stresses that it is our job as humans to look at the world and see it whole. Whole-seeing is what I and others mean by "higher." Mental mapmaking, as Schumacher describes it, is only the beginning of whole-seeing. But, he cautions us, without the concepts of higher and lower, we remain stymied:

> The ability to see the Great Truth of the hierarchic structure of the world, which makes it possible to distinguish between higher and lower Levels of Being, is one of the indispensable conditions of understanding. Without it, it is not possible to find out everything's proper and legitimate place. Everything, everywhere can be understood only when its Level of Being is fully taken into account. Many things which are true at a low Level of Being become absurd at a higher level, and of course vice versa. (Schumacher, 1977, p. 14)

Schumacher is saying that all things are relative, that to understand properly we must position ourselves—as perceivers and thinkers—at the loftiest place, the place that comes nearest to the absolute, the universal. Such positioning occurs through varied means: meditation, personal development, openness to art, dance, poetry, sculpture, mythology and so on. As we become aware of what some have termed a unitive consciousness—an unbounded state, calm and interconnected, in which we feel at one with our human powers and with others, with all the world— we feel more hopeful, friendlier toward others and even become accepting of the situation as well. This is the place of awareness we reach when we have successfully focused our attention within, or focused on some device or object used for meditation purposes. The ancients used flames to organize and hold their attention. They gazed at walls—simply looked at blank walls—to calm their emotions and gain objective capability.

Various physical disciplines are useful too for holding and disciplining the attention. For some reason, these practices bring us closer to our own strength and power. In time, the mind disciplined in this fashion develops a sort of "pattern literacy." Through this, incoherent, unrelated bits of data—among which we could not see any connection before—become whole to our perception. Maharishi Mahesh Yogi's well-known adage, "Knowledge is structured in consciousness," applies here: as we expand our awareness, as we grow more conscious (by whatever means we choose) we attain knowledge.

By developing our capacities along these lines—stretching not only our intellectual understanding but our consciousness itself into nonconscious realms—our thinking capacities and thus our human powers increase as well. We gain leverage and the creative flexibility needed to organize fragments of information into useful, whole, perceptual maps.

When we make decisions or try to act before grounding ourselves in the broadest possible awareness, when we fail to think from our deepest or "highest" insights and sensibilities, when we do not fully transcend our problems to see beyond the "impossible," we cannot possibly hope to develop clarity. Our too rational awareness cannot see the ocean for the undue attention it gives a water droplet. Common logic, unaided by higher consciousness, cannot, to use Jerome Bruner's poetic phrase, "move beyond knowledge"—cannot see, or even learn to read, patterns.

If we want to be more able, to blend our own thinking and action so that we develop the street sense or fluidity of action spoken of earlier, we must learn to manage our attention, direct it—like a laser beam—so that as fixed, passionate intention and purpose it helps us be and do and have what we desire. I will return to this theme again and again, each time in a slightly different manner, because its implied lesson is deceptively simple: To master this art we must master our mind. The phrase "master our mind" can mean to control our thought. However, I use the phrase to refer to controlling the mind's functions and processes—not just thought.

The Art of Being Purposeful

In the *Hagakure, The Book of the Samurai,* we read of the benefits of one-pointedness. Although this classic collection of aphorisms was intended as a guide to samurai ethics in the mid-1800s, its text supports those of us who wish to gain personal mastery today. The perfected samurai is self-disciplined even to the point of perceiving his own death as an art form in which he is both artist and art. The way he approaches and handles death becomes his metaphor for life.

The samurai's personal development involved meticulous training of focus, the cultivation of utter guilelessness and of mindfulness—that full, here-and-now presence of mind which precedes right action in ambiguous, uncertain situations. Ideally, thinking and acting have no distinction. Cultivation of mindfulness also helps us gain access to the nonconscious. Again, this promotes right action.

Race-car driver Jackie Stewart, quoted in Edward de Bono's *Tactics,* paints a picture of such mindfulness translated into right action:

> [I have developed] a very complete consumption of visual fact which gets analyzed very clearly. I became able to dispose very fast of the unimportant elements of a situation, and take exactly what I required as input so as to be able to see the relative advantages open to me on the track. Now if there is a slow-moving vehicle in front, a less experienced driver might say, ["Why is it there? Has it blown a tire?"] . . . My vision has become extremely

analytical. It's one of the advantages I have over other people—
that I was able to assemble what I saw, clearly analyze it, bank it
and deal with it. You're talking of microseconds of decisions. (de
Bono, 1984, p. 211)

If we can understand that this is what creative adaptation looks
like on the race track, we can extrapolate and develop this skill,
so that we have it in other parts of our life.

The *Hagakure* instructs the samurai to be concentrated in all
things, in the smallest of things. It teaches us what Stewart and
every other champion know intuitively:

There is surely nothing other than the single purpose of the
present moment. A man's whole life is a succession of moment
after moment. If one fully understands the present moment, there
will be nothing else to do, and nothing else to pursue. Live being
true to the single purpose of the moment. (Yamamoto, 1979,
p. 68)

If we ask ourselves how *we* more ordinary persons can achieve
such purposefulness and presence of mind, we are told:

It is spiritless to think that you cannot attain to that which you
have seen and heard the masters attain. The masters are men.
You are also a man. If you think that you will be inferior in
something, you will be on that road very soon.
    Master Ittei said, ". . . First intention, then enlightenment."
(Ibid., p. 46)

Earlier I suggested that Hansel and Gretel's distraction with
that luscious gingerbread house cost them: they were caught by
the wicked witch because they'd abandoned themselves, left the
demands of the moment, grown preoccupied with food. In the
same way, although the form certainly varies, we adults also get
trapped and done in by our preoccupations—and even more so
during a crisis.

During stressful times we easily grow suspicious of others'
motives, or become engulfed by negative feelings and worries, or
get confused by all the elements in a problem that require handling. We manifest less—not more—intelligence. We rely on
popular notions of what to do instead of thinking for ourselves.
We believe the gloomy things that others say and cannot erase

their negative prophecies from our minds. We think that over-powering evil resides in persons or situations. Of course, at times evil does exist in externals. This is clearly an imperfect world. However, more often than not, the wickedness we fear "out there" is in us—it is really our own darkness, our own dark side or shadow, as Jung called it. We suppress, reject and deny our dark side. Instead of accepting and harnessing it for our own use we project our lost power into externals. Jung wrote that this "dammed-up instinctual force" is terrifically destructive if we do not integrate it into our awareness; its danger exceeds anything our rational mind understands. Until we accept and integrate our own evil, or negativity, we lose thinking power and dilute our own intelligence.

Recently, for example, a friend phoned to talk about a serious business problem. A large, unscrupulous corporation threatened to undermine his small firm with underhanded negotiations. He was frantic, couldn't eat, sleep or think straight. He believed that his world was caving in, and fantasized that he'd be penniless and sleeping under a park bench with only newspapers for blankets. In fact, he was scaring and confusing himself. His attention was caught by this imagined witch or demon, much as Hansel and Gretel were trapped by sweet foods and eventually ensnared by the witch. The evil force my friend thought outside himself was in truth his own creative, potent self, which he cast out, projected, upon others. Thus he failed to use a part of himself (and his intelligences) for his own needs.*

The moment my friend realized that his competitors were not evil incarnate, that he himself had forfeited his own power by suppressing his anger, by believing himself a victim, by always being the "nice guy," he grew calm and gained much-needed determination to fight intelligently. He also started noticing his options. In other words, he regained control. In just this way, by talking with an objective, trusted friend or counselor, by writing in a journal or by using one of many "shadow-personifying" techniques such as those taught by some Jungian or Transpersonal analysts, we can learn (and not too slowly either) to incor-

---

* The poet Robert Bly lucidly describes this phenomenon in his lovely book *A Little Book on the Human Shadow*. He reminds us that the shadow, the dark side, of ourselves is simply the whole unconscious, and "if any help was going to arrive to help lift [someone] out of [his] misery, it would come from the dark side of [his] personality."

porate latent, long-buried powers into our normal awareness. Doing so we also inject multiple intelligences into daily, ordinary functioning. By managing our attention, by disciplining our minds, we stay rooted in the present and thus gain control, vigor and potency.

In truth, we have nothing but the present moment. Being true to its demands is merely being *responsive* and alive within the context of reality. This responsiveness takes practice, but such practice can, in fact must, be done in the midst of daily life simply by elevating the way in which we do every mundane thing.

Since successful creative adaptation ultimately depends on the degree to which we can figure out what to do without over-direction about "how to do it," it is counterproductive always to ask someone else, "Tell me what to do, tell me how to go about it." A better question is: "What experiments can I run *to teach myself* how to do this or that thing?"

Of course, we do not have time to conduct our life by trial and error. Recently I purchased a computer and hired a consultant to teach me how to use it; in this case as in others, it was obviously a waste of energy and time to try to figure out everything alone. But in some areas of life, in the gray, subjective areas especially, if we lean too heavily on another's rules for self-rescue or ways to live, we limit ourselves. We defeat our further development as problem solvers by failing to practice independent thinking and losing the opportunity to engage ourselves fully with problems. The intensity of our detached absorption with a matter produces insight, dynamic tranquility, revelation.

5

Learning to Let Go

Are you willing to be made nothing?
dipped into oblivion
If not, you will never really change.
—D. H. LAWRENCE

When Hansel and Gretel fell into her hands she
laughed maliciously and said jeeringly, "I've got them
now. They won't escape me." . . . Gretel began to cry
bitterly. But it was no use. She had to do what the
wicked witch commanded.
—THE BROTHERS GRIMM, "Hansel and Gretel"

Hansel and Gretel undergo several mind shifts before being able
to save themselves. For example, they come to terms with the
fact that they are lost and can no longer rely on pebbles or bread
crumbs for self-rescue. This accepted, they are then free to turn
their attention to other resources, such as their own wits or the
little creatures of the forest. Next, they realize they must curb
their wish to be endlessly gratified by the delicious gingerbread
house. Then too, they learn to substitute purposeful action for
their undisciplined natures. Still later, they discover that someone they thought was a compassionate, giving mother figure is
really a sinister demon who wants to cook them for her dinner.
This last blow seems to be the very thing they need to let go of
their conventional thinking and do whatever they must to
escape—even kill a witch. As abhorrent as this last act may be,
it is the spontaneous gesture that ensures the children their freedom. To arrive at this point of willingness each surrenders to the

realities of the situation. The children let go of who they were then they started their ordeal.

Hansel and Gretel also demonstrate their openness to the supernatural. They embrace what is logically impossible, integrate irrational episodes quite naturally into their adventure as though these were everyday events. Later in the story, when they can cross a big lake only by riding on a white duck's back, they don't argue, "I'm too big to ride this creature; its back is too small." They simply hop on and are carried to shore. If theirs is a miracle or dream rescue, so be it. The result of their faith in these magical events is their safety: they are just as secure riding on the duck as if a boat had transported them. They integrate these two worlds—logic and illogic—for their happy end, as we must do for ours. In fact, it is only the logical, conscious mind that makes a duality of these unalike thought processes: logic and illogic, conscious and nonconscious are dual aspects of our nature precisely because we make it dual, experience it in this way. Whatever problem we have today, if we can return to the depth, wisdom, experience and nondual state of being of children, our safety is assured. For this state, our advantage lies in nonentrenchment.

"Nonentrenchment," the term used by Professor Robert J. Sternberg in his writings on intelligence, describes exactly this sort of letting go. To Sternberg, the word denotes a higher-order brain function: the way the mind solves word or number puzzles, or thinks in new conceptual frameworks and applies these to old knowledge structures. By tracking an individual's way of responding to complex, illogical puzzles, researchers can understand the way that person "lifts" above common ways of seeing and creates new contexts in which to solve problems at elevated levels of perception. Such functioning agility has wider application. I use the term to define a state of psychological "nonstuckness," as well as to describe a mode of thinking.

Nonentrenchment as a life posture is made possible by our mind's ability to rise out of its conventional, well-grooved thought tracks. In this, it serves as both intellectual and psychological tool, one of our most critical survival mechanisms. Through nonentrenchment we extend our thinking, play with possibilities and thereby—in time—creatively restructure our personal reality for adaptive purposes.

Nonentrenchment relies on both conscious and nonconscious thought processes, and conscious will or volition. It is full of paradox. For example, researchers emphasize that we grow only if we keep an open mind and stay aware of our biases and blind spots. I agree. A closed mind can lead to rigid responses. However, there are times when we must consciously close our minds and screen out certain possibilities, while keeping open to the potential inherent in the options we are creating. The metanoic process described earlier, and later, involves just such conscious, controlled open-mindedness. This is tricky.

Nonentrenchment helps us with this unusual feat, as we maintain both mental flexibility and emotional objectivity toward our vested interests or what others hold in high esteem. To be non-entrenched, in this larger sense, means to transcend what we know in order to construct perceptive innovative systems. In other words, the nonentrenched mind reinvents and reconfigures its own experience. It selectively stays closed to some things while remaining open to others.

Nonentrenchment is synonymous with creative functioning. In this state we pledge ourselves to an unknown future where there are no guarantees, no predictable paths to follow. Nonentrenched thinking frees us of old, outworn ideas and opens us to the amazing notion that we create our personal reality, our ideas, our experience, even (perhaps especially) our entire belief system. To understand this, even to be willing to try to understand this, can be life-preserving, but it can also shatter us, destroy the linear, logical thought process that has defined our life. To look more closely at nonentrenchment, we should examine its opposite—a *closed* way of thinking and being.

Closed and Entrenched

A reader of my book on right livelihood whom I will call Norman wrote to me criticizing the way I glossed over what he called "the realities of the job market." I paraphrase his letter:

> You psychologists are all alike—dishonest. You lie about the realities of the marketplace. You never mention vicious competition or back-biting or greed. You ignore the fact that money, vested interest and expediency rule. Most people don't live in your world.

Norman describes his own experience to bolster his point, and reveals himself to be firmly entrenched in a failed, lonely self-view and a pessimistic world view.

As I have said, and will suggest again, attention is power. It is creative power. Norman's inner gaze is fixed on a world without hope. He has closed his perceptual doors to the open, the novel, the possible, and apparently lacks positive role models or memory.

> I doubt if you can help me, but wish you could. At forty, I've known failure all my life. I'm the chickenhearted boy from a family of chickenhearted men. Women find me unattractive, and in fact I am impotent. When I was small, I was every bully's mark. In high school I didn't date, dance or fuck. Now I can't hold a job or sustain a relationship. I've failed at everything and consider ending it all.

He continues along these morose lines, demonstrating how he retains, strengthens and selectively screens in the ideas and behaviors that maintain his status quo, while screening out those that might extricate him from his dilemma.

Norman's dwelling on lethal, unproductive memories amounts to his ongoing meditation. His hold on and fascination with negative cues and images produces negative life experiences as surely as apple seeds eventually produce apples.

Norman hammers the final few nails in his behavioral coffin when he closes his mind to the possibility of improvement or getting help from anyone else:

> Don't tell me to see a therapist. I've seen every shrink that's worth trying, and have only contempt for them all. Maybe therapists can help some people, but to me they're con artists and cheats, the dregs of the universe, right down in the bowels of humanity with politicians, pickpockets and pimps.

This is, he admits, a "sour, angry and somewhat lopsided viewpoint," but he adds that it is a fairly accurate description of himself. He closes by saying he believes that no matter how many manageable, positive steps he takes, he'll be a lost, lonely man for the rest of his life.

"As ye believe, so be it unto you"; this summarizes my response to him. Norman's mind is obviously made up at the deepest level of belief—there is nothing I can say to change it. To be freed, he must develop a nonentrenched stance, must choose to open his mind to a new set of ideas that embrace infinite possibilities, including his having a positive, productive relationship to life.

If as individuals we believe we are doomed, we are. We limit our growth and preclude self-rescue by being more faithful to our entrenched views than to life itself. Norman is fascinated with failure. He forbids change by constantly reinforcing his own negative version of his life.

From the standpoint of his adaptive efficiency (i.e., locating a fulfilling job, life happiness, establishing bonds with others) the main question for gloomy Norman is: Does this absorption with the past work? That is, does it produce the results Norman seems consciously to want? Clearly not. His attention, rooted as it is in his unhappy past, severely limits the new information he uncovers as he searches for solutions. Ironically, Norman believes he already has his solutions, his truths. His focus on his sad history may be symptomatic of his overall resistance to believing in other possibilities. This resistance—lack of faith, doubt, unbelief—*constricts* the mind's access to its nonconscious realms—the abundant domain of its answers. Instead of dwelling on the past, Norman needs to train his mind to dwell on new images and ideas.

Behavior follows along quite obediently once we firmly plant the appropriate seeds of right thinking in our imagination. The process also works the other way around: altering our behavior will help us change the images in our mind. Either thinking or behaving anew, can break the old pattern, can signify to our unconscious that we are ready to receive its inherent wisdom along the lines of our hoped-for change, idea or goal.

Digging Out

Norman is angry. But anger need not stop him or anyone else. Anger can be put to creative, productive use and can be a useful tool in letting go of an entrenched self-view. Anger can fuel determination and even resolve contradictory, negative emotions. We can work through the anger born of grief, loss or frustration by our witness, or testimony, about what we have experienced. People who lose a loved one find that they cannot resume healthy, full functioning until they speak out about the issue, and formally speak about what the ordeal has meant to or taught them. On a large scale, the Vietnam Memorial in Washington, D.C., is an illustration of how our entire country is attempting to work through its grief and its other strong emotions about family, friends and neighbors who died in that war. However, not everyone is healthy enough to reroute grief or anger willingly in this way. Some people are simply stuck in the throes of what could be likened to a child's tantrum. They cannot, will not let go of their negativity.

When we are *too* angry—and this occurs when we project, suppress, deny or have unresolved anger—we may be unwilling to forgive, to let go of resentments. Nursing old wounds is perhaps consoling in some ways, but we deny ourselves adaptive power by wallowing in negativity. We shoot ourselves in the foot when we fail to express and resolve anger. On the other hand, we can turn anger into productive, self-repairing behavior—a creative act wherein we use anger for life instead of against it.

I also believe desire for an answer helps lift us out of entrenched thinking. This desire is predicated on a belief— however frail—that answers do exist and are worth the effort of our searchings.

Our attitude, be it admiration or disdain, toward the processes of our own nonconscious mind can either open or shut the doors to helpful answers and ways of being. The answers we seek exist in our nonconscious world, in some form. At the very least our best current directions are there, waiting to guide us to answers in the external. Whether through primary thought processes, or creative incubation, or some other avenue like keeping a journal or studying our dreams, the more creative we are, the more able we are to tap into not fully conscious information. I suggest our intention to discover our nonconscious world (i.e., our desire for answers, our willingness to believe those answers exist, our trust in our own primary thought processes, our openness to many categories of the possible) is a key to our nonconscious world.

To foster change we must build a more hopeful belief system.

This is, in part, the metanoia I refer to all along—that whole-brained conversion of mind and heart stimulated by a fixed, absorbed focus on a single goal, quest or vision. Metanoia begins with our willingness to believe in the possibility of our goal or vision. Which is not to say we already believe—only that we are willing to believe, that we stay open.

If creative adaptation is a measure of the success with which our minds solve problems, then we must teach our minds to seek the answers among "an astronomical number of possibilities," namely, those answers available from our interior resources. And if creative adaptation depends on our mind's flexibility, then we must come to grips with whatever fear, anger or resistance keeps us rapidly disbelieving and thus stuck in untenable circumstances. Working with competent therapists, talking to trusted friends or religious counselors, or even exploring self-help methods (e.g., journal writing, taping a stream-of-consciousness audio journal) can help. To change our early, basic, quite solid life-shaping beliefs, and to prove to ourselves that reality is more promising than it seems at present, we may even need to find a spiritual director, therapist, teacher or guide who can, responsibly, help us court nonconscious solutions.

This route is more ancient than new. For example, shamanism, a 100,000-year-old tradition of healing and knowledge, like the healing arts practiced by medicine men and women in both South and North America, ministered to people's physical ailments by taking into account their emotional and spiritual needs.

It would seem that "primitive" rites and ancient health-care practitioners realized that all healing is predicated on both spiritual—that is, creative, nonconscious, illogical, supernatural—as well as physical processes. To initiate these processes, it was understood centuries ago that individuals must transcend their normal state of ordinary consciousness and enter some other state akin to a trance. In our century, psychoanalysis and other therapies may replicate this process, only they do so over a much longer time frame: the constant reinforcement of teaching, discussion and dialogue, and ongoing self-disclosures, dream analysis and repetitions of new ideas that are inherent to verbal therapies seem our modern interpretation of the mental restructurings (and subsequent healings) of the ancients.

A Case History:
Considering the Possible

A Vietnam veteran, Hank* is as strong-willed in his pursuit of health as Norman is in resisting it. Whereas the latter had no history of successes (making his change of mind about himself difficult), Hank's memory bank is full of successes. However, none of his past victories fostered his new objectives.

Hank's job was at stake given his abrasive, intimidating and argumentative relationships with almost everyone. He had been given an ultimatum: Either learn to get along with people or leave the company. The senior officer who referred him re-counted a litany of abuses, arguments and personnel problems that Hank had caused. People didn't like or trust him. He grilled colleagues who presented reports during meetings as if he were the prosecuting attorney and they the criminals. He used sarcasm to intimidate and control. He was close-minded, rigidly detail-oriented. "Anything to win a point," was his motto. The president of his firm told me, "He's lasted this long only because he's brilliant in his field. We've given him six months to improve or else find a job in another company."

My first impression of Hank was of a bantamweight boxer or an actor in a war film, not a business executive. He was squarely built, tightly controlled. Hank's eyes seemed *overly* focused; his jaw was clenched. He seemed to expect attack. Months later, he told me that he'd had a massive headache at our first meeting; the thought of having to work with someone of my ilk made him sick. Characteristically, he decided to do whatever was necessary to "put things right."

Hank was forthright. Had he been more manipulative, he might have managed to mask his argumentative, offensive

---

* As with Steven in chapter 3, Hank is a synthesis of many people, both men and women. Yearly I meet dozens of executives thought to be abrasive or unproductively aggressive. Their peers avoid them, subordinates fear them, senior managers look the other way—especially when they are technically or analytically gifted. In fact, these are usually sensitive people who have received insensitive treatment and training. "Hank" seems a helpful prototype, since most of these executives are well schooled in military models of management and behavior or fixated on football metaphors. Of course retired military people can be brilliant statesmen. I have worked for, and admired, several. However, without question, people like Hank need to improve their interpersonal skills, and depending on their age and motivation, this can take some doing.

attitude, but there was nothing phony or slick about him. He'd had success in his life with his present traits and mannerisms and he didn't want to change. He said he resented being asked to change, but he also understood why he had to improve.

When I explained that our goal would be not so much to "change" him as to help him learn to draw out behaviors and attitudes already present—if in latent, undeveloped form—he showed relief. He was ready to proceed, though as it turned out it was a lengthy process.

I can best summarize the work by saying that Hank had taught himself to be a master fighter and he now had to learn to be a peacemaker, a master diplomat. Hank viewed people as his opponents and enemies. He said it was almost impossible to "turn off" the images of violence he had brought back from Vietnam. In business dealings, if anyone showed self-doubt, hesitance or even gentleness, Hank's urge was to attack.

In his personal life, he was also closed. Not surprisingly, his marriage was in trouble, and had lasted, he admitted, only because his wife was intelligent, patient and intuitively knew he loved her. Hank yearned to improve his family life, especially since he and his wife had just had a son. He craved open affection and intimacy with them both.

Initially I was surprised that Hank turned so eagerly toward our development program, but I soon realized that he put the same ferocious energy and zeal into this work as he had put into his military battles. Hank's willingness to try new behaviors was touching, if a bit overdone. He was scrupulously honest, objective and above all tenacious. While his intense commitment helped him begin the program, my sense was that in time Hank's striving, his 110-percent drive to conquer problems would also have to be relinquished.*

---

* After six months, I recommended that Hank begin weekly sessions of clinical therapy and occasional visits to the Menninger Clinic in Kansas City, whose Executive Development program I have recommended to many corporate clients over the years. Often a mix of offerings (individual dialogue and feedback; ongoing psychotherapy; various seminars; books and other readings; lectures; and so forth) is the best program for adult learning problems. When a gifted, willing, but well-entrenched adult is ready to grow, total immersion in the new learning offers maximum benefit in minimum time. This total immersion more reliably approximates the self-view and world-view restructuring addressed earlier in remarks about metanoia.

Hank eventually saved himself (and his career) by his active willingness to participate in his own development. This too illustrates creative adaptation. Creative adaptors move bit by bit, positively, with little reserve or reassurance toward their goals. Committed, they choose their path, even if it is the more difficult, distasteful one. Another way of putting this is that creative adaptives take full personal responsibility for the problem they want to solve. They do not blame; nor do their normal resistances undo their overall efforts. Hank's inherent emotional health and willingness ensured his success. In time (and he is still working at it) he will stop seeing the world through a warrior's eyes. His gentle, humane side may always have sharp edges. He may easily slip back into old ways, but Hank will reconfigure his perceptual maps. He will gain the option of having an affectionate, cooperative relationship with family and work colleagues.

Nonentrenchment as Survival Stategy

Sometimes, in order to survive, more than behavior modification is needed. We must completely alter our world view. We not only must abandon what we used to think true but must also, simultaneously, build faith in a new set of ideas.

In a worst-case scenario, people who are terminally ill have a greater likelihood of surviving if they believe they will survive. Their belief in their ability to recover empowers and sustains them while they undergo treatment, and gives them the wherewithal to argue with doctors and the strength to be assertive on their own behalf. And more: their hopefulness guarantees them the inner balance to keep their wits while hearing friends, family, physicians, perhaps even the media speak about their illness in morbid images and dire statistics.

If they refuse to be victims in the course of their healing (and they must refuse if they are to survive), it is because they retain optimism in the face of a pessimistic social order. In order to go against the grain of other people's thinking and beliefs, they must ground themselves firmly in a perceptual frame of reference that supports their own best interests. Another term for such a perceptual framework is "personal reality."

Cancer specialist and now well-known author Dr. Bernie Siegel treats this subject persuasively in his best-seller *Love, Medicine & Miracles*. He offers example after example of people who had to change their entire way of relating to life (i.e., to their spouses, their families, themselves) in order to get better. He describes the "exceptional patient" as a survivor who does not participate in his own defeat. Exceptional patients possess an unusually vigorous will to live. Dr. Siegel and his patients actively demonstrate that love of life, love of self and love for others bolsters hopefulness. Their optimism may be a critical factor in their survival.

A provocative aspect of Siegel's narrative is his description of the battles he had with the medical establishment. Instead of hearing his observations about exceptional patients openmindedly, the response was, in Siegel's words, "hard-nosed skepticism, if not outright scorn."

> Each discussion turned into a battle of wits, a game of "my statistics against yours." Almost no one was willing to admit, "Well, maybe there's something there. I'll try it." As a result, even though there is now plenty of scientific data to argue for psychotherapy in treatment of cancer and other diseases, I became convinced that *statistics rarely alter deeply held beliefs* [my emphasis]. Numbers can be manipulated to make bias seem logic. *Rather than dwell on statistics, I now concentrate on individual* experiences. To change the mind, one must often speak to the heart . . . and listen. Beliefs are a matter of faith, not logic. (Siegel, 1987, p. 32)

Many will wonder, reading these lines, "What if I am not optimistic when faced with my own life traumas? What if I don't have a doctor like Siegel? What if I don't really believe I can improve things?" Then—I suggest again—we can learn to *change our minds*, alter the nature of our personal reality, and find the happiest options available to us. We ourselves can create these options over time with a bit of work. My own experience tells me we can do a great deal to repair our state of mind when we have hit the wall of despair.

The relative poverty of our knowledge about altering our reality is clear. We are not taught how to do this. There are few contemporary role models to help us along. Like Hansel and Gretel, in this learning we are quite alone. The few teachers who have such experience rarely teach or talk about it. Ancient cultures do have elders or, now, stories and legends that teach youngsters how to restructure reality in their favor. While Western fairy tales and myths cover the same subject in varied ways, they do so in more cryptic fashion. We have almost no tradition and few resources to show us how to believe in miracles. The popularity of the grass-roots best-seller and spiritual training program *A Course in Miracles* attests to the fact that today's adults are eager for such knowledge.

As a result of our spiritual impoverishment, most of us don't realize that we possess within ourselves the power to create or destroy our own belief systems. While discussing theology with a business colleague, I once disclosed that I'd actively chosen some of my beliefs. He said, with not a little disdain and finality, "We can't choose our beliefs."

We can, and unconsciously *do*, choose our beliefs. That is exactly what the enculturation process of childhood entails. We know, for instance, that as an infant the child experiences his body's interacting with the environment, and with others, and begins to get an idea of what he is like. This is the start of self-concept (Yamamoto, 1972). Onto this unconscious foundation are then built variations of all sorts, other aspects of beliefs about the self, based on whatever gradients of experiences we have throughout life.

For the most part, we grow up imprinted by what our parents see, think and do. We believe the world is largely as it is described to us. These thoughts and perceptions become belief systems—bodies of thought developed through our interaction with others and the environment. These early beliefs are gained somewhat passively (except among a minute handful of enlightened youngsters). Later in adulthood, however, it would seem almost anyone could take an active choice-maker's role in re-creating belief.

We can learn about our belief systems by asking, "Where did I learn this or that idea? How life-supportive are my notions? How productive or vital were those who taught me what the world was like? What was I taught I should or should not be, do, have, think?" We can choose (actually, *create* is more precise a word) new beliefs that better serve us and our life's overall intent.

In her Seth series, written in the seventies, Jane Roberts describes quite specifically how belief systems are formed and altered. She postulates that we can change our life experience by changing our beliefs about ourselves and our world:*

> Your experience in the world of physical matter flows outward from the center of your inner psyche. Then you perceive this experience. Exterior events, circumstances and conditions are meant as a kind of living feedback. Altering the state of the psyche automatically alters the physical circumstances. . . .
>
> You change even the most permanent-seeming conditions of your life constantly through the varying attitudes you have toward them. There is nothing in your exterior experience that did not originate with you. (Roberts, 1974, p. 11)

Nonentrenchment involves having faith in what we *can* accomplish (as opposed to clinging tenaciously to what we cannot do), then creatively reconceptualizing our ideas and circumstances. This too is grounded in the three central characteristics discussed previously: learning resourcefulness, positive self-valuation and growth toward autonomy. We can hardly build faith in an ambiguous, uncertain future or see things in a fresh, positive light if we are too easily thrown off balance, if we are confused, don't believe in ourselves or are too dependent on conventional ideas and authority figures.

A Case Study:
Seeing in a New Way

Sometimes circumstances to which we must adapt are so painful that the trauma extends beyond mere business or interpersonal

---

* More recently, the neurolinguistic approach to restructuring beliefs and reality systems has expanded on these themes. *Unlimited Power*, a popular book by Anthony Robbins, may also prove useful to readers who want specific techniques along these lines. The popular, original writings of neurolinguistic founders Richard Bandler and John Grinder are well-known to growing numbers of therapists and trainers. Their techniques, such as anchoring or reframing, are excellent tools for the reality-shaping goals under discussion. And long before Seth, neurolinguistics or modeling theory, selected theologians have taught this esoteric wisdom. For instance, the "prosperity" enthusiast, Reverand Ike, has for decades been educating his congregation in the subtle nuances of consciousness training through positive visualization and affirmation.

problems, sometimes beyond even our desire to live. When our choice is between life or death it is preferable, for most of us, to live. We vote with our attitudes and behaviors for whatever will extend life. In some cases, for instance when we lose a loved one, life as we have known it loses value. Then what?

If we can muster the will to endure the grief process, we can survive and emerge intact on the other side. In such cases, we must use our minds to help us detach emotionally from the intense pain so that we can think objectively and gain time to re-create a life worth living. If one discovered one was going blind,* it would be critical to creative adaptation to reconstruct one's self and one's life purpose within the new reality system of sightlessness. This task of reconstructing self and world means adopting a nonentrenched mind-set in a more intense, personally relevant way than would be required if we were simply playing an intellectual game. Here the very meaning of life is at stake. Here our way of relating to and communicating with others, our way of getting around, our security as persons are involved. Resourcefully solving these problems requires radically new learning. This is ground zero for starting over, where we create a fresh life strategy.

A blind woman, writing autobiographically in a psychological journal, describes how she learned to let go and restructure her whole life. Three years before actually becoming blind she was told she would lose her sight. After the initial shock she adjusted to a progressively unappealing trauma. Her sight dimmed, she underwent repeated eye surgery, she endured various other hardships—such as having her oldest son serve in Vietnam—and eventually she lost her sight. Hesitatingly, very gradually, she reconstructed her life and self-image. She passed through all those stages familiar to the dying: shock, denial, anger, guilt.

Perhaps her quickest lessons—although none was easy—were the technical ones: Braille, typing, orientation and mobility. The more profound part of her learning was the complete restructuring of self and world necessitated by sightlessness. Vision had

---

* Most of us have an intense fear of blindness, a fact demonstrated by a national poll several years ago in which adults said that blindness was second only to cancer as their most dreaded health problem.

been her "most important aesthetic experience." When she realized she would have to let go of it, she considered suicide.

Ironically, this consideration was her turning point, as it seems to be for all of us who must hit bottom before we can go up. When we willingly opt for life lived according to the realities of a new paradigm—whatever these may be—we commit to the new construct with revitalized power. We emerge from the trauma enlarged in our own eyes, if not also in the eyes of others, and we are also radically changed and recharged within.

In this woman's case, as soon as she decided to live, she underwent a transformation that brought her life potency and productivity. Today she is a therapist who helps others adjust to blindness; but first she had to die as a sighted person and experience rebirth as a blind person. She writes about her low point:

> In this crisis—which I lived through in an intensely private way—I finally decided to resume my formal university education, even though I could no longer see. It was not enough to go on living an empty life.
>
> I have discovered that . . . learning a new skill, such as orientation and mobility or typing, accomplishes a kind of functional cure, but it is not necessarily the kind of healing that leads one to confront and re-evaluate such issues as the meaning of one's life. (Lampl and Oliver, 1985, pp. 302–303)

When she decided to go on with her life, she understood what it meant to give up to a "mystery beyond self" which can be understood only symbolically. I suggest this giving up or surrender is part and parcel of nonentrenchment, although for each person the opportunity for surrender is different.

The interior readjustment made when we hit our lowest point may be exactly what allows the solutions to surface in our awareness. Then our defenses drop and we surrender to what is and must be. Those who do not give themselves over to the new in such a deep way might never adapt creatively. These deep adjustments are not formula processes. They take us beyond our conscious levels of understanding. And as noted, beyond the conscious may be our true creative power. The ideas gained in or from this state provide revitalized road maps for life; they call forth special ways of living that take on transcendent meaning for the individual involved.

Nonentrenchment as Access to Metanoia

Unlearning, or letting go, relates to changing thought patterns, habits, life-styles and even entire belief systems. Letting go of all that is dear or familiar can be our starting point of power. We surrender all we previously have clung to as worthwhile. When we leap into an abyss in order to honor life, when we die to one reality, to our self-perception or to the world as we have valued it, we experience rebirth as a larger, mysteriously expanded self. Then—and only then—is our conversion complete. In this case, we create an entirely transformed relationship with ourselves and with the world. The novel endpoint—that new life posture, which we thought impossible for us to experience given the depth of our despair—opens up to us almost in direct proportion to our willingness to let everything else go.

I have written elsewhere (Sinetar, 1985) of the need to die to our small self as a first step to living as a larger self. This "dying" enables us to consider life in a fresh, reconceptualized manner. Here we return to the metanoia phenomenon.

Joseph Chilton Pearce writes eloquently of the metanoic process.

> Metanoia restructures, to varying degrees and even for varying lengths of time, those basic representations of reality inherited from the past. On those representations we base our notions or concepts of what is real. In turn, our notions of what is real direct our perceptual apparatus, that network of senses that tells us what we feel, hear, see and so on. This is not a simple subjective maneuver, but a reality-shaping procedure. (Pearce, 1976, p. 13)

Nonentrenchment is interwoven with the metanoic process. In life-threatening situations, this mode of thinking and behavior intensifies our unlearning and erases or regroups the brain's stored data so that personal realities shift and change. Whether we die to an idea we previously held sacred, or to a self-view or world view, or whether, as Pearce describes, we touch fire without being burned, is not as important as the fact that we have this innate power. Our minds are equipped to act as architects and to engineer new conceptual frameworks for our lives. These architectures of belief are abstract and invisible, granted, but solid nonetheless. However, we can remodel these belief structures. Predictable forks appear routinely in our road of choices, especially as we move toward psychological health. It is then that we realize we can pledge ourselves freely to whatever or whomever we want. Even young children realize this freedom (Erikson, 1964). This is when souls are saved or lost. Either we commit our loyalties to truth or to falsehood. In the language of Transactional Analysis, these times are called spellbreakers, and I don't want to understate the seriousness of these turning points.

If we move toward life and truth, we turn our life upside down. We feel something akin to complete self-surrender, a letting go or giving up of all we've known or tried to control. We feel an exhilarating mix of fear and excitement. We answer yes to life without reservation. If we choose to go in the direction of the spell, the old dishonesty, the self-defeating script, then our subsequent fraudulence forces our spirit to commit real treason against itself (Buber, 1952). These choices have grave consequences, as we see daily in each other's eyes and vitality.

The world we perceive is truly our creation—not because the external, physical world is an illusion, but at least in part because we ourselves edit outer reality to conform to our preselected beliefs. When we face something untenable, it is possible to re-create our conceptual systems and engineer a way of seeing things, and living life, so that purpose, meaning and overarching universal order return. By this act, we re-engage ourselves fully with life. This choice in and of itself, regardless of outcome, can bring healing. Pearce writes of "metaphoric mutation," through which we can create new life and health where illness has existed. In sum, we can reverse causality:

> If an arbitrary and premature death is announced as your statistical imperative, why not give up allegiance to that system, and devote yourself to something less statistical? . . .
>
> Granted, the statistical world is a broad and powerful way. You would need a strong image for the new goal to break completely with the bad-news system and risk your life in a new one. . . . If you hold and serve the question, until all ambiguity is erased and you really believe in your question, it will be answered. (Pearce, 1976, p. 113)

Let me describe this matter of letting go in yet another way, this time using a story about St. Francis's conversion experience. G. K. Chesterton, in his lovely book *St. Francis of Assisi*, describes the metanoic phenomenon as an upside-down process. Before he was a religious figure, young Francis responded to a dream or vision instructing him to get up from his sickbed and immediately go into battle. As he rode out of his small hometown boasting that he would return a great prince, he took ill again and had another dream, informing him that he had misinterpreted the first dream and that he should return home. Obediently, miserably, shamefacedly, he did so. Chesterton vividly describes it as "his first descent into what is called the valley of humiliation, which seemed to him very rocky and desolate, but in which he was afterwards to find many flowers" (Chesterton, 1957, p. 51).

Francis entered a bleak period of his life. He was thought to be a fool and a lunatic. He made public gaffes that were so perplexing his own father rejected him. He gave away goods he was supposed to protect; he disrobed in public and threw all his clothes away; he wandered the streets as a rag man. Finally, dejected and crushed, Francis went into a cave for a lengthy, indefinite period. Perhaps he went there to reflect on his strange conduct and try to comprehend it. Perhaps he went there to escape the ridicule of family and friends or to grieve. Whatever his reasons for retreat, something miraculous happened in that abyss—some inexplicable experience or mind shift changed his reality, releasing all his powers, powers he then used for a lifetime of service to God.

Chesterton relates the familiar childhood fantasy of digging a tunnel through the earth and coming out on the other side to St. Francis's conversion. I find this interpretation especially helpful to our exploration of nonentrenchment and metanoia.

> We cannot follow St. Francis to that final spiritual overturn in which complete humiliation becomes complete holiness or happiness, because we have never been there. I for one do not profess to follow it any further than that first breaking down of the romantic barricades of boyish vanity. . . . But whatever else it was, it was so far analogous to the story of the man making a tunnel through the earth that it did mean a man going down and down until, at some mysterious moment, he begins to go up and up. (Ibid., p. 73)

I love Chesterton for writing this. His words teach us so much: we can survive the living nightmare. What is more, we can adapt to things that are distasteful, troublesome and unfamiliar, and in a surprising way, one much better, brighter, more magical than the old. Chesterton adds this endearing touch:

> Of the intrinsic, internal essence of the experience, I make no pretense of writing at all. But the external effect of it . . . may be expressed by saying that when Francis came forth from his cave of vision, he was wearing the same word "fool" as a feather in his cap, as a crest or as even a crown. (Ibid., p. 74)

The man went on being a fool of sorts; his whole life was riddled with unusual, even laughable acts. But he became "the court fool of the King of Paradise." In other words, he became a saint—so transformed was he at the core.

So too can we be transformed, but only if and when we become willing to accept our dilemma in a new and reconfigured light. This acceptance in and of itself is nothing short of total interior revolution. I sense this occurrence is the hallmark of optimum levels of health, the start of a unitive consciousness that reflects a much-heightened discourse among nonconscious mental processes, the conscious mind and external events.

Those who believe in saints, as I do, will say only a grace and not any action of our own permits instantaneous conversion such as this. Perhaps our ardent, keen desire to reconstruct our lives when we hit rock bottom is the grace. For surely the interior mechanics for personal reconstruction have already been given as a gift; not using this gift may be a grave error, in both judgment and appreciation. Were we not taught: "Ask, believing, and ye shall receive."*

Transformation often stems from extremes of emotion: utter desolation or ecstatic joy. These offer opportunities for growth and reconceptualization. It is not that we engineer ourselves into such situations (usually at the lowest points of our lives we wish to be anywhere else), but if we can just let go, can simply disengage, we afford ourselves a chance to see things differently.

---

* Merton's reminder that metanoia is impossible without the work of grace is worth repeating. But, he adds, "if the gift be rare, it is . . . because of our fear, our blindness, our ignorance, our hatred of risk. For after all, in order to make this leap out of ourselves we have to be willing to let go of everything that is our own—all our own plans, all our own hesitations, all our own judgments." This does not mean we abandon thought or action, but that we accept and ready ourselves for anything that God's grace gives to our lives (Merton, 1961, p. 127).

Joseph Chilton Pearce provides helpful criteria for engineering our own conversion:

· We consciously must desire the experience.
· We must detach from the commonplace. (This risk-taking behavior means thinking through data or experimenting on our own or with unconventional and unusual sources of information, experts, etc.)
· We must passionately commit to building a new construct, which involves intense study or preparation, gathering of information, a mind dominated by the ideas or solutions needed for our situation.*

A central skill in all of this involves learning how to let go of the things we think we cannot do without. I do not suggest we simulate such learning, merely that we ask ourselves what it would mean to give up something on which we now depend. Gradually, as we give thought to this question, the ways and means present themselves for appropriately and safely learning how to let go. Above all, "how" involves first our mind-set about "what"—a willingness simply to consider the "impossible" as specifically and concretely as we can.

It takes flexibility to experiment our way toward change, to work along diligently without road maps or guarantees. Our resourceful learning skills help us adapt creatively. This includes allowing ourselves a chance to rest, to retreat, to regress occasionally and recover from the challenge we have assumed, and seems especially true in the initial phases of a challenge when we wonder what our future holds. Optimism can help us overcome uncertainty. With faith in our ability to learn we gain a type of self-opinion that permits failure, yet—even in failure—clings to hope, feelings of worth, the promise of fulfilled potential. It is to these learning tools that we next turn our attention.

---

* Lynette in chapter 2, and Hank earlier in this chapter are case examples of what it takes to "commit passionately" to building a new construct. It is worth noting that both of them retained competent therapists to help them along, much as others might retain an architect to help them build a house.

6

The Creative Power in High Self-Esteem

> What good is creativity if the owner is afraid to use it?
> —Sister Grace Pilon, *Peace of Mind at an Early Age*

> Every morning the [witch] hobbled out to the stable
> and cried, "Hansel, put out your finger so that I may
> feel if you are getting fat." But Hansel always stretched
> out a bone, and the old woman, whose eyes were dim
> couldn't see it, thinking always it was Hansel's finger,
> wondered why he fattened so slowly.
> —The Brothers Grimm, "Hansel and Gretel"

Only if we grow to value our basic dignity and worth as persons can we view ourselves and our lives objectively, and then articulate our needs. These creative adaptive skills give us power to manipulate circumstances so we can control undesirable events or build options for ourselves.

Gretel goes through a period of mourning. Perhaps depressed, she blindly obeys the witch. She becomes compliant, stops seeking ways to escape or solve her problem. Similarly, denial can limit us. A woman I'll call Sara ran away from difficulty. In the early years of her life, and throughout two marriages, she denied her problems. During her third marriage, circumstances compelled her to change. Over the years, she had watched her husband drink increasingly. As his drinking escalated, so did his abuse of Sara and her sons by her previous marriages. Then, when her husband was arrested twice in one month for drunk driving, Sara was forced to look at their life, to admit there was a problem, even though she resisted doing so:

I wanted to run away. Mentally I *was* running away from it. I kept things inside. If anything traumatic happened, I'd sidestep it. I didn't want to talk about tough issues. I didn't know how.

Sara fled from stressful situations. She directed her emotions inward instead of toward the offender or her problems. Hers was a passive, not an active, life stance. Challenges mastered Sara rather than she them. Whoever avoids problems in this way gets easily stuck in a life someone or something else creates.

By contrast, some people choose to fight rather than flee their problems. Sometimes this response is useful—especially if they use anger creatively, to strengthen their resolve. A black entrepreneur discussed his way of using racial slurs and discrimination to energize himself toward success:

Although it would have been easy in the old days to let myself get discouraged when doors closed in my face because of my color and lack of economic advantages, I used my anger to propel me forward. I envisioned myself having more power and money than the people who were prejudiced against me. This is exactly what I've done. Frankly, I'm grateful they gave me a reason to push myself.

In this vein, I recently heard a true story about two young men who had each been rejected by their girlfriends. One was so crestfallen that he drove to a lonely, high bridge and jumped off, killing himself. The other was also depressed. For days he remained alone in his bedroom, feeling his pain. On one long, sleepless night he composed a song about his loss. The following day he took the song to a publisher, who bought the song. It turned out to be a huge success. Over time, a work written in grief and desolation earned the man a million in royalties. As this story and Sara's case illustrate, it is not what happens to us that makes or breaks our happiness, but how we respond that counts for so much.

Anger, feelings of loss or rejection and all other emotional obstacles can be useful creative allies if we stubbornly tend to our life purposes. While there are no guarantees that we will meet with success, increased effectiveness is almost assured if we bring commitment, positive energy and growing competence to our tasks. However, we can transcend problems only if we believe *we* have more power than they do.

To act powerfully, we must deem ourselves worthwhile, competent, deserving. In other words, our self-esteem must be at least healthy enough to let us endure, choose or behave productively. During a crisis, we must function. Some pale at this.

Feeling insecure, they believe that as adults they cannot improve their self-esteem. Yet high self-esteem is only an idea—a self-judgment made in childhood—that permits us to feel we know what to do, that we have what it takes, even if we don't know exactly how to do this or that thing. We change these self-ideas at any age if we can learn how to build new idea systems for ourselves. A solidly grounded, prudent program that combines productive thought with small, safe actions (that support the hoped-for, enhanced idea) imprints our mind. These can help us change our minds about ourselves.

Some of us are taught, and this begins early in life, to be dependent and incapable in many areas of endeavor. Some parents *do* everything for their children. Others overcontrol with words, body language or even illness. Soon the children learn to be ultrasensitive to nonverbal cues, in the process forgetting their own internal cues for living. A friend of mine whose parents were overgenerous now complains about her inability, as an adult, to earn a good living. Another, a man whose father handled all the family finances, protests that he cannot possibly invest his money wisely. Each of these persons can strategically devise a way to improve competence in the specific underdeveloped skills area.

Similarly, each of us has pockets of deficiencies. These are not truly inabilities, but rather latent abilities we've never needed to use fully. As adults, we can carve out new powers in precisely those areas where we now feel inept or helpless. But before we do, we must believe we can learn. Additionally, it is helpful to hold the conviction that we are able actors—that our actions on behalf of our needs will be productive. This conviction lets us try new steps and persist even if our initial, small steps fail. Sister Grace Pilon—a pioneer among educators, long interested in the link between high self-esteem and creative, resourceful learning—sums up this idea well:

> It is not enough to have creativity. People need human powers and skills to be brave enough to live their creativity. That takes courage, initiative, fearlessness in risking independent work, fearlessness in making mistakes and willingness to share bursts

of excitement for what is happening—all of this without fear of being "laughed at." (Pilon, 1978, p. 4)

The powers and skills Pilon speaks of are abilities that adults can learn, no matter what their earlier life experiences may have been. Those we call "late bloomers" or those who learn how to read and write in adulthood prove this daily. High self-esteem can be developed through *prudent risk-taking, self-trust* and *courage*. Both high self-esteem and low are learned ideas about the self and can be changed.

Prudent Risk-Taking

For most creative people, errors are just ways to find out what doesn't work, signposts to what does work—not a self-defeating comment about their worth as persons.

Sister Grace Pilon has created innovative methods for teaching knowledge skills and human skills to primary school children. To help them learn what works and what doesn't, she teaches them to expect to make mistakes and provides an environment where they can do so safely, without recrimination or harsh self-judgment.

We can learn how to correct old, self-defeating patterns by studying Pilon's methods. She rewards children for their efforts, not for the "right" answers. Her methodology is based on the ideas that each child is unique and that each must believe he or she has value as a person. Feeling their own value, the children gain peace of mind, that is, inner order, self-respect, sharpened senses and perceptual skills, and the feeling that they can learn. "I have self-worth" is not simply an intellectual affirmation; it is grounded in the individual's subjective experience. Pilon writes that if one is convinced one can think and learn—can even make mistakes while learning—then that is a formula for peace of mind (Pilon, 1978, p. 53). It is also a formula for adapting creatively.

While there may still be some who equate high self-esteem with narcissism and unhealthy egoism, most parents and teachers now realize that without it and without a feeling of safety, children cannot grow psychologically and intellectually.

This is also true for adults. To learn how to create better

options we must first believe in our own worth. We earn this belief through the small things we consciously choose to do each day (see Sinetar, 1988). Earned self-esteem is that quality of self-respect and positive self-valuing which is born of mastering the practical problems life presents us with. As we triumph over each level of challenge, we gain inner security. This enables us to move on. In time, we come to believe in our abilities and our worth, at which point we don't have to possess material things, look a certain way or fulfill someone else's idea of perfection to have value in our own eyes. We evaluate ourselves positively because we experience ourselves as striving, sincere and possessing those qualities we admire.

We see this progression of self-valuing in Sara, whose story opened this chapter. I met Sara when she was a new secretary in a respected multinational corporation. The first year I was associated with that company, Sara was promoted twice. The next year she gained another promotion into an administrative position. By the third year she was shouldering enormous responsibilities. Steady increments of tangible success gave Sara fresh insight into her capabilities.

At work she sailed through obstacles, but at home she avoided grappling with her problems. Sara's pocket of underdevelopment was clear. She had to build skills in assertion and in intimate, family problem-solving.

When she realized that her home life was falling apart Sara consciously chose to ask for a reassignment back to a secretarial position. This choice was not easy but now, precisely because of her career successes, she had gained enough inner confidence to allow herself "regression." The healthier we are, the less time we spend denying our needs. Sara realized, then freely admitted that she needed to spend time on her family concerns.

> I simply didn't think I could do a good job at work *and* untangle the mess at home. Even though my husband was the one who had a drinking problem, somewhere in me I knew I had a problem too, and that I'd have to unravel the mystery of my involvement in this dysfunction. I knew this process demanded time, energy and all the attention I had to give.

Sara had to master the skill of dealing with sensitive communication problems in those areas where she was emotionally and

intimately invested. For her, this was the true test of growth—
not whether she could advance at work, though the self-respect
gained at work helped pave the way for her willingness to tackle
home problems. Although initially she resisted talking about or
even facing family problems, Sara learned to give weight to her
feelings and perceptions. Self-questioning and talking things
out with her family were the result.

> With the crisis of alcoholism in our family, I was forced to face
> things I didn't want to face. I wasn't willing to admit my part in
> the problem. I relied on old habits of thinking and reacting.
> At first, the situation itself forced me into a learning mode. I
> had to go to counseling, or my marriage wouldn't have lasted. I'm
> not sure I could have survived. So this wasn't so much my taking
> the risk of going as much as my having the sense I *had* to go. . . .
> For more than a year and a half, I fought the program I'd enrolled
> in. Then, all of a sudden it seemed, the pieces fell into place.

Her "all of a sudden" change began with *small steps*—low-
risk choices and decisions Sara knew she wanted to make.

> I understood what I needed to do, and yet because I was so afraid,
> I would try only a piece of the action. Then my understanding
> would take me further. Each time I saw myself take a productive
> action, my self-esteem grew. This let me try a little more.

Children often need rewards from authority figures to encourage positive behavior, but as adults our understanding, heightened self-regard and increased self-esteem may be in themselves
sufficient reward. If we move steadily and faithfully in the direction we know we should go, our smallest step will encourage
another small step. Even continual setbacks become less and
less significant when we put our attention on our forward, positive steps. Hansel initially discovered a way back home and
reassured and calmed his sister. His second try was muddled
and failed. But perhaps something in his first success gave him
the power to keep on trying. Hansel's attempts to get out of the
woods and, later, fooling the witch were his risks: he took these
because, no doubt in part, he had a memory that at least some
of his earlier risks had worked out.

Our first goal may be simply to learn that our risks pay off, succeed, get us what we want. If we have watched effort after effort

produce counterproductive and energy-draining results, then we may need what amounts to private tutoring in risk taking. We must build a memory bank of personal success in the very area where we believe ourselves inadequate. There may be underlying forces that hold us back and lessons we have yet to learn. This is where a competent, caring therapist can prove helpful.

Our long-term goal is to shift and stretch the boundaries of our central idea of self—changing it from "I am not powerful, competent, worthwhile" to "*I am* powerful, capable, worthwhile." In Sara's case, her desire for enhanced self-esteem involved scrutinizing her typical response to family problems—especially the way she avoided communication about what she termed "the tough issues."

> When I was upset, instead of backing away from the conversation, I would try to explain my feelings. If the person I was talking to was closed, at first I closed down too. Then as I saw myself try, I felt hopeful. Something within me, faith in my ability I suppose, grew. I had to start with myself. I had to have faith that my abilities would develop in time.

Perseverance is essential. The creative process demands tenacious effort and disciplined will, and it involves countless starts and stops. Creative people stubbornly cling to their unique experiences. Their acute intrinsic interest in a matter drives them. Sara's passionate involvement with her newfound learning helped pave the way for developing needed skills and answers. So too with our own hopes for improved self-esteem: we must press on, despite setbacks and regressions. Trying is itself a victory; our smallest success can be a triumph if we construe it correctly.

Suppose we are afraid of doing something, such as admitting our shortcomings to a close, trusted friend or talking to people we don't know at parties. One day we decide to take a chance, test ourselves, use what little courage we have to get closer to a friend or to meet someone new. Whether or not our friend returns our gesture of intimacy, whether or not we become instantly popular with strangers is less important to our development as persons (and to the enhancement of our self-esteem) than the fact that we have watched ourselves being brave, being in our own corner, being inspirational to ourselves.

If we can know ourselves as brave and inspirational in small things, even when we do not achieve the end results we want, we grow. We reward ourselves by increasing our self-esteem, or by gaining more courage, wisdom, improved judgment because we have objectively seen ourselves acting in a way we respect. However helpful such steps forward are, be assured that I am not encouraging anyone to take high risks or skate on thin ice as a method of building feelings of self-worth. Only gamblers, self-defeatists and amateurs expect an immediate and positive payoff when they take risks. Not every risk is even worth taking. As theologian and author Dr. Richard W. Kropf wrote in a letter to me, intent is a crucial factor:

> Risk-taking for its own sake is hardly a commendable quality, for one can take risks even for the basest of reasons: "What then will a man gain if he wins the whole world and ruins his life?" Risk-taking is admirable and wise only when a worthy goal or an altruistic purpose is in mind. It is then . . . that risk-taking comes to the fore as the very leading edge of life, and the old security quest is seen for what it is—the formula for stagnation and death.

There is little growth involved when one plunges into foolhardy, impulsive acts, poorly thought out and executed. However, unlike Kropf, I sense solid adult gains result even from our impulsive acts *if* we ask ourselves what we have learned from an ill-timed or poorly calculated risk. Although these are costly lessons, experience will teach us to be prudent and proceed slowly. One successful entrepreneur I know enjoys projecting a public image that he is carefree and that he takes dangerous business risks. In fact, he does a lot of preparatory homework:

> I study worst-case scenarios. I ask myself if I can afford that "worst case" and look at every eventuality to see if I can survive it. Only when I'm convinced that it is worth my effort do I go ahead. I've discovered, however, that *not proceeding* with a choice, once I see there is value in going ahead, is my real danger.

More than simply "worst-casing," any serious risk-taking requires that we develop a proven track record: we have to know that we possess sound judgment.

On a practical level, the president of a financial institution trains his staff in taking risks and making mistakes by asking them in meetings, "Where did we go wrong this month? Where should we correct matters? What did we do well this month?" Earlier in his career, he learned from his mentor to evaluate both achievements *and* errors openly and objectively. Such a method lessens the sting of failure and sounds much like what Pilon teaches her young charges. Although this executive probably didn't know, care or think much about it, he has helped himself and his staff realize the Zen precept of nonattachment: If we detach ourselves from craving praise and adulation, or cringing from criticism, we are free to act spontaneously. We will then be liberated from slavish dependence on desiring a particular outcome. My client isn't much interested in Buddhist ideals, but he does want to shake the fears that might hamper his and his staff's decision-making processes. Each time he responds appropriately to the requirements of the moment, instead of intellectualizing about imagined criticisms or problems, his self-opinion is enhanced.

Much earlier in my career, I overcame a fear of public speaking by designing a step-by-step desensitization plan that allowed me to speak in front of larger and larger groups. The breakthrough did not occur until I enrolled in a brutal twelve-week public-speaking seminar with 200 other adults. All of us were intimidated by the thought of public speaking. My self-opinion and confidence soared after each presentation—whether it was technically successful or not. By the end of the first weeks, speaking in public seemed tolerable, no matter what the audience size. Because I knew in advance that seminar leaders would criticize me, their criticism stung less. Looking back, I see that I desensitized myself to praise and criticism. Focusing on the opinion of others—and failing to keep my attention on my message—had been the nub of my problem.

The less we care what others think, the less attention we give to the by-products and prizes we are aiming for through our efforts, the greater focus we can give our primary target. This allows us to concentrate unemotionally on the results we want. One of Father Thomas Merton's translations of the Taoist poet Chuang Tzu speaks directly to this point:

> When an archer is shooting for nothing,
> He has all his skill.
> If he shoots for a brass buckle
> He is already nervous.

> If he shoots for a prize of gold
> He goes blind
> Or sees two targets—
> He is out of his mind!
> (Merton, 1965, p. 107)

We can be more effective risk takers if we examine our motives and ambitions for taking the risk in the first place.

Of course there are different types of risk. Some people risk their lives by choosing one thing over another. My client who heads a financial institution faces both emotional and financial risks. When Sara confronts her husband she risks both his wrath and her feeling of safety. We too risk rejection, ridicule and inner turmoil when we first move out of an all too familiar comfort zone. Whenever we speak up for something we believe in, or change our minds, jobs or habits, we disturb the status quo as we, and those important to us, have defined it.

Persons with high self-esteem have an easier time with all this. When taking an unpopular stand or going against convention, they feel they are just doing what they consider important. Their inner sense of worthiness and their own degree of positive self-valuation allows them to survive trauma, change or confrontation. Their "yes" stance in life allows them to retain their uniqueness, to conform and equivocate less and, consequently, to gain more of what they want in life.

Self-Trust

Another hallmark of high self-esteem is self-trust. In his book *The Antecedents of Self-Esteem,* Stanley Coopersmith highlights the crucial link between self-esteem and creativity:

> To explore ideas and strike out in new directions requires the belief that one can discriminate between sense and nonsense, that one can impose order where disorder apparently exists. An essential component of the creative process . . . is the conviction that one's judgment in interpreting the events is to be trusted. (Coopersmith, 1967, p. 59)

Self-trust allows an individual to have staying power during times of uncertainty, when the success of a risk or new behavior is unknown. Here too, time and patience are required. Sara's support group helped her endure:

> I was reinforced by a support group and by a sponsor. In time, I learned to listen to my instinctual good sense—I came to see I had this sense. I'd known how to use this ability in business. Yet in my personal life, I've discounted myself.
>
> No one in the group tells you what to do or how to do the things you know you must and want to do. But they ask questions. These questions seem largely unanswerable at first, but as you dwell on them, you realize you are questioning yourself. This becomes a productive habit. Still later in the process, I found myself asking those questions and getting some of my own answers.

One of the most helpful questions Sara learned to ask herself when family crises came her way was: "What would I be doing if this circumstance hadn't come up?" Another set of questions involved reviewing what she had or hadn't done for herself during a day or week.

Growth in self-trust translates into new behaviors. Sara began to exercise and lose weight, she gained the courage to go into the city alone for shopping or entertainment (something she had never let herself do), and she changed the way she relates to others:

> Lately when I ask myself what I've done for myself this week, I'm happy to see that I *have* done some things that I value. For one thing, I no longer "react." I stop and think. I have learned to put myself first. Although it might sound selfish, actually it has the reverse effect. My relationships are now calm and peaceful.
>
> Getting my life back under control is something I am learning bit by bit. I also see that no one can do these things for me; *I* have to do it and that means taking action.
>
> These are skills—thinking and acting skills—that I have been teaching myself over the last few months. I've had to learn to figure out what I want. This has, I'm amazed to say, been a major lesson for me.

Sara didn't know what she wanted because she had learned to satisfy the needs, expectations and demands of others. As she'd been heavily motivated by externals, learning to identify her own goals took practice. However, she soon saw that doing something for herself didn't mean shutting people out; with greater self-trust came the understanding that she did not have to control other people and situations. She realized that she used to create bigger problems by trying to get *the* solution she wanted. Also, increased self-trust brought increased respect for others. She found her husband and children could solve problems without her interference and direction: "Now, because I'm taking responsibility for myself, I figure other people can take care of themselves. And they do."

In order to alter our frames of mind, even to think clearly, we must believe in ourselves and be capable mapmakers. These attitudes are also thinking tools. In *The Antecedents of Self-Esteem,* Stanley Coopersmith takes us one step further in understanding how this works. He too views the self-esteem/creativity connection in terms of both thinking and behavior, and identifies two stages in this link.

The first requires conviction that what we desire or must do is worth doing and that we can do it. When we trust ourselves we also trust our ability to set goals and to plan. If we think we can solve problems, if we have seen ourselves solve them in the past, then we have trust in our future ability to do so. Because our perceptions flow from our well-developed, higher-order thinking skills as well as from our emotions, our subjective life is the context in which all intellectual operations take place.*

The second stage of the self-esteem/creativity connection is *assertive action.* To shed its old skin, a snake will rub up against rough surfaces; to shed ours, we may have to rub up against rough spots too, but in our peculiarly human way. If we don't take steps to carry out our solutions, what good are they? If we are prone to perfectionism, if we think too much about others' opinions, if our mistakes provoke inordinate anxiety, we stay stuck: we overanalyze, intellectualize, procrastinate, develop maladaptive habits or physical "symptoms," sink into apathy or depression, become inert, do *anything* just as

---

* Of course, self-perception, our notions about the efficacy of our mind, our optimism about our future well-being, safety and success all color our perceptual maps. In a real sense, we *are* our perceptions. A Hindu saying, "The world is as we are," sums up my point that intellectual mapmaking is governed, or at the very least influenced by, self-perception.

long as we don't have to act. The Hamlet syndrome is natural when we first confront a problem, but it also can become permanently addictive and lead to atrophied assertiveness.

Courage

Creative actions require courage. But having courage does not mean we feel no fear; it means acting *despite* fear in the most prudent, effective way we can.

There are ways to promote action when we're stuck. One is to admit what we are feeling. Yet many of us go through amazing contortions just to deny our feelings of fear. We try too hard, act impulsively to bury these feelings, brutally criticize and depreciate ourselves, or blame others. Such self-abuse tells our nonconscious selves that we—our emotions, for example—have limited value in our own eyes. This is a significant self-betrayal, since everything we say to and about ourselves establishes the tone of our relationship with our inner being.

A sweet encouragement for sound mental health is found throughout "Hansel and Gretel." The tale is ancient testimony to the notion that admitting feelings doesn't mean being overcome or crippled by them. Neither child is afraid to feel, weep, admit despair or helplessness. Each is completely transparent to the other.

Hansel screams in protest when the witch imprisons him; later, dismayed, he cries out to Gretel that they can't possibly make it across a big lake. Yet overall, Hansel is a veritable rock throughout their ordeal, a helpmate to Gretel and someone on whom we know we ourselves could rely. Gretel weeps bitterly when mistreated. She mourns and cowers. She too admits to fear and helplessness. But like Hansel's, her self-disclosures of helplessness coexist with her obvious strength and competence. It is, after all, Gretel who ultimately destroys the witch and gets herself and Hansel home. Their example reassures readers that none need think that feelings necessarily overpower right action. The Brothers Grimm further teach us that awareness of what we feel is a precursor to being in control of ourselves—that perhaps we can better overcome feelings of powerlessness if we can admit to having them.

Many of us learned long ago to deny our interior world. When children are afraid, parents often tell them not to feel frightened. Men and women tell each other not to feel jealous, angry or anxious. British psychiatrist R. D. Laing describes the resulting self-alienation in his book *The Politics of Experience:*

> Much human behavior can be seen as a unilateral or bilateral attempt to eliminate experience. A person may treat another as though he were not a person, and he may act himself as though he were not a person. . . .
>
> Our capacity to think . . . is pitifully limited: Our capacity even to see, hear, touch, taste and smell is shrouded in veils of mystification so that an intensive discipline of unlearning is necessary for anyone before one can begin to experience the world afresh, with innocence, truth and love. (Laing, 1967, pp. 25–26)

After we acknowledge our feelings comes the inevitable question: "What can I do about this?" Our answer, if we have courage, lets our feelings exist, lets us exist. Even if we do not act on them, if we can face and accept our feelings, we further our growth because in the process we show respect for our own emotions.

Growth occurs as we *use* our experience on behalf of life, whether our own or others'. This takes any number of forms. Perhaps we will write an article about our experience, or join a community group, or simply minister individually to someone who is going through a similar situation. Our experience can knit us back into authentic, multifaceted relatedness with others, highlighting the themes that once caused our avoidance or withdrawal. Even a negative experience can help us create ourselves anew and give a fresh meaning and purpose to life.

Following this route is not easy. It runs contrary to behavior patterns most of us learned all too well in childhood. Indeed, not falling into well-worn habits is a separate struggle during which we are best served by patience. It takes courage to accept what we feel and to let ourselves authentically be who we are.

We need to cultivate our courage if we don't have it, but even a sliver of it can start our growth process. If we can risk taking a glimpse into our own darkness and admit that we see no light, the very courage it takes to do so gives us added power to begin mapping our next steps. Giving up what seems safe, choosing to move on—because we know that our long-term survival depends on it—takes what Father Richard Kropf calls an act of faith:

> To accomplish this requires faith: a belief in something that takes us out of ourselves and a commitment to the conviction that we are called to be something more than our ego-pleasing selves.

Perhaps the most crucial article of faith when first stepping onto this ill-lighted path is that even the smallest act of courage is its own reward. I like immensely the poetic way Ruth Gendler writes of courage:

> Courage is not afraid to weep, and she is not afraid to pray, even when she is not sure whom she is praying to. . . . The people who told me she is stern were not lying; they just forgot to mention she is kind. (Gendler, 1984, p. 12)

Two sets of pulls are at work in us: weak, unhealthy, fearful, regressive pulls, and wholesome, positive, life-oriented ones. The more well-developed our creative adaptive response skills, the more we embody and give evidence to what Abraham Maslow termed "Being Values." These are the values of health and growth; aesthetics and play; the sacred or eternal qualities of life, including courage and truth-telling. Maslow's point that actualizing adults are better *choosers* than others would seem to have merit. (See Figure 2.)

As Sara develops her creative adaptive skills, her first concrete and courageous action toward solving her problems was to allow herself to retreat from the pressure of her job. By having the courage to make her job a secondary priority. Sara was able to conceive of altered and improved ways of being a wife and mother. Everyone's authenticity takes a uniquely personal form. Not everyone takes Sara's "step back" in order to go forward.

A woman whose mother was dying of cancer chose to stay in a demanding corporate position, because for her the job was an island of sanity amid the chaotic turbulence of her mother's illness. When she didn't feel able to cope with the sadness of seeing her mother die, her work helped her creatively adapt. Both she and

FIGURE 2

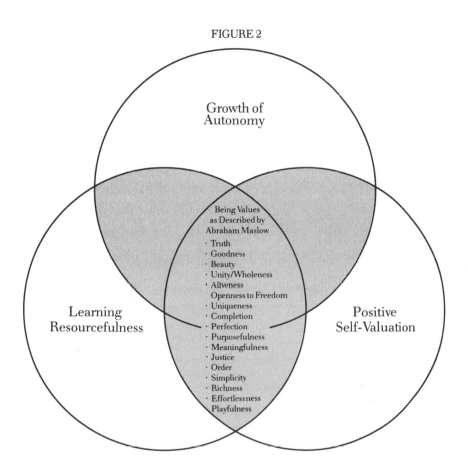

Sara accepted themselves as they found themselves, acting out what they observed and felt to be true. Each had the courage to face her truths squarely, regardless of what others said or thought.

By contrast, in a crisis situation the person with low self-esteem may be split, denying his deepest needs, limited energy or the elements that would contribute to his sanity and good health. This person forges rigidly ahead. Already cut off from his inner realities, he severs himself from creative ideas—from the part of his brain that might, in a more accepting, relaxed, organic mode, imagine solutions, play with possibilities, intuit what his best directions might be.

As we regain authority over our lives, we accept our feelings as having validity for us, given our unique perspective or circumstances. We then give ourselves freedom to be real, to act on these and proceed authentically with our lives.

Finding the Exit Door

I have suggested that we improve problem-solving skill by improving the quality of our thinking—that as we repair our inner processes, we make outer strides. Now I suggest a backward route: We can also move from outer to inner—change our behavior in order to reorganize and repair our states of thinking and feeling. This too we do cautiously—by taking small, authentic acts in the desired direction. Even small acts enhance our verdict of ourselves.

The core self—the one some call the soul or higher self, or, to borrow author John Cantwell Kiley's phrase, "the part-that-knows"—has our answers. In us, the part that knows is capable, can create options, can pave the way for right responses, but only if we can get that lesser, resistant, stuck, hesitant, insecure part of ourselves to cooperate. Patience, acceptance, moving gradually help us accomplish this.

When we see ourselves behaving genuinely, we can mentally editorialize, "I'm a truthful person, capable of honest action." This commentary serves as a reward. Like Sara—who saw herself choosing from ever-widening circles of empowered alternatives–when we choose in the direction of our highest values in small things, we gradually improve our self-opinion. Then our inner dialogue grows positive. The behavioral component of enhanced self-esteem is clear: however small our action, by acting in line with our most esteemed values—by acting as we know we should—we demonstrate value for ourselves. In time, valuing ourselves, we can believe we do have what it takes to handle life.

As a result of wholesome movement from outer (behavior) to inner (feeling), progressively useful, creative solutions pop up in our minds. By our own behavior we impress on ourselves that we are capable of doing that which we respect. We then also reward ourselves with smooth-functioning, "cooperative" thinking. Now instead of a sluggish mind, we have increasingly powerful insights. When autosuggestion is healthy, something positive is always gained: ideas, courage, enhanced feelings about ourselves, insight, added willpower, optimism. I am speaking about tiny, incremental improvements, not megaleaps of courage or spectacular genius. Small improvements build exponentially as we reprogram our inner computer through self-styled and valued behaviors.

Both routes help us. We can move from improved thought processes to improved behavior, or from improved behavior to repaired self-opinions and states of feeling. As we systematically and strategically improve our thoughts and daily actions, life improves.

Of course this is all obvious. Yet many people remain stuck. Even Confucius reputedly was perplexed by this and asked, "The way out is through the door; why is it that no one will use it?"

PART THREE
Creating Joy

HE old woman [upon whose house they came] appeared to be most friendly, but she was really an old witch who had misled the children, and had built the little bread house only in order to lure them in. When anyone came into her power she cooked and ate him, and held a regular feast day for the occasion. Now, witches have red eyes and cannot see far, but like beasts, they have a keen sense of smell and know when human beings pass by. When Hansel and Gretel fell into her hands she laughed maliciously and said jeeringly, "I've got them now. They won't escape me." . . .

[But cleverly, Gretel foiled her plans to eat them.] Gretel flew straight to Hansel, opened the little stable door, and cried, "Hansel, we are free! The old witch is dead!" Then Hansel sprang like a bird out of a cage when the door was opened. How they rejoiced, and embraced each other, and jumped for joy, and kissed one another! And as they had no longer any cause for fear, they went into the old hag's house, and there they found, in every corner of the room, boxes with pearls and precious stones. . . . Then they set off at a run, and [found their way back to the familiar part of the woods and to their own home and father]. . . . Thus, all their troubles were ended, and they all lived happily ever after.

7

Optimism:
Learning to Relish Challenges

Whatever it is which drives the dozens of young aspiring dancers who stream in and out of the famous dance
studio near where I live and compels them to exert
their bodies and wills until they can't anymore,
it is not pessimism.
—Lionel Tiger, *Optimism*

"Creep in," said the witch [as she tended the oven
from which firely flames were leaping], "and see if it's
properly heated, so we can put in the bread." . . . But
Gretel saw what she had in mind and said, "I do not
know how I am to do it. How do I get in?"
—The Brothers Grimm, "Hansel and Gretel"

Optimism is essential to the creative process. It supports our
faith in ourselves and in our abilities. Optimism stimulates fresh,
imaginative thinking and lets us take tough or desperate steps
when we don't know what else to do. When Gretel stalled the
witch, saying she didn't know how to creep into the flaming
oven, she may not have known exactly what she was going to do,
but some life impulse stirred her brain, giving her just the words
she needed for that instant. And that was all it took to escape
death. Optimism bolsters self-acceptance, especially as we come
to recognize ourselves as the authors of our own answers, de-
signers of our lives. This hopeful state permits—indeed urges—
experimentation, risk taking and assertiveness, filling us as it
does with special intrapsychic energies. Optimism naturally and
spontaneously directs us toward our highest goals and values

(even when these are unattainable). It is our buffer against fear, obstacles and disquiet.

Optimism lets us believe in the future, as we want that future to be. When asked what it takes to live a long life, George Burns, America's elder statesman of comedy, replied, "You have to fall in love with your future." Burns captures the essence of optimism. As we shall see, it is unlikely that we will fall in love with our future without faith that we can take steps to create a future we prefer, a future worth our effort, without faith that *we* ourselves are worth something.

Let me underscore this faith/self-worth issue. The critical factor in problem solving, as discussed in the last chapter, is not merely how we initially structure a problem—not just our intellectual entry point to it—but also whether we have sufficient faith in ourselves to take action on what our intellect and intuition say must be done. If we mistrust ourselves, if our "realistic" weighing of the odds undermines faith, if we believe there is nothing we can do and feel all forces are against us, our will becomes paralyzed. Then imagination becomes the servant of panic, hesitation or inactive helplessness.

Having faith produces not so much clear-sightedness as it does prudent boldness: we choose to act judiciously despite risk. These positive impulses on behalf of life stimulate productive, forward movement. This is optimism. It is more than merely mood.

In the nineteenth century, William James framed optimism as a leap of faith, rooted in life itself. He stressed that our faith in happy outcomes despite uncertainty is the only factor that makes those results possible. Suppose, he said, you are stuck on a mountain and your only escape is to take a long leap. If you mistrust yourself, you so fiercely hesitate that in the end only fear reigns.

In everyday life as well, if we mistrust ourselves during uncertain times, we are doomed to failure. If we move forward despite fear (acknowledging it nonetheless, so as to hearken to its warnings), at least we have a chance. What we feel about the issue may not matter as much as what we must do.*

---

* As we saw, Sara learned through her support and therapy group to ask herself, "If I didn't have this problem (i.e., if my husband weren't an alcoholic, if my family life weren't disintegrating) what would I be doing?" She taught herself to move toward her life's superordinate goals despite heartbreaking concerns. Optimism helped her consider such questions.

To define and delineate our choices more clearly, James quoted Fitz James Stephan:

> In all important transactions of life, we have to take a leap in the dark. . . . If we waver in our answer, that . . . is a choice: but whatever choice we make, we make it at our peril. . . . Each must act as he thinks best; and if he is wrong, so much the worse for him.
>
> What must we do? "Be strong and of good courage." Act for the best, hope for the best and take what comes. . . . If death ends all, we cannot meet death better. (James, 1956, p. 31)

In most instances, fortunately, matters are not so severe. Usually, a positive act opens up a way for life to continue, perhaps in a better fashion than before.

Optimism also is the belief that the world is good and, as the *New Webster's Dictionary* defines it, is a "building toward the ultimate in excellence." With the obvious evidence against us, with all the pain felt in a lifetime, how is this idea possible? How can sane, reflective persons possibly believe that the world is "building toward the ultimate in excellence"?

Simply because through us as individuals, the world has its chance to move in that direction. Our smallest act gives the world a chance to progress, however infinitesimal the chance. It is precisely sane, reflective persons who resolve this paradox, who put into practice the notions that life is worth their effort, that they are worth it, that there are purposes, values and tasks worth doing. The saner the person, the more this resolution is possible. Despite pain, defects, ugliness and even evil, life itself is sacred. Personal actions do count. Right action and creative, conscious choices trigger feelings that the world will go on, with or without us, and will do so honorably precisely because of people like us who demonstrate integrity and faith.

Right actions form the very matrix of our hope. But while optimism floats amid thought, action and outcomes, inclination and spirit of action differ from person to person. Some people look circumstances right in the eye, "realistically," denying nothing. When ready, they move ahead. Others have what has been termed an "illusory glow." They turn away from the ugliness, but nonetheless they act. Whatever their adaptive strategy, true optimists proceed in the direction of their highest values—toward an affirmation of life.

Lionel Tiger, researcher, biologist, author of *Optimism*, defines his topic broadly:*

> [Optimism is a] mood, attitude and mode of perceiving life [which] has been central to the process of human evolution; it determines to a degree not yet charted the way humans think, play and respond to birth and death. (Tiger, 1979, p. 15)

Optimism gives our brains the go-ahead to play with solutions. It drives us forward, though we are immersed in fear. As noted, to be creative our mind must be open to its own primary, nonconscious processes. There are messages for us here—messages that can save us. Optimism helps us open the doors to these clues, making it, as Tiger suggests, an evolutionary key.

The evolutionary key, however, perhaps is found as much in what we *do* as it is in what we say and think. What we do illumines our belief that life is, indeed, worth it.

Anticipatory Strategies
of Hope or Horror

Anticipatory strategy and emotional set differ among individuals as they face predicaments. Some people may indeed be pessimistic. Perhaps one individual doesn't have a track record of success in a particular area. Another may simply be disposed toward melancholy—as a friend of mine admits he is. But if their underlying conviction is that they must, no matter what, move in a chosen direction, even if and when they waver, they are optimists.

If we act hopefully at all, we gain hope. If our choices are self-affirming, then however pessimistically we structure the challenge in our minds, we still function under the sway of predominantly positive thought. Thus even pessimists may be optimists (much as some hate to admit it): it all depends on what they do.

A friend of mine says she never rules out a gloomy outcome, calls herself "realistic, not optimistic," but acts "as if" all will

---

* Those who want a comprehensive discussion of the gradients of optimism can do no better than to read Tiger's book.

work. In the previous chapter, I quoted an entrepreneur who said that he "worst-cased" risks before he took them. Such practices are doubly helpful: first, they help us form a plan of action in case things don't work out the way we'd hoped; next, they help us protect our self-esteem if we fail. We create a nifty fiction for ourselves that softens the blow should we not make it.

I did this in college before exams when my pessimism was well founded. I rarely studied, skipped most lectures and had to steel myself against the worst: poor semester grades; barely passing test scores; embarrassing, ego-bruising comparisons with friends' scores. Pessimism beforehand was my ego's protective device.

Aggressive optimists, on the other hand, imagine no such outcomes. Some have actual track records of success. Others simply have such strong self-esteem they don't require advance shielding from failure. These people strive for pure success from the start, without buffering themselves by magnifying obstacles or lowering their expectations. They face challenges naturally, impervious to failure because their minds dwell on previous successes if they have had them (and usually they have). Or they absorb themselves fully in the challenge. If they do fail, they repair their self-esteem later—*after* the results are in.

Either of these strategies—self-protective defense mechanisms or boldly forging ahead—can move us toward our goals. At their roots, both are motivated by a belief in the goal and in the possibility of reaching it. Only depressives seem self-defeatingly inert. The absence of optimism is not pessimism, but rather depression: lack of life, vitality and effort. When we don't try, we thwart creative power. This was the case of a man who wrote to me describing his debilitating resistance to change:

> I used to love going to therapy, but no longer do. Now, I watch myself resist change, resist making choices. Also, I see how I internalize pain. I turn difficult situations inside and pretty soon I have a migraine or a back spasm or a neck pain that debilitates me.
>
> The famous "pain in the neck" gets me through my own choice to do nothing. I hurt myself rather than take action on my own behalf. It's all so destructive and such a waste of time.

A pessimistic outlook per se is not enough to make one a pessimist, it may be just a protective device. Studies measuring the effects of pessimism or optimism on performance (a test, for example) show *no* difference between the two: both pessimists and optimists can achieve positive results; both pessimists and optimists can fail.

However, optimism probably gives us an endurance edge, especially when others, maliciously or misguidedly, try to sabotage us. Doctors, teachers, "helping professionals," parents, friends may direct us toward or away from a particular choice. But we alone will live with the consequences of that choice. Perhaps others simply erode our hope when we most need it, for example by feeding us gloomy statistics to prove why we should or shouldn't act. When one is ill, or trying to escape a dispiriting commitment, or changing careers, then the "You've got to be realistic" message saps life and energy. How many people could have improved their lives, left inner-city poverty or hopelessness, for instance, if they had been "realistic"?

Optimism is not just holding happy thoughts and uttering affirmations. It has countless variegations, some quite deceptive. Still, whatever its hue or form, optimism injects us with the vigor, stamina and staying power to adapt creatively.

No doubt physical strength begets at least a degree of optimism, although I question whether it alone helps us when society, experts, those we love—or even we ourselves—imagine our demise. To combat that, we must cling tenaciously to joy and love of life. Then our hope can dull the impact of external forces working against us. Hope gives us power to endure, even enjoy, the battle. In the final analysis, we must love and relish our battles or we rob ourselves of the strength to do what is necessary. Optimism both supplies and is a by-product of this love.

Sometimes, however, all we can manage is just to "make do." In this case we savor ordinary life. If we have been near death or otherwise traumatized, little friendly things take on great import. These unspectacular anchors bring reassurance and security and epitomize life as we have always known it, and always want to know it tomorrow. The sun shimmering through the trees in our yard in a certain way, our first cup of coffee of the day, a walk around the block—these are enough for us.

But comforting habits alone do not always sustain us for long. We may need to push beyond what we know, to free ourselves of fear or self-doubt or the restrictions and expectations that addict us while our unique life goes unexpressed. A friend taught me what it means to "push beyond." An active journalist, he suffered a severe stroke in his fifties; his left side was affected by brain damage (not muscle or nerve damage), so that he had to concentrate on both the mental and physical aspects of minutiae, as if he didn't know how to do the simplest things. He became intensely aware of small things—like how many buttons his dress shirts had (seven), and that some buttons were extremely hard to fasten singlehandedly. When he asked himself why he bothered with those particular shirts, he realized that he wanted to learn how to deal with them. He interpreted his relearning ordeal as "a great opportunity to test my limits and perhaps even stretch them a bit." *Interpreting problems as a challenge is one of the key differences between being depressed by problems and overcoming them.* Creative problem-solvers explain negative events to themselves in positive ways; this influences their achievements and their health positively.*

After twenty years of study, researcher Martin Seligman believes that the way we interpret what happens to us may be more significant than the events themselves. Seligman cites a study of mastectomy patients: Five years after surgery, 75 percent of those who had reacted to the disease with a fighting spirit (or who denied they even had cancer) were still alive and had no recurrence. Only 35 percent of those who had interpreted the event stoically or helplessly were still alive. Apparently, "a feeling of helplessness appears to impair the body's ability to combat the disease" (Trotter, 1987).

I suspect many physicians in years to come will sing praises to the power of optimism in the healing process. Some of them may even have once sung in the "You must be realistic" choir. But times change. The idea that optimism helps physical healing seems here to stay.

My own focus remains on the psychological boost we get from optimism:

---

* Bernie Siegel's account of "exceptional patients" in *Love, Medicine and Miracles* describes this trait more fully, showing how their positive attitudes bolster them in lifesaving ways. Norman Cousins's book *Healing Heart* stresses how critical positivity, hope and laughter are to health. Indeed, in many instances, optimism may be *the* key to physical survival.

· It gives us the ability to pull through uncertainty,
· It supports our faith in ourselves and in our ability to find answers and strength needed for the struggle,
· It lets us act, gives us that willingness to act—and then to accept the consequences of our acts,
· It breeds in us inner joy, energy, vitality—elements that sustain us, even allow us to relish our struggles.

One of the best ways to cultivate the feeling of power is to begin believing in oneself—in the body's ability to heal itself, in the availability of answers from within, in our creative power to renew and restore ourselves to full functioning. This is precisely what my friend John discovered when he lost a prestigious job. For several years after his loss, he struggled for stability. Finally he realized that when he searched within for answers, self-approval and direction, he also found increasing stores of joy:

> My optimism started growing when I got the idea that the longed-for answers were in myself. I was, previously, always searching for mentors: teachers, the clergymen I knew in college, a professor of philosophy whose protégé I aspired to be. I was definitely looking for direction and validation from outside myself.

When John examined his mind and heart, he found useful insights and felt: "My answers are in me after all. It's okay to feel positive about the future." After that, healing emotions emerged, if only gradually, and John's growth as a person brought him his first experience of real joy.

In his book *Inner Joy* Dr. Harold Bloomfield analyzes the way joy comes out of struggle. Bloomfield suggests that just as our body passes through definite stages in healing a wound, so our thought processes pass through "recognizable stages" as we recover from loss or emotional wounds.

The first stage is shock and denial. We are temporarily unable to cope. Next come anger and depression. We feel betrayed, hurt or grief-stricken. Crying, fatigue and listlessness can be signs of this stage, and many of us get stuck here simply because we do not fully allow ourselves to experience the pain we feel. Finally, understanding and acceptance arrive, and with them inner joy wells up:

[It was] a painful event, but you have survived. Now it's an opportunity for you to learn something about yourself and the world. Energy and strength return, often in greater measure than before. Albert Camus summed up the crowning insight that marks the completion of this stage when he wrote: "In the midst of winter, I finally learned that there was in me an invincible summer." (Bloomfield, 1980, p. 250)

By optimism, then, I mean that quality that lets us forge ahead and *feel* our invincibility, as a reality, in the midst of fear, anger, sadness or hesitation. Like an underground spring, this living capacity runs through us *for* our use. It influences and expands our life.

Creating Self-Challenges

Creative people create contests and problems for themselves. They interpret challenges as battles of good and evil, or as struggles in which they can show what they are made of, or as a trial to remind them that the odds are against them and that they can survive anyway. I have watched my most creative clients and friends create personal problems for themselves when their work bored them or if they felt stultified by what they were doing. It is almost as if their creative minds need complex projects to work on. Lionel Tiger puts it in these terms:

> Apart from contests, other more explicitly artistic activities share the important characteristic that they challenge human limits and fix human experience and perception—immortality the artist hopes. . . . Like athletes [whom artists resemble in their attitudes, energies and efficiencies], creative persons, and the greatest ones the most, drive themselves to the extra bit of music, action, color, logic, assessment or whirl which creates the difference between those who leave their environments as they find them and those who make a difference. (Tiger, 1979, p. 256)

When we act out of our courageous, optimistic fighting spirit, we also act creatively. We make a difference—if only to ourselves. Making a difference always involves creativity—no matter how subtle its form. Ordinary persons can and do profoundly affect us. Each core self is unique and "special" and, regardless of achievement or lack of it, affects us simply by its existence. What we do individually matters to all of us collectively.

Even in life-and-death cases, when we engage our will to live, survival still is not the deepest issue. Then, to paraphrase the genius of Nikos Kazantzakis, our action amounts to a throw of dice on which, for a moment, the entire fate of our race is gambled. And our throw of the dice—that is, our action in any direction, based on our intention to live on expressively—enriches our entire ancestral body, because we energetically proclaim our selfhood. That is why we root for heroism, no matter how small the heroic act: the struggle becomes our struggle, the victory becomes our victory in our own battles. Through each others' courage we take tiny steps, frail, incapacitated and crippled though they may be, toward greater life.

Bruno Bettelheim suggests that the inclusion of white birds in "Hansel and Gretel" symbolizes the presence of watchful, benevolent powers over the children's entire ordeal:*

> Hansel claims to be looking back at a white dove that is sitting on the roof of the parental home, wanting to say goodby to him. It is a snow-white bird, singing delightfully, which leads the children to the gingerbread house and then settles on its roof, suggesting that this is the right place for them to arrive at. Another white bird is needed to guide the children back to safety: their way home is blocked by a "big water" which they can cross only with the help of a white duck. (Bettelheim, 1977, p. 164)

In other words, from problematic beginning to happy end, the whole adventure may have been "arranged for the children's benefit." Just who arranged this adventure? No one will say. Perhaps God, Fate or Mother Nature. And this feels right. If we list those lessons we want any child to learn, certainly this tale transmits a key precept: that we experience some higher mystery of being by facing challenges courageously and creatively. When we realize that each ordeal can be a vehicle through which we find higher levels of understanding of ourselves and the world, we remain optimistic through our trial.

Optimism is linked to our creative drive; our creative adaptive responses increase as we willingly enter life's contest. When we strive to express meaning or purpose or virtue in our life, we

---

* Different versions of the tale contain different sorts of white creatures. In one version, for example, Hansel looks back at a white kitten. In another, he turns back to watch white chickens.

simultaneously meet our power. We can all learn. We can begin
by interpreting events—even negative or stressful ones—as challenges that demand our ingenious, creative solutions. Uncertainty, the stressful event, the unknown can and do become
allies when we surpass and inspire ourselves by our own optimistic acts. One sweet mystery of life is that such acts, inconsequential though they may seem to us, inspire others, lift them,
whether or not the outcome is successful. Understanding this,
Kazantzakis wrote:

> Your first duty, in completing your service to your race, is to feel
> within you all your ancestors. Your second duty is to throw light
> on their onrush and to continue their work. Your third is to pass
> on ... the great mandate to surpass you. (Kazantzakis, 1960,
> p. 74)

8

The Autonomous Adult

The one most important goal of family systems therapy is to help family members toward a better level of
"differentiation of self."
—MURRAY BROWN

Then Gretel gave her a shove that sent her right in,
shut the iron door, and drew the bolt. Gracious! How
she yelled! It was quite horrible. But Gretel fled, and
the wretched old woman was left to perish miserably.
—THE BROTHERS GRIMM, "Hansel and Gretel"

Autonomy means independence. The term is generally used by
social scientists, theologians or psychiatrists to refer to the individuated, self-actualized or authentic human being, a self-
governing and self-defining person, subject primarily to his own
laws of being and deeply sensed goals and values. This does not
mean that autonomous individuals reject social customs out of
hand, but rather that their locus of control, their reference point
for decision making, rests within. A woman named Catherine
describes her independence in this way:

> Most social codes exist for the greater good. But some rules seem
> absurdly stupid; these I consciously choose not to go along with.
> If after going against the system, my judgment worked against
> me, I'd take the consequences.
>   For example, I live on a ranch in what the county calls a "non-
> code" house. This means it is illegal. I choose not to renovate it.
> I take my chances with the building department. I can and will
> handle the penalties if I'm caught.

Some criticize such statements and this viewpoint. Fearing anarchy, they wonder, "What if everyone did that?" If Catherine's stance troubles us, we can keep in mind that autonomous persons typically keep their own counsel, have their own life agendas and privately know what rules they will and will not obey. They guard and protect their intentions in order not to be subjected to needless debates on issues they have already made up their minds about. Despite this apparently anarchistic position, autonomous individuals are thoroughly responsible. To paraphrase Abraham Maslow, only to whole, autonomous persons can we confidently say, "Do what you will, and it will probably be all right."

Maslow's interviews reveal that in psychologically healthy persons, duty and pleasure are highly correlated, self-discipline comes easily and self-interest coincides with altruism. The autonomous are good-choosers. They know when and how to strive for achievement, and also respect their own needs for rest, security, protection and play. Developmentally speaking, these adults are not stuck or fixated at an immature level of growth. Such persons may have been in Aristotle's mind when he taught, "It is the things that are valuable and pleasant to a good man that are really valuable and pleasant."

Autonomous persons consciously author their own lives. They sense a deeply felt interior injunction to be, do or experience life in a particular, distinctive way. In other writings, I have called such persons self-defining. By this I mean they effortlessly and spontaneously extricate themselves from clichéd and stereotypical behavior (Sinetar, 1988).

Hansel and Gretel's father lacks autonomy. He cannot go against his wife's wishes, cannot protect his children or what he knows to be his family's greater good. Despite their young age, Hansel and Gretel are able to defy their parents. They also defy the witch, who, at least in the early stages of the tale, is a mother figure for them. They can question or go against authority because they have a drive for autonomy (and through their trials progressively gain more of that drive).

Gretel gains strength and freedom for herself and Hansel only after she chooses the difficult but necessary course of action. She pushes another being into a flaming oven; the act is at once so understandable and so unthinkable that we have to wonder whether, if put to the test, we could make such a choice.

After this bold choice, Gretel seems newly empowered. She

becomes the reassurer for the two on their journey back home. She becomes the team's decision maker, telling Hansel how they will cross the big lake. Moreover, both Hansel and Gretel are energized with an almost supernatural degree of joy, enthusiasm and loving kindness at the end of the tale. These two youngsters, having undergone—and survived—a fantastic ordeal, and having disentangled themselves emotionally from their previous problems, now possess a permanently altered reality, wherein each has personal power. Torn from the safety of their parents' protection, separated from the conventional home life every boy and girl expects to have, they now quite consciously develop into autonomous, full-functioning persons. In this outcome also lies their power to be happy forevermore.

Those whom society calls normal often follow roles scripted for them by external agents—parents, peers, church or political groups. There is obvious irony to this: normal may not be the healthiest, most desirable state of being. For instance, respected psychoanalytic tradition teaches that psychological health and the dropping of masks are practically synonymous. While many who call themselves normal prefer to wear masks, believing success, social skill and happy adjusted living will follow, the autonomous elect to drop their masks. If they have a social face, it is an authentic replica of who and what they are. The mask they drop is the false, perhaps socially "correct" self. The person revealed is the true self, that self they experience themselves to be—the core self, as psychologists and theologians often call it. Responsible, autonomous persons are ever aware of these choices, and are willing to live with the costs and consequences of these mask-dropping acts. This is a far cry from simply accepting (submissively or unconsciously) a destiny handed down by authority figures—or bad witches.

To live creatively, we must first discover our core self, then live that self in our life. This usually demands a sacrifice of security, the security once afforded us by our social masks. Identifying what is important to us, truthfully disclosing ourselves (perhaps at first only to selected, trusted others) helps us become real to ourselves.

Psychologist Sidney Jourard suggests that we reach psychological wholeness only by disclosing our real self to at least one other human:

It is not until I *am* my real self and I act my real self that my real self is in a position to grow. One's self grows from the consequence of being. People's selves stop growing when they repress them. This growth-arrest in the self is what helps to account for the surprising paradox of finding an infant inside the skin of someone who is playing the role of an adult. (Jourard, 1971, p. 32)

People who speak up for the first time for something they value while with friends who think differently are sometimes happily shocked at how strong and bolstered they feel afterward. "I didn't know I had that in me," or, "I felt good about myself when I stood up for my viewpoint," they will often report proudly. This realization stems from their "emergence" as distinctive individuals. They also feel as if a barrier, or block, to their real self has lifted. While previously they may have submitted to convention or social pressure, now at last they let themselves out. The "it" they say they didn't know they had in them is themselves. Through concrete, conscious, authentic words and acts they grow more alive, and aliveness resides at the heart of the creative process.

Autonomy and Social Transcendence

Usually we face some personal cost or sacrifice in autonomous choice-making. My interviews in the mid-eighties with a wide variety of self-actualizing adults, living vividly unconventional but positive, contributive lives, demonstrated that as autonomy increases, one grows willing to make these sacrifices. Increasing autonomy brings with it increased social detachment or objectivity, transforming such sacrifices into what I have termed "social transcendence." For example:

· A sacrifice of adherence to collective opinion, custom, vanity, security, guarantees, in favor of identifying and expressing the deepest life values: truth, love, health, beauty, compassion and so on.
· A sacrifice of living unconsciously, of not knowing who one is or what is right, in favor of bringing the law of one's being into existence through conscious expression.

· A sacrifice of direct and "safe" or predictable routes of accomplishment in favor of those which may be more demanding, risky, ethical, illogical, unpopular and so on.
· Sacrifice of the individual's peculiar, risk-avoiding tendencies (e.g., withdrawal from or avoidance of difficulty) in favor of reliability, commitment and responsibility in relationship to self and others. (Sinetar, 1986, p. 23)

Social transcendence carries with it the heightened ability to look within for guiding values and answers as well as the tendency—I believe the need—to detach ourselves responsibly when observing society or our own life. Mature autonomous persons are characterized by a love of freedom. This trait contrasts sharply with the need and desire for sameness, safety, structure and societal directives that most people possess.

Catherine, quoted earlier, illustrates the autonomous person's love of freedom: judging herself worthwhile, she also trusts her perceptions and uses them for her long-range life planning. She does not submit her ideas, decisions or internal experiences to others—except as she chooses and then certainly not for approval or validation. As a result her life is distinctive and personally meaningful; however, it is not one that others would find easy, secure or even desirable.

Catherine lives alone at the end of a nine-mile dirt road on a 360-acre homestead. She had a clear vision about how and where she wanted to live. She was able to create this life for herself. Incrementally, her life is evolving into what she feels is her best option despite hard work and uncertainty.

In order to survive economically, Catherine periodically divides her time between the ranch and northern California's Bay Area, where she free-lances as an editor and researcher.

> I didn't have any illusions about being totally self-sufficient here. This land is too water- and soil-poor for farming. I knew that before I moved here. I have a lot of homesteading skills, but my talent is with the written word. I want to make a life here that reflects and is supported by that.

Catherine knows her strengths and limitations, her preferences and dislikes. This characteristic is another benchmark of self-defining, autonomous persons—they have a capacity to look unflinchingly at their own and external realities and then get on with the best available course of action.

At age forty-four Catherine doesn't wish to hold two jobs and live in two locations forever. Ideally she wants to find a way to live full-time at her ranch and stop commuting. Until then, she keeps her city jobs going and waits to figure out her next steps. This response is a sign that a creative mind is at work in the real world. Catherine has no instant answer but does know that her own practical steps will help her find a long-term solution, in everyday terms.

Growth toward independence is an evolutionary process as well as a creative one. Autonomy does not occur overnight, although, as Hansel and Gretel show us, some young children seem born "mature." In most cases, years, even decades, of thoughtful, personal exploration precede that level of independence we associate with full human functioning and living, creative expression.

Autonomous, creative adaptation means finding our own answers. This requires we think strategically and that we tolerate long-term experimentation. Because of this we must be willing to assume our growth and goal tasks without any guarantee that things will turn out as we envision. This lack of guarantee terrifies many—if not most—people and keeps them locked into commitments and ways of life that are far less fulfilling than they might ideally want.

Autonomous adults are engaged in a creative process that involves, at least partially, asking the world to adjust itself to them, rather than merely trying to fit themselves to it. They demonstrate a deep fidelity to the law of their own being. Therefore they maneuver around obstacles, keep their own counsel, maintain their inner balance and sense of purpose even—indeed, especially—during times of adversity, all the while trial-and-erroring their way along an uncertain route. But those whose actions and choices are influenced by their inner core are also tenacious in their ability to stick to a private agenda, as Catherine demonstrates. It is as if their *intentions* part the seas of their chosen life's voyage.

A young, energetic executive I will call LW has similar clarity about his goals. LW's decisiveness, willingness to be patient, his creative adaptation are identical to Catherine's although his goals are completely different. LW too is growing toward mature autonomy; he too experiences himself to be a wholly separate, distinctive person; he too lives a creative process. LW loves business. When he was in his twenties, his career goal was to be a CEO; today, in his mid-thirties, he *is* the CEO of an aggressive, publicly traded corporation. LW has always had other personally meaningful objectives, and these have kept him on what some call a fast and driven track. In truth, LW retains control over his life and career while sustaining a good deal of balance and control over both his personal and professional life. His sense of destiny guides his decisions. He demonstrates in a vividly urbane manner what personal clarity looks and sounds like.

When I first met him, LW was a junior executive in a multinational corporation in Los Angeles. His work ethic and intelligence, his ability to stick with a task until it was properly completed, his eagerness to devote long hours to company projects and his political adroitness brought him early recognition from top management. In a very short time he was made a vice-president of a major function. Senior officers tried to be his mentor. They counseled him to slow down, to enjoy his position and success and to be satisfied. "What is he trying to prove?" was their common refrain. Only his wife and one or two close business associates understood his urgency. LW knew his own mind and kept to himself the fact that his desire to become a CEO quickly was based on his intention to amass a good sum of money and then enter the diplomatic service.

> I see myself as having two or three careers. I have the talent to run a business. I also have a great desire to be responsible for certain improvements in international relations. I've always intended to make that level of contribution, ever since I was a boy.
>
> I wasn't born into a family with political connections or fabulous wealth. I'm going to have to create the context of such assets myself. For this, I need to move relatively fast. Others can't understand this, and I choose not to explain: explaining means only that you're justifying yourself. My wife understands, and since I know what I'm doing, that's enough.
>
> There's no guarantee that I'll make it. But given my capabilities I'd be crazy not to try. I know what I want for my life, and it's my life after all.

LW's or Catherine's specific personal goals aren't the issue here. Rather, it is the ingenious, creative power they, as self-defining individuals, exercise when making choices.*

High self-esteem is an essential ingredient in the growth toward autonomy. It gives us the ability to sustain ourselves emotionally when things are not going our way. Almost everyone has been heavily imprinted with society's values and expectations. Ignoring the demands of others, making simple requests or expecting somehow that the world will conform itself to us is nearly impossible if we are preoccupied with pleasing people or "adjusting." Self-trust, our feeling that we can get what we need from our own depths or by our resourceful behaviors, lets us accommodate externals as long as we must—say, while we are waiting for our answers. Yet we still keep our long-range goals intact. In other words, we may conform to the world's way of doing things but still work toward our own private goals.

Catherine's sense that she doesn't know right now how to support herself economically while living full-time on the ranch is offset by the deep conviction that she will know how eventually. This conviction allows her to adapt herself continually to surface necessities and events while holding fast to her inner plan:

> I go with the flow. If things don't go my way, I don't have fits about it. I just wait, or adjust myself somehow. I'm capable of making long-range plans, but until the goal is in my hands, I don't actually count on it. I act as if it were available, but I don't bank on it until it's reality.

Carl Rogers wrote of the newly emerging self as someone who becomes whole to the extent that he becomes congruent—that is, lives so there is no discrepancy between the inner self and the outer self. As we open ourselves to the inner word of what our life is meant to be, no doubt we gain new power to express that life.

To create a distinctive life, to grow in self-trust, to love freedom does not mean to become so wedded to our own idiosyn-

---

* Lynette, Hank and Sara, quoted earlier, demonstrate these same traits in their earlier stages of formation. Catherine and LW illustrate the traits of autonomy at more advanced, mature levels.

crasies or plans that we fail to interact responsibly with society or with those around us. Autonomous individuals enhance their own and others' lives because their own lives and goals are motivated predominantly by a love of life.

Catherine's willingness to be known through her choices gives her unusual staying power: she is able to sustain the effort required for her life's journey. LW's willingness to express his core self, to do those things he senses he must, makes him unusually well equipped to sustain responsibilities, an arduous work and travel schedule and the duties of a husband and father. Gretel's desire to live gives her power to commit an unthinkable act of self-defense. Nor should we interpret her self-defense too literally either. We also become emotionally capable persons when, and only if, we separate ourselves from those who would hurt us, thwart us or create dependencies in us. Looked at through this lens, Gretel's act against the witch can be interpreted as a symbolic gesture of rebellion—the *positive* separation from authority that serves life.

It is safe to suggest that people who retain their inner equilibrium during crises have developed a core self from which choice, conviction and responsible action flow. Conversely, when we pretend to be something we are not, we crack under pressure or life crisis.

Catherine's self-acceptance, her own support of what she is, wants and needs, enables her to tolerate what others could not.

> I have high tolerance for what many people consider adversity— no phone, no so-called services. In winter I have to maintain a dirt road and in late summer I run out of water. But things a lot of people take in stride, or even relish, are really abrasive to me—things like crowds, traffic, locks, shopping (I genuinely *hate* shopping), cement where trees should be. I can cope perfectly well in the city, but it eventually triggers an urgent need to escape and regroup my forces.

Her self-acceptance opens up other unusual talents (and each of us has at our disposal similar sensitivities) such as a sureness about her own rhythms and timing. This sureness connects her effectively to the real world:

> I watch the sun, moon and stars a lot—much as someone else might glance at the clock from time to time. These orient me and

provide a rhythm I've grown attuned to. I can lose track of what day of the week it is, but rarely of the phase of the moon. It's just the opposite in the city. Artificial constructs like "Saturday" mask time, just as skyscrapers distort space. I'd rather measure my life by the coming and going of birds and flowers and mushrooms than by when the new McDonald's on the corner will open. It's good to know that there are forces other than "man" at work in the world, and that they are very strong indeed.

LW's self-acceptance gives him a similar sureness as well as distinctive awarenesses and skills:

I seem to know about groups, their rhythms—if I can call them that—some invisible hum or cue that the entire group gives off. I am able to read this language like other people read a book. I can walk into a group of strangers and know what's happening, know who has the power, know what needs to be said and done for the greatest good to emerge.

I remember seeing *Chariots of Fire*, in which one of the heroes is a long-distance runner. He says at one point that he can *feel* God's pleasure when he runs, that it's in his blood to do this. Well, I relate to that. I feel an almost visceral pleasure when I build something, like a business, or when I have responsibility for people's welfare. I'm not religious, but I too feel God's pleasure when I use myself as I know I was born to be "used."

The life process of autonomous choice-makers can teach us *how* we can make creative adaptations in our own lives. There is a pattern to their behavior that we can read and interpret for our growth lessons. Autonomous adults fluidly, perseveringly and strategically experiment. They keep on going. They adjust to the unexpected or the novel. They wait when necessary, while holding fast to their inner plans. If we want to create a life context that lets us express ourselves distinctly, if we hope to function productively, we first have to take responsible action toward expressing the best in ourselves.

In sum, we can reclaim our lives. We can learn to live according to our highest personal dictates and inclinations, and can begin to do so at any age. Whenever we strengthen our self-acceptance we begin to recover. From our recovery point, our growth toward autonomy begins.

9

The Positive Side
of Rebellion

How can we have the courage to wish to live, how can
we make a movement to preserve ourselves from
death, in a world where love is provoked by a lie and
consists solely in the need of our having our sufferings
appeased by whatever being had made us suffer?
—MARCEL PROUST

Gretel flew straight to Hansel, opened the little stable
door, and cried, "Hansel, we are free! The old witch is
dead!"
—THE BROTHERS GRIMM, "Hansel and Gretel"

Gretel's power to save herself and her brother ultimately results
from her ability to rebel, to protest, to trust her basic instincts for
survival. To save herself and Hansel, Gretel refuses to be victimized. This part of the tale and her growth parallels the natural
tension that exists between the individual's need to grow and
society's need for order and control. We can think of the witch
as a symbol of well-entrenched forces, both outside and within,
that threaten our personal growth. Ideally, at some point in the
life of every organism (individual, group or community), this
tension must be resolved so that the whole and its parts can
survive and prosper.

Every effective, creative individual, every innovative, viable
organization and community does, in fact, resolve this antago-
nism between individual and group need. But not all persons or
groups are able, or willing, to reconcile this pull.

A degree of rebellion against the dictates of external forces is in fact normal and necessary if we want to grow properly into self-expressive, whole persons.

In an excellent article in *The Atlantic,* Michael Kerr (1988) clarifies Murray Bowan's work on family systems therapy. Kerr points out that healthy adult functioning requires *emotional* disengagement from family or society. This seems precisely right. Our ability to be objective to those dysfunctional, or maladaptive, processes within our family structure—with which we have been involved since childhood—enhances autonomy. Individuation, that ability to differentiate ourselves from family or social influences, furthers creative adaptive skills. When we can afford emotionally to stand alone, as distinctly separate individuals, with our own feelings, values and life's purposes, then we can freely function with inner direction and authenticity even when living within family, group, community or social structures.

Psychiatrist Robert Lindner, who championed the cause of individuality over thirty years ago, encouraged us to view any and all "adjusted" persons as killing their own spirit, even as impeding human progress. Lindner was adamant about this; his books have a hard, inflexible edge:

> *You must adjust* . . . this is the motto inscribed on the walls of every nursery, and the process that breaks the spirit is initiated there. . . . Slowly and subtly the infant is shaped to the prevailing pattern, his needs for love and care turned against him to enforce submission. Uniqueness, individuality, difference—these are viewed with horror, even shame, at the very least they are treated with disease, and a regiment of specialists are available to "cure" the child who will not or cannot conform. (Lindner, 1952, p. 169)

To recover our own best instincts, Lindner supported a kind of positive rebellion—those modes of protest, being or behavior by which we preserve our core self and our healthiest, life-supporting instincts. He believed that by the time we exit childhood, most of us have extinguished the flame of our own spirit, killed our life-giving impulses.

Implicit in my own use of the term "positive rebellion" is the idea that our wholesome protests affirm life, move us closer to being who we are, in a way that, ideally, preserves the rights of others. Instead of being born of anger, or a negative move against law, order, cooperation and the like, positive rebellion helps us develop the strength to contribute to human advancement and cultivate what Fromm calls our "productive" side. Positive rebels (when they can be found) protest in whatever way is possible and natural to them. They do not so much protest against as actively resist encroachment of who they are and what they value. Positive rebels fight for their own values or their own well-being as well as for those of others. They strive toward authenticity and autonomy.

Nevertheless, despite my gentler interpretation, the idea of positive rebellion is greeted with suspicion. One reason seems to be that almost any striving to live vibrantly means that we must give up much of what, since childhood, we have learned to regard as safe and acceptable behavior. Lindner believed that all persons become successful rebels as they overcome the obstacles all societies construct to contain those "with the greatest capacity for positive, affirming and rectifying protest":

> In this group . . . apart from the few, rare, soaring souls who are members of the estate from birth forward—Socrates, Lao-tse, Christ, Gandhi, and others—we must include those who have somehow recovered from a negative condition—be it a neurosis or even a psychosis—and re-entered the evolutionary stream in a manner [in which they give it] impetus. . . .
>
> [This group is literally superhuman] because of their ability to express their human potentiality to an extent and in a manner hardly conceivable by the remainder. (Ibid., p. 226)

The rebel, for Lindner, is a catalytic agent, someone who is inwardly and psychologically successful. The rebel's life-affirming manner leads him or her to freedom while simultaneously leading the group toward evolutionary progress.

Not all "rebellion" is antisocial, although most of society's elders regard it as such. Sometimes our unwillingness to acquiesce is our bid to preserve our life. When Hansel and Gretel hear their parents plotting to send them away, they in turn plot to find ways to return home. When Gretel realizes the demonic witch plans to cannibalize them both, she instinctively takes steps to thwart the witch's plan. Then, when that red-eyed witch orders Hansel to stick out his finger so she can test it for plumpness, he tricks her. By cunningly putting out a thin bone instead of his chubby finger, Hansel saves his own life. He continues his deception for four weeks. By his trickery and rebellion, he survives. Are we to say, as some might when talking about adolescent rebellion, that Hansel is a troubled, delinquent child? Sometimes people, regardless of their age, must operate in opposition to others. *Not all rebellion is a reaction against all authority. Some rebellious acts, like Hansel's, like Gretel's, perhaps like ours, may be specific acts of protest against a specific danger.* These acts flow from a highly defined self that loves life, that has the power and centeredness to say, "I protest on behalf of who I am and so that my spirit might live on." Dietrich Bonhoeffer, the German pastor and Christian martyr executed by the Nazis for his part in the "Officers' Plot," fits this discussion as a case in point. His words—"If we want to be Christians, we must have some share in Christ's large-heartedness by acting with responsibility and in freedom when the hour of danger comes"—and his willingness to rebel during his own hour of danger cost him his life. He serves as an example, with few modern-day peers, of "positive," autonomous rebellion.

With reference to Hansel and Gretel, Bettelheim interprets the witch as symbolizing the threatening mother. This calls to mind another point: that many abused, victimized children and adults could do themselves good if they learned how to rebel in a positive way. In reality, sometimes protest is—at least on the surface—unattractive. Perhaps those who too coolly judge adolescent rebellion as inappropriate would do better to empathize with adolescents. We need only recall those instances when we spoke up on behalf of something we considered important, or asked for what we needed, or prevented someone from imposing on or demeaning us, to underscore the productive and quite organizing dimension of positive rebellion.

Molding the "Well-Adjusted" Child

Children are rewarded, coaxed and helped to perceive selectively along the lines of their elders. To perceive the world as adults do, children must distort their own perceptions when these contradict adult expectations. Methods differ for teaching children how to suppress their emotions and themselves. Some adults threaten and abuse. Some manipulate. They use praise, rewards, combinations of a sweet voice and conditional approval and/or mild to vicious punishment. Initially, Hansel and Gretel thought the witch was warm and friendly: she housed them and kept them warm, she fed them a delicious dinner, and she prepared two beautiful little white beds for them. They felt "as if they were in heaven" when they went to sleep at night. But all her kindness was really a lure; she wanted them for *her* dinner. On the simplest level this tale transmits the simplest lesson: Don't be deceived by false kindness. Adults too can be taken in by pretense and manipulation. A misguided manager once proudly confided to me that he kept his employees on their toes and in line by training them as he did his dogs: "First I hold up a little food so that they'll jump high for me. Then, when they've reached it and are busy eating it I step on their toes so they don't feel too secure."

Adults mold children and thwart their growth toward autonomy by creating guilt. The child is told, "After all I've done for you, now you go and say [or do] this?" Or, "Look at Johnny, *he's* not crying—be good, be like him and stop your crying." The child soon realizes he can gain praise and esteem if he suppresses his tears. He obeys by rejecting his own feelings, then by denying his overall awareness of what he feels. In time, he is unable to say *what* he feels. Those who intellectualize about their emotions instead of experiencing them have effectively learned to deny their feelings. Robert Bly (1988) reminds us that in the 1800s, adults distrusted "exuberance" in children. Child-rearing experts of that era believed that exuberance could be trained *out* of children by keeping the severity of a punishment unrelated to the child's offense. Adults who remember their own dysfunctional childhoods may productively review how they were rewarded and punished. This review would seem especially helpful if they do not feel joyful or happy now.

Sometimes people grow up feeling ashamed of what they are and are not. They remain so throughout adulthood for reasons they can hardly remember. One man expressed his shame in these terms:

> I learned from my parents that I was "worth less" than others. I learned this mainly from their nonverbal messages, from the way they parented me. I now realize that the core cause of adult dysfunction is shame—the feeling that we get from our parents that we are not satisfactory to them.

Children are also bribed or browbeaten or patiently taught to repress their self-protective hostilities. First, their awareness, feelings and defenses become submerged when these don't meet their parents' expectations. Then they must quell the anger and hostilities they feel as a result of their initial denial.

The strongest, healthiest children (the luckiest children probably) rebel. How they rebel is an individual matter. The more creative child may, for instance, simply "know" what he or she feels or thinks (e.g., that she doesn't like someone, that someone is manipulative, dishonest, dangerous, unwholesome, etc.), but usually the child has learned prudently to keep such feelings silenced. Other children may more directly refuse to play the adult's game. They might use their temper, their wits or sarcasm to keep adults from undermining their sense of reality. No matter how a child rebels, if it is done with the purpose of preserving his or her private, psychic self and spontaneous, healthy, instinctual life, we can be sure the rebellion is preferable to the passive surrender of soul and life force.

My friend Tom grew up in a dysfunctional family. Among other problems, his mother expressed only conditional love for him: if Tom met her stringent specifications, she accepted him; otherwise, she withdrew love. Unlike the man quoted above who carried his shamed feelings into adulthood, from the youngest age Tom felt his mother's conditional love was fallacious and he would not accept it as "love" or her as "loving." Tom sounds much like the woman quoted in chapter 1 who learned to respect herself because she didn't respect her abusive parents, when he describes himself as always having known, instinctively, that love meant something far more generous than merely conditional approval. But he stopped talking about his feelings, did not cry ("would not cry" may be more accurate) and kept his own counsel:

> I put my feelings on hold. I simply decided to wait until I was old enough—then I would leave. I was seething inside but there was nothing I could do about it as a boy. What I knew, though, was that conditional love was not love at all. This I knew from the time I knew anything at all.

Tom also gained much-needed privacy by simply disappearing. Even though he lived at home, he found ways to hide.

We had a downstairs bathroom, and I'd go in there with a three-year-old newspaper and lock the door and just while away the time by myself. I'd stay in there for hours, and my mother couldn't bother me.

However, Tom's most powerful tool was his temper:

I envisioned my anger as if it was pure uranium—hellfires in me. There happened to be a comic-book character at the time who epitomized this feat: he could burn obstacles down with his inner flame. If anyone got too far under my skin, if they cracked my normally complacent shell, they saw the hellfires burning. Usually they stayed away.

Today Tom is productive, creative and successful by anyone's standards. He has made peace with his parents and has actively forgiven them. He has built a solid, happy marriage of his own. He is an innovator in his profession and an active contributor in his community. His refusal to submit to the *idea* that he was unacceptable may account for his centered, empathic way of being.

Early Lessons in Self-Betrayal

Children have minimal power. Their size, economic dependencies, and emotional vulnerability put them at the mercy of the adults around them. When faced with the choice between accommodating their parents' expectations and rebelling in favor of their own, most children deny their real feelings. They think, speak, feel and behave—project themselves as persons—in any way that authority figures expect or think is correct and acceptable. Children's need for love and approval, for safety and belonging is so great that to gain it they will trade their true selves for false ones. Stories abound of children who, though severely abused by their parents, remain faithful, loving offspring, eager to stay near or live with their parents. Sometimes, after years of torment, they crack and turn their wrath against others or against their parents.

Reading Erich Fromm's *Escape from Freedom*, we can perhaps re-experience our own youthful powerlessness and remember what led us to self-betrayal. Fromm convincingly reminds us how children so easily suppress their thinking, insights and love of truth:

> A five-year-old girl, for instance, may recognize the insincerity in her mother, either by subtly realizing that, while the mother is always talking of love and friendliness, she is actually cold and egotistical, or in a cruder way by noticing that her mother is having an affair with another man while constantly emphasizing her high moral standards. The child feels the discrepancy. Her sense of justice and truth is hurt, and yet, being dependent on the mother who would not allow any kind of criticism and, let us say, having a weak father on whom she cannot rely, the child is forced to suppress her critical insight. (Fromm, 1965, p. 217)

In a short time, the child will no longer realize that she has a mother who is insincere, so fully will she have suppressed her observations. Along with the prohibition of truthful insight, the child will censor her own critical thinking skill since it too endangers her, puts her relationship with her parents at risk.

Pessimism and a lack of independence can result from such suppressed awareness. We learn to depend on others and cannot understand why we experience a pervasive feeling of sadness or hopelessness. We must not fault ourselves if as children we adopted such behavior or gave in to society's devotion to maintaining the status quo. Almost all adults eventually have to forgive themselves for having made this sort of bargain. The real betrayal begins much later in life when we have the power to see and speak our truths and don't cultivate the skill to do so. When we have the strength and the means to repair our early damage but choose not to notice that damage has been done, we betray ourselves.

Dr. Arno Gruen's book *The Betrayal of the Self* describes how hidden or suppressed rebellion becomes self-crippling. He sees autonomy as that state of being in which we live in harmony with our feelings and our needs. Positive rebels (although Gruen does not discuss rebellion with this term or in this way) accept and integrate their needs, authentic feelings, truest values into their lives in such a manner that they honor themselves, not betray themselves. This is indeed a creative adaptive achievement. As Gruen proves, not everyone can muster this achievement. The costs are steep. Most people back away from an autonomous life, not because this life does not beckon them but because they still are afraid and lack the strength to reach for autonomy. Back away though they might, a subterranean protest lives on nevertheless.

If our protests are overly vehement, if we lack assertion skill or adequate self-understanding, or if we don't know how to express ourselves so that others support our perceptions and needs, our autonomy has gone underground. Mental institutions and prisons are full of people whose protests have backfired. They have much to learn about the art of (and the love inherent in) positive rebellion.*

Rebellious children, those who refuse to follow the dictates or preferences of parents or other adults, may be attempting only to establish some protection for themselves or some minimal freedom so that they can defend themselves against self-deception, disrespect or an unhealthy life.

I have spent much of my professional life working with children, and I have seen youngsters of all ages (even adolescents and those children who get categorized as "delinquent") be quite willing to develop solid citizenship skills if given half a chance. One group of preteen "problem" youngsters whom I taught was in the same class for two years in a row. They had a terrible reputation—were labeled "bad," were called troublemakers and were believed to be unintelligent, low achievers. They were mostly boys, and none were academically inclined in the traditional sense. Their notoriety had spread to the school district's main office with the result that the principal rerouted his school tours so that visitors would not have to see our classroom. My sense was that the class misbehaved out of a desperate longing for attention and recognition. Convinced

---

* In her book *Sweet Suffering (Woman as Victim)*, Dr. Natalie Shainess provides readers with a compelling look at how our communication patterns set up self-punishments. Shainess focuses primarily on the way women have learned passive, masochistic responses, but I have shared this text with my more passive male clients with good success. Inherent in Shainess's work is the idea that it is in childhood that we learn not to "resist, refuse, offend or insist upon limits"; this learning is rooted in the abuse of power in parent-child relationships. This is a widespread learning and seems, to me, a genderless matter. Readers might be surprised if they knew how many men, as boys, have been brutalized by their mothers and fathers, and thus, as adults, suppress their own life instincts. When we love ourselves correctly, we trust our instincts to lead us in productive protest when necessary.

that positive recognition would be the best medicine for curing their low self-esteem, I persuaded our administrator to visit us the next time he brought dignitaries from the county seat to tour the classrooms. When our guests finally came by, these students were exemplary. They conducted themselves as well as any teacher could wish. In exchange for this cooperation, they needed protection. In their case, protection meant respect—the respect of school authorities and of the other teachers (who referred to them as "animals" and with other such terms of endearment).

Usually, children who protest need and want shelter from adult insensitivity, domination or intrusion. Children are quick to smell a rat; lacking power and sophistication, sensitive children easily lash out destructively or hold back enthusiasm and effort when threatened. Parents, teachers and community authorities often misunderstand this behavior and vehemently overreact, making matters worse. Disrespect begets more disrespect. A student spoken to in a disrespectful tone will generally speak back in an equally sullen or disrespectful tone. Impoliteness escalates until someone, usually the child, is punished.

Tactics of delay, refusals and resistance can be interpreted as healthy statements of growing autonomy or—at the very least— as practical good sense. What would we do if we were in their shoes?

Donald, a young participant in a study of children's adaptive responses, was highly guarded when his mother brought him to the psychological center to participate in intelligence tests. Writing about Donald, clinical psychologist and Harvard professor emeritus Robert W. White tells us that initially Donald refused to leave his mother's side, was uncooperative, said little and wouldn't do anything that his mother hadn't done first. He would do only what he found interesting—not what the psychologist prescribed.

White cautions adults not to jump to the conclusion that Donald has "problems" or needs psychiatric help. He suggests we look at Donald's behavior from a child's viewpoint. Suppose, for example, that like many children Donald has visited doctors, dentists and other "helping professionals," and has found a discrepancy between what his parents told him would happen and what actually happened:

> If such conditions existed for Donald, he exhibits commendable common sense in sticking close to his mother, the one familiar object, until he can figure the nature of the racket. (Moos, 1976, p. 21)

Compared to the child who happily and speedily surrenders to the will of adults in an unknown environment, Donald retains far greater personal autonomy. Yet adults might, and do often, overreact to children like Donald: they feel easily threatened or think their authority has been disrespected, or they come from a school that teaches: "When I say, 'Jump,' you say, 'How high?' " Their military model of parenting or teaching has little place in sound early-childhood methodologies. If we want to cultivate positive self-valuation and a growth toward autonomy in children (or in ourselves), along with our directives we had best show respect and proper dignity. In adulthood, people like Donald may well be the more prudent, effective adaptors since they assert their wills, even if only minimally, in the face of the unknown until they know what's what.

Donald has adapted creatively to the demands of adult society. He effectively retains his power, although to most adults this may not be readily apparent. Many children, however—perhaps most—cannot even imagine their own power. The result, as demonstrated in studies of children with below-grade reading achievement, is passivity, submission and a total inability to conceive of themselves as victorious over conflict situations.

When as adults we lack power over our circumstances, it may well be that we too cannot imagine ourselves triumphant over the problem. As inconsequential figures in our own mind's eye, we may have learned to be overly submissive and retain outmoded feelings of inadequacy. To repair the damage, we need to learn to respect our feelings and ourselves.

Adults who (either early or late in life) develop the coping and "protesting" skills that children like Donald portray are often cautious in the face of the unknown. They pay attention to what they fear, need or want. They move at their own pace. They cooperate with rules and authority when they are ready—after they have appraised the situation as best they can in their own way. They can imagine themselves powerful, achieving and ultimately successful despite the fact that the odds seem against them.*

Parents as Role Models for Rebellion

Children who resist, delay or refuse to do a thing may be quite commonly found today, but those who insist on boundaries in their parents' or other elders' treatment of them are still rare. However these unusual children manage to set their own standards and boundaries, they are probably developing skills which, in adulthood, allow their true talents and strengths to emerge. They learn proper timing, how to be politically adroit, how to gain persuasive advantage or information. If such lessons are disruptive, to supervising adults, they can help children foster appropriate ways of protesting. The most democratic processes within each family structure are in fact designed to teach just this. Both LW and Catherine told me that their parents rewarded them for expressing their own opinions. Catherine said that her parents actively taught her to think independently, and that independent thinking was something she also saw in them. Unless we observe our parents embodying these skills, we are unlikely to learn in childhood the smoothest, most practical ways to resist encroachments. The road to this learning may then be bumpy in adulthood.

Opinionated, independent parents are more likely to produce opinionated, independent, expressive offspring. Yet such children rarely rebel against their parents, even when cultivating the

---

* It seems clear that the Nazis understood quite well authoritarian techniques for squelching rebellion. The techniques they used in concentration camps (and in what Bruno Bettelheim terms "that larger concentration camp called Germany") focused on establishing powerlessness. Their primary objectives were to produce, in concentration camp residents, childlike attitudes and dependency and to erode their individuality and autonomous thinking. "Successful" residents retained their humanity and their own authority, even though they appeared to conform. They refused to steal food from other prisoners. They resisted—in whatever way they could—those things that undermined their individuality. They tried not to behave in an animal-like way. Sounding like Nikos Kazantzakis ("When you rise to a valorous deed, all of your ancestors rise with you"), Bettelheim writes that for the survivors of concentration camps, life was not meaningless. Rather it taught them that there is meaning to life, despite all outward appearances and brutality to the contrary (Bettelheim, 1952).

skills of speaking up for their values and needs. In a study of 400 creative, eminent persons, Victor Goertzel and Mildred Goertzel found that the bulk of the parents of the eminent were highly expressive about their own opinions and often conflicted with established ideas and mores. Their offspring were more likely to emulate, not rebel, against their parents. The children learned by example how to appraise society, how to respond to convention and political events, how to respect their own sense of reality, from standards of fair play, and trust their own opinions. Margaret Sanger, for instance, was quoted as saying that once her parents felt their children were old enough to have an opinion, they were then given room to express it. Similarly, my own parents valued both politeness and honest intellectual debate. I had clear understanding of what "grown-up" behavior was and had my parents' permission and encouragement to express myself in grown-up ways. In our home, this meant expressing independent ideas, contributing responsibly to conversation and respectfully allowing other people to express themselves. Mine was by no means an idyllic home, but it was cultured, respectful and humane. These simple ingredients go a long way in nurturing a child's spirit.

In the early years, firm parental guidelines and structures generally are needed to produce children with high self-esteem. Children whose parents expect them to participate responsibly in discussions respect their opinions. They listen and encourage the child's input to family- or community-related discussions. These methods develop individuals who tend to think for themselves, act responsibly and use their minds and influence productively. Because they are *expected* to behave in this way, these children may find it easier than others to rise to the occasion of debate, self-expression and independent, accountable action.

Looking back, I am certain that something in the democratic structure of my parents' child-rearing practices also enabled me to acquire a sense of timing, self-monitoring and assertion— skills that furthered my own growth toward autonomy. In chapter 1, I described how a distant cousin helped me return to boarding school after my father died. My cousin knew that I did not want to travel around the world with my mother. I am sure now that negotiating to remain in boarding school was my way of meeting my needs for inner balance and even emotional and physical security. I was thirteen—old enough to know that I was making a move against my mother, but I also knew I craved stability, however distasteful the packaging of that stability may have been to me in other ways. Continual hotel-, school- and country-hopping, no matter how elegantly managed, would have somehow undermined my emotional growth. Rebelling in this way was my instinctive survival tactic—a positive act undertaken for self-protection—although for years I felt guilty about my "treason."

Teaching Ourselves to Rebel

The process of growing into autonomous persons capable of positive, life-affirming protest and expression need not be initiated only in childhood. There are turning points all through life when a small choice can symbolize, for us, what we value and who we are. Affirmation in adulthood can begin simply, unassumingly. This means our choice or act may appear insignificant to everyone but ourselves (see Sinetar, 1988). We need not put ourselves into high-risk situations or suicidally and aggressively bite off more than we can chew. At almost any point, wherever we are in life, we can further our autonomy by asking ourselves about our daily choices. "Am I expressing my core self in this choice? Am I rejecting or affirming my life's spirit by this or that act?" In time, and often with professional help, it will be increasingly clear to us what we must do to resurrect our innate ability to protest so that we can live productively. Moreover, it is in our small day-to-day choices that we save or lose our life, since these add up over the years to be who we are.

Self-acceptance is best developed in childhood, but relatively few are so lucky to gain it then. Nonetheless, the techniques for nurturing it can apply equally to adults. Carl Rogers believed that a child's core self can be bolstered (and healthy development enhanced in the process) if parents do three things:

· accept their child's feelings and strivings;
· accept their own feelings (e.g., their own anger, disappointments, joys and sorrows) and their child's unacceptable behaviors;
· communicate acceptance for their child as a person. (Monte, 1977)

As adults we inherit the job of parenting ourselves. Even if we have not known emotionally whole, completely nurturing parents, our task in adulthood is to develop our core self just as ideal parents might have done for us if they were able.

To liberate our unused, hidden powers we must first free ourselves. This freedom is sometimes referred to as "wholeness": a psychological integration or centeredness, an interior spaciousness devoid of excessive fear, stress or conflict. In this state we gain access to the wealth of our inner resources, stir up and stimulate that magic synthesis spoken of earlier, and generate the answers and acts of creative adaptation. As we saw happen with Gretel, when we mine our inner wealth our own answers give us the power we need to save our lives.

10

Freedom's Strange Logic

The Way of the individual is the microcosmic reiteration of the Way of All and of each.
—JOSEPH CAMPBELL

Then Hansel sprang like a bird out of a cage when the door is opened. How they rejoiced and embraced each other and hugged for joy and kissed one another.
—THE BROTHERS GRIMM, "Hansel and Gretel"

The image of Hansel, liberated and ecstatic, no doubt reminds us of our own wish for personal liberation. Reading how the children free themselves, everyone empathizes: if only we were free of life's confinements, how we too would rejoice, how we would embrace those we love, how happily we could then live out our lives. But just as Hansel and Gretel discovered, there are tasks each must face and master before liberation is possible. These relate to meeting the often harsh realities of life and achieving individual wholeness. The healthy, integrated emotional state is a way of being that transcends fear, domination and self-imposed limits.

We soar perceptually at first, then—despite problems—we somehow sense a way out through our choices and acts. Personal freedom such as this, and the answers we seek, can be attained. The great mystery of all time is why so few choose to travel the path that leads to freedom. Perhaps one clue lies in the fact that this path involves trusting irrational forces.

Befriending Freedom

Before we become whole and gain the upper hand on problems, we must befriend freedom—that open, intricate, infinite landscape of our nonconscious world. This interior freedom is the wellspring of creativity, the ground of being from which we inherit, and grant ourselves, external freedoms. A line from scripture, "What you loose on earth is loosed in heaven," may serve as a universal rule for those who yearn for solutions. Before we find these special answers we must become comfortable with freedom, right here on earth.

When we meditate, daydream or pray for answers (and are willing to let these come of their own accord, in their own time), when we stop trying to force our answers into existence, we embrace freedom. We release our stranglehold on our own thought processes. We allow our various intelligences to work things out without our logical, too structured interference. On the other hand, when we chase the quick fix, or organize our lives rigidly around preconceived notions or idealized images of how we "should" live; when we follow too obediently convention on matters important to us, or passively make life choices along the lines others have convinced us are correct; for "our own good"; when we deny ourselves time to think, dream, grow, explore, experiment, play and pray, we also deny ourselves the freedoms we need to create our own lives anew. Then our cage stays shut.

This denial permeates adult life in any number of ways: We refuse to take responsibility for our choices, blaming others instead for our inability to do this or that. We let others think for us, let them tell us who and what we are. We force ourselves to have mind-numbing conversations with people we dislike or find toxic to our health. We deprive ourselves of hearing, or seeing, external cues and feedback that could help us find much-needed answers and directions. We say yes to "opportunities" that we hate or that kill us. We convince ourselves we are too old, young or inept to do something we'd enjoy.

While open minds freely spot split-second insights as they leap into view from every conceivable source—twenty-four hours a day, both while we sleep and while we are awake—the closed mind is ever caged, heavily defended from itself.

Life, autonomy, experience, the intrinsic mystery of the nonconscious world, feelings—all these elements threaten to undermine the tidy self-view and world-view construct that the closed mind creates, then invests in heavily to keep itself intact. Boundlessness, ambiguity, instinct, spontaneous feelings are fearsome precisely because the individual, even if utterly miserable, depends on fixity, the evidences of "logic," and previously chosen structure. His closed mind bars itself from its own primary thought processes and lives on in its little jail. The closed mind hates freedom just as it hates life itself.

By vivid contrast, healers, artists, mystics and all exemplary leaders continually demonstrate their enjoyment and pursuit of freedom. Abraham Zaleznik, professor of management at the Harvard Business School, has described eloquently how, in childhood, those who later become leaders learn to rely on their own problem-solving skills, and on their own minds and feelings, to solve early life problems. Trusting their instincts, intuitions and most private realities, they are strengthened in a way that later serves both them and others (Zaleznik, 1977).

A friend and colleague, D. Patrick Miller, a poet since childhood, and now a gifted writer and graphic artist, describes how he communes with his nonconscious self and thus gains a creative edge. For Miller, feelings serve as entrance to his nonconscious world:

> I've discovered that in facing my feelings for what they are, I tap my creative power. This is a meditation of sorts. I allow my feelings just *to be*—I experience them, carefully observe them.
>
> I had to find my way back to this ability, which I had abundantly as a child. During a recent serious illness, I recovered this skill and found, initially, that my fear of my own feelings made me shut myself down in other ways. Now, the more I observe or experience my own feelings moving around in me, the more creativity flows through me into the world.

Miller is convinced that we create problems for ourselves in related areas. For example, we deny ourselves permission to think for ourselves:

> Society may not encourage us to think independently, but we turn its lack of encouragement into denial. The big creative ideas that succeed generally come from those who stray out of the mainstream just one time at least. They may get back into the

mainstream later, but hanging out there on the edge is what keeps them in contact with that creative source.

Trusting Our Illogical Self

We can assess our willingness to befriend freedom by simply observing our speech patterns. If we ignore or suppress our need for protest, if we fail to teach ourselves appropriate ways to communicate our discomfort (to the extent that we prefer to deny we feel uncomfortable or angry than to express ourselves authentically to others), if we pretend we don't have this inclination or experience, we further subvert ourselves from the way of wholeness and erode our creative power. We block our options. Like children who try to communicate their feelings and needs with temper tantrums instead of words to protest their unhappiness, we lock ourselves in a self-styled prison. Unproductive means of expression generally create unproductive results.

Our alternative is to educate ourselves and, in some cases, seek professional help to identify, then express, what we think, feel, need or want. We can learn to be authentic without putting others off and, simultaneously, can discover ways to protect our own interests. A by-product of this learning is that we eventually realize that our assertion, protest and search for understanding are just natural human impulses for selfhood and unconstrained living.

Emotionally healthy persons exist in all ages, genders, socio-economic and cultural groups. They share an ability to think for themselves and are able to express what is real for them. They tolerate their own inner chaos. This means healthy persons in every walk of life establish a rapport with their nonconscious, illogical selves. When something within says, "I am scared," or, "I am distressed," or, "I enjoy this, want that, need this other thing," at the very least healthy people honor that instinct by paying attention. Whatever the outward form of their lives, the emotionally healthy respond to problems with similar ways of thinking: they attend to their own insights, feelings and directives.

For creative people, the illogical self becomes a trusted ally. Daydreams, dreams while asleep and personal symbology (e.g., certain music, art, poetry, words, phrases, colors, animals, natural sounds, environments) contain nuances that they know benefit them. They may not know why these things help direct or heal them, and no teacher has taught them how to use these psychic processes or why some elements have power to influence their lives, yet still they trust these inputs. Creative people use a host of irrational means to further their rational, conscious goals, possessing an intimate connection with that ineffable aspect of self most others commonly ignore. In this way they are enlarged. The quality and development of their life is furthered and enhanced.

When a friend of mine reviewed these thoughts she said, "True, no one taught me how to know myself, and true, I do use many parts of myself in solving problems, but it took me thirty years to learn it was okay to have access to my illogical self. I have also had many teachers along that road." Others are more fortunate, perhaps more precocious in gaining this awareness. They learn alone and at an early age that they can fully trust themselves.

Whatever our age, we too can befriend our nonconscious, irrational, subterranean worlds. To do this, we must first align ourselves with the part of us that wants to become autonomous, authentic and whole. A support group facilitated by an able therapist, sensitive to this nonlinear, seemingly irrational underworld and its images can help us. Meditation, dream analysis, dance, art or music therapy, outside readings, walks in nature, time alone, making notes to oneself in a journal or diary—all these are ways to begin communicating with our interior selves.

To learn to understand the special language of our nonconscious, it is best not to struggle to push things along on a preconceived and usually quite irrelevant timetable. We must minimize our desire to tame what is essentially the brilliant wilderness of our own nature. The seemingly incomprehensible language of our infinite inner space communicates in its own way. As a friend told me:

> I'm aware that within me exists a mysterious dimension. This part serves my entire life if I'm receptive. The less I try to structure or impose my lower "logic" on this, the less I crave tidy ways to exploit this aspect of myself, the more I receive. When I make an effort to control my unconscious for purely material gain, or according to my own daily time frame, the less I receive.

Our nonconscious world invites us in on its own terms, in its own way, using a language that is inextricably tied to our life's purposes, emotional states and our own makeup and self-acceptance. When we fear autonomy we make ourselves anxious about certain necessary ambiguities that might otherwise produce creative, helpful insight. An entrepreneur told me that when she started her business, she hadn't a clue where or how to find clients. She proceeded anyway, as if she knew. She wrote up a business plan, located the required working capital and rented an office. The clients did surface, but not until she completed much of the groundwork. Had she lacked an independent spirit, the vagueness of her circumstances might have produced inordinate, crippling anxiety. "I was nervous about it, but I figured the worst that could happen was that I'd have to get a regular job again if things didn't work out."

To befriend freedom is to entertain that in us which is hidden, mysterious, often only fleetingly available. This freedom asks us to relinquish our dependencies and overconcern with safety. For some, freedom demands a release of unthinking, robotic habits that may have been mindlessly adopted. For others, something else entirely is required. The less autonomous we are, the harder it is to let go of our craving for security and to tolerate uncertainty spontaneously, cheerfully. Cravings for predictable, routinized, often lifeless approaches to problem solving make us nonproductive, whatever our daily habits.

Dr. Arno Gruen (1986) writes that we fear such freedom because it reminds us of our original helplessness. Gruen suggests that since we learn in infancy to view freedom as a threat, we as adults believe we are disobedient if we desire liberation. We then put our faith and trust in the power of others, and in familiar external things. We think that these can protect us from the helplessness we so fear and despise in ourselves. Our adaptation then lacks all creative power: we live involuntarily, "in accordance with the will of other people." Gruen stresses that when we live this way what is really dangerous is that we fear the smallest breakthroughs of our own self. Emotional blandness, lack of feeling, and weak expressive skills are all symptomatic of low creativity quotients. On the other hand, vibrancy, intensity or high emotional and expressive "color" seem qualities creative adults have in common. In other words, they are alive.

Erich Fromm has argued persuasively that nonproductive

people are concerned predominantly with safety, while productive persons flow with their life forces and circumstances without demanding excessive guarantees or rules. Chronically nonproductive people hate freedom and will go to any length to avoid it. They are unalive in the sense that they habitually choose against themselves, acting self-defeatingly and perhaps even mechanistically.

Each of us has, within, a mix of all human traits, but highly adaptive people generally enjoy and predominantly express whatever is alive in themselves. They prefer people, wildlife, nature, beauty, creation and creating to gadgetry, technique, technological devices and mechanical formulas for how to live. Earlier I wrote that I often meet people who seek ready answers for how to do almost everything, who become irate when the instant answer is not forthcoming or when they are asked to consider paradoxical or unsettled, unanswered concepts instead of dogmatic, doctrinaire solutions. For them, everything—all ideas and problems—must be answered, closed immediately and settled. Ironically, real life is rarely neatly manicured or ordered like this. Their mechanized reality—as well as mode of thinking—is deathly because it excludes life and life's own spontaneous, instinctive process, which is an ever-changing flux. Organizations with nonproductive leaders do not meet change smoothly and easily become extinct. Only living, creatively intelligent people and groups can adapt. The living dead cannot: they are dense, thick, hard to stimulate to novel responses.

If this seems harsh, we have only to observe in ourselves reactions that are obviously nonproductive. If we are honest, we can each find within ourselves pockets of ineffective, entrenched habits that thwart our lives and deprive us of satisfactory, truly intimate, lively or healthy connection to the world. Perhaps we cling to a form, an outward shell, of relationship—a "perfect marriage," for instance, or the right club or community affiliations. Or we preserve old routines with people with whom we have patterned, predictable conversations but little real relationship. Perhaps we try too hard to figure things out logically or seek endless reassurances from others and then feel angry or thwarted when their reassurance is unsatisfactory or leaves us feeling empty. Reassurance and logic are never routes to safety: safety exists only when we are comfortable without it. Our control is most perfect when we feel free to relinquish it.

Perhaps as parents or teachers we attempt to transform our children into what Fromm calls "unalive." By observing what we do to our children, we can discover what was done to us. As suggested at the opening of this chapter, most of us have been schooled away from our own depth and breadth. This is why restoring creative skills in adulthood so often involves some confrontation with authority, as well as major unlearning and reconceptualizing of the past. Because as children we were taught to deny certain "inappropriate" responses, such as protests or our awareness of social and parental hypocrisies, as adults we may need to resurrect our abilities to feel in precisely those response areas we killed long ago.

When "No" Means "Yes"

Learning to say no constructively is a fruitful step along the path to recovering our suppressed selves (Maslow called this the "recovery of delight"). People who feel confident, worthwhile and secure can let themselves say no to jobs, relationships or invitations that disinterest them. Their no really means they are saying yes to life. Since they are not overwhelmed by anxious feelings when faced with the disorder of a problem, they retain an inner balance that then allows them to manage the chaos of that problem bit by bit. As a result, they steadily order their lives and free themselves from stereotypical or frantic responses. In other words, saying no selectively, problem-solving abilities and refusal to be a victim are simply healthy defenses resulting from a healthy, self-valuing inner state. A bright young client of mine told me, in happy amazement, that he gains strength and added power when he refuses to compromise in small business or personal matters. "When I say no to some shortcut or shabby choice I feel better than when I say yes to that and gain the advantage I'd wanted."

Coherent problem-solving results from possessing an inward unity—even during ambiguous or chaotic, uncertain times. When a problem is overwhelming (and problems overwhelm almost everyone at times), we need to give ourselves time and permission to retreat or rest, even to regress. It is simply intelligent to leave ourselves alone when we have had enough for a day. Responding with self-respect, defending ourselves appropriately, enhances our ability to trust ourselves to take on more the next day. It is also simply practical good sense to say, "I'll feel better in the morning after a good night's rest—I'll deal with this then."

A friend told me recently that he was "bone tired" after a trip and planned to take a few days to do nothing. He gave himself permission to rest, retreat and be self-protective. While doing "nothing," he was in fact growing stronger, renewing himself thoroughly.

It takes persistence to reinvent ourselves even under the best of circumstances. Change is difficult no matter what our temperaments, and even those who thrive on stimulating projects and who enjoy fast-changing environments preserve what futurist Alvin Toffler terms "stability zones"—patterns, habits or routines of sameness and familiarity. If we are overly anxious or self-doubting, our barriers to change loom extra large. Then we have an insatiable craving for reassurance. We seek external definition for what to do. We need outer support to such an extent that we become unhealthily dependent on strong, controlling authority of others.

I am struck again and again by the lack of ingenuity I find in some perfectly bright, well-educated and financially secure persons. They seem unable to look at themselves and their life situations in imaginative, resourceful ways, or to create a means of escape from their predicaments. My corporate clients, for example, are often faced with mergers that uproot them occupationally. During such times, many are incapable of seeing all the opportunities open to them. They do not appreciate just how well-off they are. I believe they have been indoctrinated to be ultraobedient, and are too respectful of what others think. They view themselves through cultural or organizational eyes and cannot see themselves as people with talents outside those narrowly defined as accounting, finance, planning and so on. They are so keenly sensitive to how the majority culture lives that they don't experience themselves as individuals within society's flexible context. In fact, our culture allows people a wide range of personal options. Similarly, the organizations that retain my services are progressive. These companies provide tremendous leeway for individual decision-making. Yet many employees are distrustful of this fact and rarely take advantage of their freedom. They behave like prisoners in the old fable, who spend years locked up in a dark dungeon, only to find that the door to their escape is open and has never been locked.

Those of us who have thought for decades about leaving a job, a relationship or a particular way of life may find it comforting to blame others for our indecision. In truth, it is we who fail ourselves, we who have not attempted protest, we who remain behind an unlocked door instead of walking out to the life we prefer. To adapt creatively to our circumstances always means that we must invent ourselves anew, ask ourselves what we want to do with our human power. Creative adaptation does not imply merely that we accept a little crumb of a job, relationship or project that someone deigns to throw our way. When we are satisfied with crumbs, when we make do or agree to exist like things in boxes rather than insisting we be treated as persons, it may be because we need the security of things or the approval of others more than we need to live our lives.

The heroine in Erica Jong's novel *How to Save Your Own Life* honestly admits she has clung to security instead of "letting go":

> With no children to "tie me down" (or anchor me to reality), with a profession and livelihood of my own, leaving was still the hardest thing I ever did. . . . I tried everything I could think of to postpone the decision—or reverse it—and the process of leaving took years, not months.
>
> [My reluctance to leave] was a far cry from what one overhears from a neighboring lunch table. . . . "And then she just up and left him." That classic line is inevitably pronounced with a mixture of contempt and envy—but vicarious elation underlies them both. Another prisoner has escaped! . . . The line stirs us, no matter how many times we've heard it repeated. Freedom, freedom is the theme. (Jong, 1977, p. 57)

Men too, with hopes of living up to society's definition of "manly" or to family expectations, suppress their real selves and live restricted lives rather than create solutions more in keeping with their true needs.

Psychologist Herb Goldberg writes of what he calls the myth of masculine privilege. He speaks passionately about how the traditional idea of masculinity narrowly boxes men into unfeeling, linear and overcontrolled lives. In his book *The Hazards of Being Male*, Goldberg describes how the typical overachieving male usually rejects feelings, his irrational or "feminine" side and, therefore, his creative powers. Goldberg reminds us that while it is in style today to urge men to feel, this is much like encouraging crippled men to run.

Many of us—men and woman—are incapacitated in our ability to create wished-for solutions for our work, relationships or life in general. To become more able we may need to develop a new, and sometimes unusual, set of muscles. As a culture, we have made strides. We are more sensitive to the needs and abuses of children and the elderly. In addition, we are getting conscious of the realities of what it means to express human values in a complex, demanding world. Still, there is so much more to be done if we as individuals would recover and develop our true human values and capabilities.

As a start, each of us can learn to say no to those things that stifle our best instincts. We begin this by sensitizing ourselves to what those instincts are, then learning to trust them. Furthermore, we can say yes to the things that bring out our love of ourselves and others. We can teach ourselves to befriend freedom, in the process learning to trust our own ineffable interior life. In this way we cultivate an experimental manner that promotes creative solutions.

Occasionally, these acts produce feelings that we are going against the grain of what has always been. In fact, this is exactly what we are doing. Just as Hansel and Gretel must plot against the witch in order to get free, we too may have to plot against our internal demons whose subtle voices tell us to comply, accommodate, always "be nice," or change instantly to keep up with others whom we admire.

It takes hard, persistent work and not a little courage to develop our full humanity. Our bids for authenticity easily arouse fear, anger or at the very least concerns in family, friends or coworkers. People close to us may not want us to change. Certainly for many of them our growth introduces inconvenience. At a deeper level they may believe we will grow away from them the more we cultivate our strengths and uniqueness.

I recall one man timidly saying that each time he tried to do something for himself, like read a book quietly or attend an evening lecture, his wife and children became perturbed. "They say I'm selfish, and that I should think of them first." A woman struggling hard to become an artist reported that her husband disliked and seemed jealous of her ongoing need and enjoyment of time alone. Since solitude is essential for the development of any creative talent, she found herself pulled between her growing desire for silent, uninterrupted blocks of time and her need to keep the peace at home. One hardly knows how to respond to these basic but poignant interpersonal concerns. Certainly bringing one's family along—one would hope far, far in advance of actual changes or alterations in schedule—is one way to minimize problems. Another practical approach is to talk with a counselor or minister when we first notice that our goals and our family's expectations and comforts may collide. Even books or adult education classes on this theme can help us learn to phrase our needs in such a way that we elicit cooperation from those we love.

Initially, as we attend to our needs, we could well make too much of ourselves or cause undue trouble for others. If we pattern ourselves after heroes or heroines who always did for others, those around us may resist our coming into our own. Here too practice makes perfect. Loving and patient repetition of our objectives, our calm reassurances to them help us merge our interests with theirs. As mentioned in a previous chapter, resolving the tension between our individual needs and those of others is a central task of mature, creative adulthood. However, like the man who said he had spent so many years being an ideal father, husband and provider that he no longer knew what he needed for his own good, we too may require a lengthy period of time to experiment with our goal setting, our assertiveness skills and our objectives toward peace of mind.

On the other hand, if such freedom terrifies us, if we have overgroomed ourselves to be a Good Soul, to borrow Dorothy Parker's term, then we have to wonder if we aren't setting ourselves up. We can try to see whether we have "victim" or "masochist" stamped on what Parker calls our "unsuspecting backs." She describes the Good Soul as one who gets identified in early childhood:

Can you get a good look at the child whose precious toys are borrowed for indefinite periods by other playful youngsters and are returned to him in fragments? Do you see the child upon whom all the other kiddies play their complete repertory of childhood's winsome pranks—throwing bags of water on him, running away and hiding from him, shouting his name in quaint rhymes, chalking coarse legends on his unsuspecting back? Mark that child well. He is going to be a Good Soul when he grows up. (Parker, 1973, p. 577)

Whether or not we are Good Souls, it is likely that our deepest self waits patiently to be set free as it does in almost everyone. Since we alone choose to free ourselves, this can seem an overwhelming, frightening task.

If we place our faith in dominant but unsupportive others, if we reject our finest sensibilities, if we steadfastly refuse to experience the consequences of our acts, then the logic of this freedom will seem incomprehensible to us. On the other hand, there is good reason to expect happier days as we develop our humanity. Joy's strange logic equips us with exactly the skill we need to slay our private demons.

11

Slaying Our Demons

Desire reaches out beyond itself. To sin is to deliber-
ately halt along the way.
—Father Jean Sulivan, *Morning Light*

And as they had no longer any cause for fear, they
went into the old hag's house, and there they found, in
every corner of the room, boxes with pearls
and precious stones.
—The Brothers Grimm, "Hansel and Gretel"

From all we know of Gretel, attack is not in her nature. Neither
is she an angry, hostile person by any stretch of the imagination.
Nevertheless, this gentle, loving girl—long intimidated by the
witch—manages to strike out in violence. It seems that not until
Gretel faces a do-or-die situation does her spontaneous desire
for life prompt her right action. Her obvious crisis and her gradual, evolving realization that without action both she and Hansel
are doomed prompt her lucid, courageous act.

In like fashion, over time our predicaments make or break our
ability to reach out beyond ourselves and face reality squarely.
Throughout this book, we have seen that adults can grow. They
can learn that personal reality is malleable. They can develop
quite practical lifesaving skills. They can also gain developmental health, true self-appreciation and enjoyment of life. We cannot separate these elements: *our ability to act on behalf of our life
is tied into our developmental readiness.* In turn, this, at its height,
relates to a heartfelt regard for life. Maslow's remark, "When
[healthy persons] *know* what is the right thing to do, they *do* it,"

sums up this point as well as Gretel's uncharacteristic behavior. Had Gretel not been ready to act, she could not have. Had she not loved life—felt it somehow sacred and worth protecting at all costs—she could not have acted. Had she failed to act, it would have been through no fault of her own. While we often blame ourselves mercilessly for inaction, in some ways this is like being angry at a child whose first teeth have been slow to appear.

In terms of development, several qualities and traits prepare us to know what to do. In this chapter we examine what we can do to gain the wherewithal to slay our dragons. Namely:

· We can take responsibility for our acts and their consequences.
· We can face problems directly, as much as we are able.
· We can let things be at some natural moment.
· We can cultivate archetypes and recover our demons, for added power and insight.

We can help ourselves grow up. Children's learning patterns teach us exactly what sorts of lessons we need to learn—regardless of our age. Hansel and Gretel learn that loved ones are capable of hurting them. They learn not to linger too long at a stranger's house. They learn that while some food and rest are necessary for survival, indulging indefinitely can bring catastrophic results. They master discernment: this teaches them, as it has no doubt most of us, that just because someone seems pleasant or generous doesn't mean that person is trustworthy or has our best interests at heart. Hansel and Gretel begin to look beneath the surface of things. They grow in the ability to take care of themselves. Their development includes a heightened capacity to face facts and take proper responsibility for their actions. In part the children's real-world effectiveness parallels their ongoing emotional education.

To solve complex problems, we too need to be developmentally ready. Then, as we prepare ourselves for growth, the exploration, experimentation, affirmation or discovery routes we see that we must take simply become those next, quite logical steps along life's way, inconvenient or intimidating though they may be. Then, as with Gretel, our need and desire for life will exceed our need and desire for safety. This is because, in some deeply personal, subtle way, we already feel "safe." This security is more a developmental (or subjective) acquisition than it is worldly, and it affords us the sense that we can move on, solve problems of greater complexity. This may be one reason why some of us spend years thinking about a problem before we can act. In truth, we are preparing ourselves for the inevitable. The unhappy spouse "suddenly" leaves the loveless marriage. The bored, stagnating employee abruptly changes jobs or careers. The self-defeating habit falls away. We say, "One weekend I just threw all my cigarettes away. Just like that." In truth, we may have been building up to this turning point for years. Similarly, life's serious predicaments are easier to solve when we complete our psychological homework, when we prepare ourselves, subjectively, for what we must do. Although we steel ourselves against possible pain, rejection or deprivation and against any criticism, once we are ready to move into a new stage or activity, we often find ourselves doing so with an easy grace because we know our choice supports life and is right for us.

Developmental readiness provides both the emotional and the mental power to accept consequences, to stick with the results of our choices and to create our best, most workable options. I once heard a gifted therapist tell a client who wondered why he couldn't leave a loveless, joyless marriage, "You don't feel enough pain yet. When it gets worse, you'll have no trouble deciding what to do." In other words, when our desire (our love) for the thing we want (growth) surpasses our fear (i.e., misgivings about the pain of change; avoidance, etc.) we realize we can find our way out through the necessary, most obvious exit.

A friend told me that after a serious personal crisis she learned that there always had been dragons all around her. Some people have the strength to face these dragons, and others don't. A woman I'll call MT shows us what some of the factors are that help us face reality squarely. MT was a single parent raising her teenage daughter when her doctor informed her she had breast cancer and recommended a mastectomy. He gave her a weekend to think about it.

MT's grandmother and father had both died of cancer, and her main fear was death. She had to convince herself that she could survive the disease. But along with this torment was the thought that if she died, her seventeen-year-old would be left alone in the world. Ironically, these two demons and MT's background of having overcome other obstacles may have provided her with both the emotional and the mental power to create the best outcome possible: health.

> I had never seen cancer have a positive ending. I had to tell myself that life after cancer was possible for me. I told myself that my life was not finished. "I have cancer," I said to myself, "but I'm going to fight it and I'm going to win."
> I had a life to live, I had a daughter to raise, and I simply wasn't going to die yet. I wasn't done yet—there was still too much to do. My faith, my determination, my friends—these things saw me through a dark, dark year.

A point worth noting, as it relates to both problem solving and developmental readiness to face facts and choose responsibly, is that much earlier in her life MT had had serious difficulties and managed through them. Much of her childhood had been spent alone, and she had learned to fend for herself. She had surmounted an earlier bout with illness and had observed herself regain strength. Then, as a young woman, she lost a set of twins. "When I compared the death of my twins to losing a breast, I realized the breast was nothing.

> The realities of my life had taught me how to face what had to be done. I knew if I just put my mind to it, if I truly intended to survive, if I made my choices from the base of my love of life, my love of my daughter and my faith, I would win.

MT thinks about what tools she would want her daughter to have so as to be able to face and conquer any demons that might come her way:

> I'd want her to have faith in herself—trust that she can do anything she puts her mind to. I want her to know that fear does not have to win. We don't have to surrender to our fear—sometimes you have to go against your fear, act courageously even when you are frightened. The main thing I want my daughter to have is an ability to fight for her life.

Many people wonder how they can gain similar strengths, especially if they have not previously learned to be self-sufficient. If we are to move along on our own, a first step is to encourage and teach ourselves to feel unthreatened by the risks we know we want to take in the ordinary realms of life. We must not wait for the big problems to surface—say, an illness, a personal loss or economic reverses—before we practice the skills that accompany emotional maturity. Regardless of age, we can learn to take responsibility for our tough choices and their consequences. We may not be immediately successful, but initially the important lessons come from observing ourselves try, from gaining feedback from our mistakes and from the practice of facing our personal demons in everyday, ordinary life. This practice, this self-observation relates to productive modeling, described in an earlier chapter. In effect we become our own positive models.

Taking Responsibility: A Sign of Readiness

Taking small steps into the unknown in low-risk areas of life, ensuring our privacy and safety, obtaining practice and experience with the growth step we want, retaining a feeling of protectedness and comfort—these constitute our best route to growing more responsible. Plowing ahead insensitively without regard and respect for the fears we do have just won't work.

The small, low-risk step to growth also affords us another valuable lesson: we learn how to be responsible, how to examine what we are doing objectively, so that we can see which of our actions, if any, are working against the results we say we want. If we recognize our irresponsible streak, we can modify our behavior for the better.

The responsible person asks himself, "How is what I'm doing [or being, or thinking etc.] now helping me get what I really want? Is what I am doing right now helpful? Is it harmful—to me or to others? Is it productive or unproductive?" Our job is to upgrade our own ability to be discerning, primarily about our behavior and our ability to function effectively. Then we can correct ourselves as we see we must.

Often, counseling or attending a support group is required to move from a stuck, fearful and entrenched position into a more assertive, courageous and nonentrenched one. But just as often we first need help to see our own irresponsible behavior clearly. Self-defeat is maddeningly hard to spot in oneself: almost everyone has a blind spot as far as personal defenses are concerned. Responsible action toward creative growth can be avoided for years (if not for a lifetime) if we do not get help to break through our irresponsible behaviors.

Dr. William Glasser's approach to promoting responsibility is to prompt the individual with such questions as those above, to help him see how his own choices cause unhappiness. The question "How is what I'm doing now helping me get what I truly want?" reveals irresponsibility when the person is acting against his own interests. It assists in the upgrading and correcting of behavior. The overeater who asks himself this question, for instance, can readily spot his problem and may then choose to push away from the table. This approach, which Glasser twenty years ago termed "Reality Therapy," has continued to prove useful to teachers, social workers and counselors alike:

> In psychiatric treatment, strengthening the patient's recognition that his present behavior is wrong or irresponsible is a powerful motivation towards positive change. When we point out what the patient is doing which may be wrong instead of helping him look for excuses, he finds out that therapy is not an intellectual psychiatric game. . . . He discovers that we really care about him, an essential step toward gaining the involvement necessary for therapy. (Glasser, 1976, p. 71)

More recently, another psychiatrist, Garth Wood, put the notion of responsibility in slightly different terms, writing that when our lives do not work we seek endless ways to explain this away instead of assuming active responsibility for our actions. Such intellectualizing alleviates our distress and guilt but does little to improve our behavior. As the witch quite cogently observes to the weeping Gretel, "Just keep your noise to yourself . . . it won't help you at all."

Like Glasser, Garth Wood suggests that real self-help comes not from having our problems solved for us by a therapist but by learning how to solve our own problems, thus removing the unhelpful illusion that we lack power to resist doing this or that thing or that our past is to blame for our present inability. Wood calls his brand of therapy "moral therapy," and he too stresses the importance of helping patients rid themselves of excuses and alibis:

> When such individuals become aware that they are going to be asked to do things which, inevitably, they will find difficult—to

undertake hard work, to give up many unprofitable pleasures, and to lead a strict moral life as dictated by their own consciences—they may shrink from the situation and return to more comforting but less helpful philosophies. . . . In this "caring society" it may seem hard that help can only be given to those who show a genuine willingness to help themselves, but in the real world it has always been thus. (Wood, 1983, p. 21)

Signs of Unreadiness:
Blame, Envy, Anger, Fear

Of course, not all irresponsibility requires therapy. Sometimes we can simply monitor our own negative habits and attitudes for insight into our less attractive qualities. For example, if we notice we feel bitter or jealous about the good fortune of others, we might discover by paying attention and digging a little deeper into our feelings that the underlying dynamic is that what we say we want and what we are doing in life are mutually incompatible. People who say they want business success but who spend no time preparing themselves for it, who want to leave work every day at 5:00 P.M., or who devote little energy to reading in their field often experience pangs of resentment when someone else gets promoted quickly. When we envy someone else's supposedly effortless creative choices or success, it may be a signal that we have avoided being responsible to the goal we say we want for ourselves.

When we admit our hostility, we can find that like the older son in the parable of the Prodigal Son, we too will wonder why our brother is a blessed, adored child when he has done so little to earn that status, while we—who, after all, have given up so much, who have been obedient to the rules and expectations of parents and society—are not praised and rewarded accordingly. In truth, it is not so much the other person at whom we are angry; we are angry at ourselves for failing to embody effort, courage, or responsible action in our life.

Fear hinders creative choice-making, and often explains why our actions lack power. If we have not learned how to protest wisely, if we have not taught ourselves how to assert ourselves so that those closest to us hear what we say, or so that we are better able to create life circumstances that we want, if we have not had to pay for our choices (for whatever reason) or if we have lacked early life experience in problem solving, then—as adults—it is natural for us to believe we can't do things. We may feel held in check by fear when we want to create new solutions for ourselves. Our minds then tell us that this or that choice is simply too complex, is out of reach, could never be ours, or that we have no experience, are too old or too young. In other words, it is we who keep the creative option out of reach.

If we are not ready to take on the hard choice developmentally, we cannot imagine ourselves free of the burden that we feel is real. We can neither imagine searching for solutions nor affording the inconvenience of exploration. As yet, we are too anxious, too much in need of safety or approval to probe beneath the surface. Although people hate to hear this, if we do not push ourselves, if we care for ourselves properly (i.e., are nurturing and self-accepting, build stability and capabilities in ourselves, etc.), these anxieties often fall away of their own accord. Everything just clicks into place, as it does for someone who can "suddenly" stop smoking or overeating. As one woman told me, "When I stopped trying to *force* myself into the changes I desired, my true growth began."

On the other hand, we may have to prepare ourselves consciously first, to lead ourselves up a ladder of readiness (much as we prepare children to read or to do some other complex task). In time, with experience and self-trust, we can choose creatively despite fears, and do so successfully without excess force, without shooting ourselves in the foot.

David Viscott's helpful book *The Language of Feelings* discusses the value of fear. It is a sign to pay attention, often a beneficent signal from within that we are going about things incorrectly, an SOS from our unconscious to slow down or be more careful.

In an earlier chapter about learning resourcefulness, I discussed educator Sister Grace Pilon's work with children. Pilon's philosophy that children cannot succeed as learners without inner safety fits adults as well. Pilon (1978, p. 11) suggests that children must satisfy several needs before becoming able learners; these include:

· the need for intellectual safety;
· the need for inner order;

· the need to feel they can create and organize;
· the need to do satisfying work at their own pace and not in competition with others;
· the need to feel at ease when relating to peers and to those in authority;
· the need to feel a healthy sense of cooperation.

How safe do we feel, intellectually, when thinking out novel answers for ourselves? How much inner order do we have when choosing what we prefer over that which others want for us? How calm are we when in the company of authority figures? How easy is it for us to ask for what we want from significant persons, peers or family members? Are we cooperative or competitive with ourselves (and our colleagues or friends) when striving toward a goal? How nurturing are we to ourselves when we feel fear or panic?

Too frequently we don't even realize that we are afraid: along with other unwanted feelings, our fears have been buried for so long, so deeply suppressed that we don't know what fear feels like in our bodies. People who start their own businesses, or try to have an intimate, long-term relationship without sufficient readiness may find themselves repeating certain predictable self-defeating patterns. At some level of their being, they are ill prepared for the challenges inherent in the task of next-stage difficulty. If we do nothing about our fear, it is likely that we will keep ourselves from exploring new behaviors, but we can try small explorations and create experiences in just those realms we now feel are out of our reach.

Sometimes we fear our good, become numb or anxious or withdraw into a depression when facing crisis or trauma because we have not been prepared to tolerate either pleasure or pain. We give up much of our humanity by paying too much attention to preserving a lukewarm, acceptable life instead of living vitally and fully. Having the freedom to choose makes us anxious. The price we think we will have to pay for what we want terrifies us, and we believe we are bad for even wishing to create new options for our life. A letter from an acquaintance frames this dilemma:

Joe is an accomplished businessman with a keen, if unexpressed, desire to break away from the life he has and create one more in keeping with his actual needs and instincts. Joe feels stuck, and he wrote to me of his reaction to one of my books:

The freedom of choices, the options, the opportunities you write about are crucial for our welfare. I agree. But making such choices is different for someone who already controls his time and someone else who is a bureaucrat or corporate "drone," under somebody else's gun.

For my money, I'd like to read more of people whose choices *cost* them (in the way Bonhoeffer means when speaking on the issue of "cheap grace." Unless something costs me something, it's cheap). I want to know of people who walk that existential edge, never knowing if they are listening to God's still small voice within, or to their own twisted psyche.

I find Joe's letter irresistible. His complaint is that I use too many artists and entrepreneurs and not enough traditional types in my choice of interview subjects. Whatever merit his criticisms have, he has identified a universal truth: Some people are easily able to choose what they want because they are in a less encumbered place. As I am attempting to show, that different and unencumbered place is both mental and developmental—not necessarily material in nature.

Facing Problems

It helps to know how others have managed this developmental step away from fear. They provide models for our own creative adaptive choices.

Nora, a sculptress, expressed disdain for the idea that artists are psychologically similar or that they are different from "normal" people. She believes it is a myth that all artists have an easy time with creative and complex life choices:

Artists come in all varieties. We are people first. Some of us feel scared when moving into untried areas in our personal lives, and some don't. If we seem to have broken free of the conventions that hold others, it may be because, individually, we have learned that external things don't really count. We may be directed by our interior experience instead of outward things.

In an artistic sense, we create our own problems all the time—not just solutions. The block of clay, the empty canvas, invite creation. Artists enjoy imposing order on chaos. In our art, and sometimes even in our personal lives, we *choose* the creation process. But not all artists solve their problems with ease or with-out fear—it depends on the person.

Nora added that her world doesn't end if some external thing does not work out. The creative process itself reflects who she is and how she lives her life:

> I personally do not put too much value on the opinions of others, or in the symbols others use to measure *my* success. What I feel, value and experience—these count greatly for me. When I am true to these, I feel successful.

Sounding much like artists, professional athletes also often come at their problems from a well-developed emotional stance. They too frequently show themselves to be responsible to the goals they undertake. In an intriguing book, *Mental Toughness Training*, athletic coach James Loehr sketches out the way in which top-performing athletes view problem solving:

> Competition is nothing but a continuous presentation of prob-lems. Your emotional response to problems will bring you either success or failure as a competitor. If you expect to enter the com-petitive arena and have everything go smoothly, you're in for performance trouble. "Competition" and "problem" are closely linked, and to be successful, you must be a good problem solver. You must learn to control your emotional response to problems. (Loehr, 1982, p. 75)

Loehr might just as well have been talking about creative adaptation, for it too demands that we adjust to a continuous array of problems in a way that addresses our preferences and, at least in the long run, elevates life as well.

Using phrases almost identical to those of Sister Grace Pilon, Loehr stresses the importance of inner peace, positive self-valuation and learning as keys to superior athletic performance. His book reinforces the idea that we cannot force anything we hope to do well.

> No one ever told me that trying *softer*, not harder, might be the key or that inner calmness would bring strength. [My] anger, frustration, and disappointment were not so much from losing as from knowing that I performed considerably below what I was

capable of doing. When I wanted it most, I was incapable of performing well. And the reason is now clear—I tried *too* hard; I was forcing it. . . .

Performing well . . . occurs naturally or it doesn't occur at all. For me, *trying* to play better, *trying* not to get angry, *trying* to concentrate, or *trying* not to be nervous made the situation worse. I was fighting the current rather than going with it. (Ibid., p. 5)

Even without guarantees, even in our darkest hours, we still can choose creatively. We choose boldly in the direction of what we ideally want, because family, life or commitments mean so much to us. When we find meaning, we also locate the wherewithal to choose courageously. When we hesitate to reach for what we desire, when we see ourselves stuck in unacceptable situations, perhaps we should ask ourselves whether we care enough about our lives, families or long-term pursuits to act in their best interests.

Cultivating Archetypes; Recovering Demons

Just as we have looked at folktale heroes for indicators of creative adaptation, just as we use real-life, ordinary people as role-models and for encouragement, so too can we cultivate and use archetypal images for our maturation and our creative needs. Reflected upon properly, these point the way to the action, choice or value that is characteristically our own instinctive way.

The archetype is an instinctive pattern or way of being—not personality, not "form." It is an abstraction and as such can be used to represent our highest life purposes and finest characteristics. More than this, archetypal images help us find our way to that in us which lives. These images give us energy for new, vigorous growth. Archetypes suggest ways we can behave, choose and be if we would rediscover our life's intent, delight and power.

Throughout his amazing life's work on mythology, Joseph Campbell stressed this single point: All humans share a common ground of experience. People the world over and through the ages have had the same conflicts, desires, fears, strivings, griefs, joys. From this universal seedbed have sprouted common stories—myths, symbols, motifs, folktales, fables, rituals, each

complete with intrinsic values and sacred lessons—and fundamental, universal ideas.

The archetype is an idea or image without specificity, stem-
ming from nonconscious commonalities within the human race:
Life and Death, God and Devil, Light and Dark are examples of
archetypal ideas that represent polarities each of which we can
identify. These elementary ideas are rich in imagery, personal
meaning, characteristics and mood. Each has its own "tone"
within our individual consciousness; the image or idea strikes its
own chords, energies and purposes in us. Carl Jung taught that
the archetype was a *living psychic force*. The concept can become
overly vague and confusing because he also repeatedly cautioned
against personifying or making too specific a form for the archetype:

> Not for a moment dare we succumb to the illusion that an ar-
> chetype can be finally explained and disposed of. Even the best
> attempts at explanation are only more or less successful transla-
> tions into another metaphorical language. . . . The most we can
> do is to *dream the myth onwards* and give it modern dress. . . .
> The archetype—let us never forget this—is a psychic organ
> present in all of us. (Jung, 1953, p. 43)

The less we try to concretize this notion, the more likely the
archetype can remain a universal type or "psychic organ" in us,
which, in its most general, hazy and incomprehensible state,
offers optimism and information. In its very abstraction lies the
archetype's potential to empower.

I believe that when we substantively reflect on and understand
this force, the archetypal image acts on and in us as an instinctive intelligence, bestowing all the benefits of those multiple
intelligences discussed previously. These suggest answers that
cannot be found through normal, rational means, and stimulate
our intuitive defenses, our spontaneous insights and inclinations, our life paths or destinies when course work or blueprints
for living cannot help us. These stir up our courage and innate
wisdom when we are weak or are dumbfounded by events, by
fear, by circumstance. Archetypal images with which we each
identify or resonate revitalize us when we are stymied by blocked
energies or negativity. Somehow, mysteriously, the ineffable stir-
rings prompted by these primordial ideas and images remind us

what it means to be alive and human while also prompting us to reach for the divine.

Be assured that archetypes represent both good and evil energies or instincts. An inordinate fear of evil, life lived for the approval of others (or from only the sweet side of ourselves), a manner that displays predominantly polite or acceptable responses—these all rob us of vitality. If we are always "nice," we may have rejected our own dark brother, projected a piece of ourselves onto others and with this projection given away much-needed power. Robert Bly's treatment of this phenomenon, mentioned earlier, clarifies:

> Every part of our personality that we do not love will become hostile to us. We could add that it may move to a distant place and begin a revolt against us as well. . . .
>
> Our psyches are then natural projection machines: images that we stored in a can we bring out while still rolled up, and run them for others, or on others. A man's anger, rolled up inside the can for twenty years, he may see one night on his wife's face. A wife might see a hero every night on her husband's face and then one night see a tyrant. (Bly, 1988, pp. 20–21)

Any rejected, disowned aspect of ourselves is also rejected energy. When we learn to accept our dark, embarrassing, negative or unattractive sides, we recover power and vitality in the form of energy, emotional integrity and even creative insight. For example, those who reclaim and start to use their anger for their life (rather than directing it against themselves or self-defeatingly toward others) report increased vigor and health. Furthermore, we then gain a good chance of slaying our demons—much as Gretel was able to slay hers—since the energies inherited for this task come in precisely the same type and form needed to bail ourselves out of trouble: the bland, too nice guy helps himself by shows of occasional ferocity; the ever-innocent Goody Two-Shoes saves herself by smartening up a bit; victims protect their turf by punching out bullies when it's called for; and so forth. The teaching of Isaiah 65:25 that "the wolf and the lamb shall graze together, and the lion shall eat straw like the ox" gives testimony to this quite natural combining of powers in the developmentally whole. This is not to say that we become evil or dark forces, but that we use all shadings and degrees of our power on behalf of life.

Fairy-tale or folk heroes and heroines, people we look to with admiration (or with dread, envy or loathing), recalled stories from childhood or from film, drama, mythology all contain elements of our personal psychic motifs. If we can read their patterns, these elements help us identify or rediscover our lives and live as we know we were meant to do.

Jung taught that the deeper and more archaic the archetype within our psyches, the more likely it is to be a universal type, rooted in the collective unconscious of humanity. Whatever route they take in us and however deep they are, archetypal images contain the seeds of our own psychic reality: positive and negative. Like Hansel and Gretel, who clung to the idea of their beloved father and their home, we can hold fast to our own images (of life, heroism, courage, home, safety etc.) to remind us of our sacred wished-for values and our inherent powers.

The archetype colors our personal psychologies, provides clues about how to create meaning in our lives. Or it leads us, experientially, into our lives, so that we feel vital (instead of simply intellectualizing). This must have been what Joseph Campbell meant when he wrote:

> People say that what we're all seeking is a meaning for life. I don't think that's what we're really seeking. I think that what we're seeking is an experience of being alive, so that our life experiences on the purely physical plane will have resonances with our own innermost being and reality, so that we actually feel the rapture of being alive. (Campbell with Moyers, 1988, p. 3)

Jung also taught that the archetype unconsciously animates the creative process. He believed that the creative process happens in two modes: the psychological and the visionary. Within the psychological mode, ordinary human consciousness spurs a creative product or end result, but the final product lacks transcendent qualities and does not contain that ineffable seed of the archetypal image from the collective unconscious. Within the visionary mode, the creative process is spurred by an extraordinary consciousness, a timeless unconscious that produces something with its own shine. Here creative people are stimulated by primordial experience that transcends normal understanding. Whatever their lives may lack outwardly, whatever insufficiencies they exhibit or experience, their creative process—linked as it is to "mystical participation with ancient sources," to use Silvano Arieti's phrase—animates the archetype driving it:

> In the visionary mode, the creative person is at the mercy of the re-emerging content. He is, according to Jung, in a passive situation. "The work brings with it its own form, what he [the author] would add to it is declined; what he does not wish to admit is forced upon him." ... Especially in the visionary mode, the emerging product of creativity is an *autonomous complex* ... [whose] psychic energy has been withdrawn from conscious control. (Arieti, 1976, p. 27)

A good friend, a superb writer, told me recently that he goes on "automatic pilot" when he writes his books. This seems to be the sort of passive process described by Jung, wherein the person creating just lets the process flow.

Love, Courage and Creativity
Are Your Rewards

Our deepest, most committed and responsible love—the love we experience for life, for others, for ourselves; the love that stirs us to find meaning in humble things—flows primarily from our fully developed, autonomous self.

The greater our inner readiness, the more likely it is that we feel we can afford the costs and consequences of reaching for those things we consciously value, even when there are no guarantees.

Research on highly creative people indicates that they describe themselves as courageous. It seems likely, as one researcher put it, that "the courage of mind and spirit" necessary to bring something new into existence gives each of us a sense of what true heroism is—certainly it is more than physical courage, although we must not devalue that.

Powerfully creative persons open themselves to change. They are able to confront the "This will hurt" choice even without assurances of success. Once we, like Gretel, become willing to pay that price, somehow our courage increases. This does not mean we are unafraid, but simply that we are no longer immobilized by fear.

Developmental readiness to make a move, any move, is especially crucial in crisis situations. People who find themselves immersed in a problem may sometimes find they have only painful alternatives to choose among. None of the alternatives is attractive, but doing nothing will cost them something too.

Professor Donald MacKinnon's research reveals that creative people are not spared personal turmoil. Indeed, part of their high psychological health is a keen and rich inner awareness of the entire spectrum of feelings, their own and others'. Their awareness invites profound emotions:

> The kind of psychological health that creative persons have is not an absence of conflicts but rather a troubled awareness of them. Unusually sensitive to what is not right, what is not fit, what is incomplete, the creative person has a strong drive to resolve that which is disquieting, either through a direct attack upon it or through finding a medium through which it can be given symbolic expression. (MacKinnon, 1979, p. 13)

Admiral Elmo Zumwalt, Jr., who so poignantly lived through his own son's struggle with cancer, wrote in his book *My Father, My Son*, that it was not so much optimism as a willingness to fight that kept Elmo III going. It is one thing to say we will accept what life gives us, and another thing entirely to live that acceptance. The Zumwalts, as a family, also demonstrate that this kind of adversity tends to clarify true values. For them, commitment to family won out every time, and this seemed to inject each family member with strength to fight, to retain a fragment of hope and to press on. While our usual choices may be designed to bring us worldly power and create neat, tidy, structured lives, in the end—when we are struggling with a critical decision—we are forced to look at who we are and what we have created by our daily choices. Sometimes, like Elmo Zumwalt III, we find ourselves with our back to a wall, fighting for something primary—such as our lives.

The more we understand how archetypes energize and motivate us, what these images and ideas mean to us, what special ideas about ourselves, what lessons and world views they hold for us, the more our creative adaptation is served. And as it is served, we gain powers, even added desire, from our real talents and strengths to slay our demons and serve our lives and the lives of others. Identifying archetypes, growing up emotionally, staying with tough decisions—these factors help us face our battles and win. As we subsume the wicked witch of our fears, envy and self-doubts, we find the pearl of great price within our hearts. From our riches we give to others.

12

Returning Home

Remember not the former things, neither consider the
things of old. Behold I will do a new thing; now it shall
spring forth.
—Isaiah 43:19

Gretel said, "I, too, will bring something home," and
she filled her apron full. . . . Then they set off at a run,
and bounding into the room, threw themselves round
their father's neck. . . . Gretel shook out her apron so
that the pearls and precious stones rolled about the
room, and Hansel threw down one handful after the
other out of his pocket. Thus, all their troubles were
ended, and they all lived happily ever after.
—The Brothers Grimm, "Hansel and Gretel"

By the story's end, Hansel and Gretel discover what it takes to
live happily ever after. In coming to terms with this fragile understanding, their education, perhaps like our own, arrives in
both instant and gradual fashion. In exploring the children's
development, I have woven the ideas of many other theorists
with my own to help explain how, and why, adults grow into
resourceful selfhood. For instance, how might some of these
theorists explain Gretel's critical burst of insight, when she realizes in what can be called an "Aha!" flash what must be done,
and then does it? Intelligence researcher Robert Sternberg could
well call Gretel's insight a product of the nonentrenched mind.
Silvano Arieti might describe Gretel's burst of creative power as
a "magic synthesis": everything she knew (consciously and un-

consciously) melded together into right action or answers. Jung too, who wrote about this mysterious blending of forces, felt it was enhanced and governed by our openness to the process itself. For him, we amplify the very insight that enables us to deal with evil as we embrace our own unconscious. Our embrace invites inner forces to point us toward the unconscious answers of the race. Erich Fromm may have described Gretel's lifesaving action as an impulse from her productive side, from the part of her being that loved life more than death, as a transcendent instinct rooted in her life's inclination to create its own values and continuity.

Rootedness in life—the instinct to love, work and live productively—Abraham Maslow taught, is experienced primarily by the self-actualizing person, the one from whom creativity "emits" like sunshine or radioactivity. The fully developed person's creative force floods everything it touches, much as light floods the dark and makes things bright and clear.

I have introduced the idea that three basic synergistic skills—the complex constellations of positive self-valuation, learning resourcefulness and growth toward autonomy—provide us with a helpful instinctive "fusion," wherein both right impulses and choices stimulate creative adaptation to life. This lets us meet demands of the present moment. Ultimately, creative adaptation results in our serving our own lives and the lives of others.

Leaning on ageless wisdom, I have stressed the simple yet still unconventional idea that objective and subjective reality are mixed. These are more completely integrated than we now imagine. We live in an interactive universe, one in which we ourselves contribute actively to the substance of our experience and life outcomes. What we think of as our tangible world is neither fixed nor finite. Rather it is a quite malleable and interconnected affair, a fusion of subjective and objective reality, in which material outcomes are softly but powerfully influenced by consciousness (not forced into place, but sung, danced, played or courted into new forms, experiences and results). This awareness, this belief that we live in a manifest world molded by the subjective, invisible or not manifest, adds to creative power. Often the awareness arrives in a flash; more often it comes slowly, in its own sweet time.

Over time and the long haul of their personal development, Hansel and Gretel receive other advantageous lessons. They understand gradually that life success is achieved primarily through independent struggle and clear, objective thinking. When at first they find themselves abandoned by their parents in the forest, they manage to find their way home. Empathize though we might with the children's need for parental protection and a secure home, we soon see that their return to the familiar doesn't improve or solve anything.

Before long, their parents repeat their ousting, force them back out into the deep, dark forest, where, abandoned, they must face their realities much as each of us must face our own. They learn they must struggle independently with the deep, dark issues of life if they are to survive. During their second abandonment, again they try to get home. Their efforts to return fail. Bruno Bettelheim interprets Hansel's decision to leave crumbs as markers as a "fixation to primitive levels" of problem solving. He suggests that the crumbs represent an instinctive, primary inclination to rely on oral satisfaction as a source of security, that maturing means elevating our sights and skills to higher levels of solution finding. A reflective friend who called Bettelheim's interpretation "arcane" proposes this alternative: that Hansel, enveloped in fear, perhaps superficially overconfident, probably just got stuck on a single solution. He had to learn that an answer that works once does not necessarily translate well when circumstances change. Whatever the cause, Hansel didn't think things through and paid dearly. In rethinking and in learning from his error, Hansel became a better problem-solver.

Later in the story, a white bird leads the children directly into the witch's lair. As noted, Bettelheim suggests that each episode, the entire cast of characters, in fact the whole stimulating adventure seem to exist for the sole purpose of developing the children into able, autonomous persons.

In typical adult fashion, our love of wonder dead, we may ask what relevance all of this has for us: after all, how can a mere fairy tale hold any wisdoms for our lives? These stories are so unreal. Bettelheim's insight may soothe our skepticism: "The child intuitively comprehends that although these stories are *unreal,* they are not *untrue.*"

Each of us can easily interpret our life events (and all the strange, wonderful people in our lives) as existing for our developmental gain. While it is true that at some point we will stop believing that we are the center of the universe or that everyone and everything exist solely for our interests, the developmentally youthful are incapable of this level of humility. So it may help to view people and events as helping us grow. Very few adults, for instance, so fully transcend their own "evil witches" that they live fluid, spontaneously effective and generous lives. Various forces—interior blocks, specific negative persons, troublesome external challenges—continue to threaten progress and security in adulthood just as witches threaten children. Like Hansel and Gretel, we grow more able and autonomous as we learn from our mistakes. We help ourselves to *be* happy to the extent we master, then rise above, our own negative, subversive elements. A joyful future is more likely if we outgrow denying, regressive tendencies, and cultivate instead an abiding faith in the possibility of practical escape. Then we can act boldly on our own behalf.

To accomplish this, we may need to give increased respect and attention to the extraordinary (albeit irrational) assists available to us from our nonconscious world. In any event, each of us will find our own lessons on very individual paths to happiness.

Each Life Can Be Viewed
as a Unique Heroic Adventure

Creative life-mastery demands different things of different people. Each of us probably has one or more uniquely personal tasks to face and master. For someone with "entrenched" thinking, such as Norman, in chapter 5, creating even minimally satisfactory life solutions requires the repair of significant childhood damage. Norman states that up to now, friends, family, self-study and other efforts—including several therapists—have not helped him find happiness. Norman's hard task is to reopen the now tightly shut doors to his own positive emotions and acts. If he cannot do this, with or without help, his own "wicked witch" will triumph. Death will reign over life—even while Norman lives.

Others, like Sara, whom we met in chapter 6, are more fortunate than Norman. Apparently, while she was still young, Sara learned certain basic skills that now enable her to move fruitfully beyond problems. She reminds me a bit of Gretel, whose learning resourcefulness prompted her to locate just the right solution, just when she needed it most.

Sara is now an active problem-solver. She confronts—instead of avoiding—family problems. Somewhere in Sara's inner imagery must exist an archetype or heroine who is bold and resourceful, who has the power to succeed and solve critical problems, and who can move on as an enlarged person. Sara's problem-solving mode helps her become more—rather than less—accountable and responsible to life in all its forms and variations. This too is a key to sustainable happiness. She is also one of many effective people who report that sometimes life just "presents us with circumstances from which we cannot run." Like Hansel and Gretel, whom circumstances placed repeatedly in the deepest depths of the woods, Sara found herself unable to avoid problems.

Not everyone is disposed to face his problems even in the face of potential disaster. Our mental health clinics and drug and alcohol centers are full of adults who deny their problems. Sara herself admits running away from problems in her past. Now she realizes that she possesses both the psychological strength and the skill to face and master the things that upset her. At this writing, Sara's marriage is improving, and she is considering starting her own business. She experiences her newfound happiness as nothing short of a miracle. Unlike Norman, who—fully captivated—learned to identify closely with, and to project, his internal witch, Sara actively fights hers. As a result, she now takes every opportunity to grow stronger and healthier.

LW and Catherine, whom we met in chapter 8, are two other examples of persons who have effectively developed creative adaptive skills. They seem to slay any and all witches encountered and quickly find their way home. Both LW and Catherine possess those synergistic sets of skills and attitudes I have described throughout this book, and they demonstrate how these skills have become functioning assets. In other words, their learnings are sophisticated. Like graduate or postgraduate students who rely on basic knowledge in order to advance to higher understandings in a particular field, Catherine and LW rely on their creative adaptive skills to advance their overall life goals and vision.

This seems indeed a worthy objective for any of us: to develop, then apply the skills and attitudes of creative adaptation so effectively that we can forget about them. Losing all self-consciousness, we grow better able to use our talents to get on with life's most meaningful projects and purposes. In any endeavor involving problem solving and creativity (be it tennis, poetry or a relationship) the more we can let go of trying, and instead act fluidly out of our best instincts, the more elegant our solutions. On the other hand, the harder we try to walk a balance beam, the more likely we are to fall. Every great leader or hero and heroine makes things look easy. Even when they use themselves up on behalf of their visions and dreams, they still serve others tirelessly from the wellsprings of their being. We seek to do just this whenever we read this kind of book, join self-development courses or attend skill-building programs that promise to improve our functioning and life fulfillment.

Life purpose or vision generally flows from a clear call of destiny. This call, or interior prompting, makes creative adaptation and self-realization almost inevitable. Yet those who feel this pull may be mysteriously cursed and blessed at the same time. Their road is rarely comfortable in the conventional sense of that word, but neither do they wonder what they should do with their lives. If we reflect on Elmo Zumwalt III's life, in which he grappled with his own terminal illness, we see that his choices consistently reflected his values, his sense of destiny and his mature love of family and life itself. In the final analysis, he must have known he did everything in his power to live fully. He chose to live up to his *own* standards. Even if people face some personal disaster, they are elevated in their own eyes, if not in the eyes of others as well. When choices are made in line with our own values and highest standards, we have the skills to cope with whatever comes along. We know our behavior is motivated by courage and the will to live, and this knowledge gives us the courage to face anything.

It is naive to think evil never triumphs over good or that death never wins out over life. Our own observations and experience tell us differently: nightmarish forces do have power and victories. Yet I am naive enough to believe each of us has a choice about how we live with this. Making the choice can be a struggle, and harder for some than for others.

A powerful drive to live fully and successfully becomes ours whenever we sense our life's critical values and most meaningful goals. Then our life's route becomes clearer; we gain the fortitude to endure what we first think we cannot. Just as Hansel and Gretel's yearning to get back home fueled their courage and tenacity, our archetypal forces and deepest inner purposes fuel ours. We find and create mental maps or blueprints for that which we feel impelled to do; these illumine the way when mere rational thinking fails.

These maps emanate from instinctive intelligence that is activated the more fully we know ourselves and the more readily willing we are to surrender to our good and *act* on what we know. A friend of mine comments:

> The inner call also tells us what we will *not* do. To compromise, for example, is always tempting and often destructive when dealing with a chosen path. My inner sense will not allow compromises that go too much against the direction I know my life must take.

Passionate Belief in Life's Potential

To believe passionately in life's potential is to believe passionately in ourselves. Our conviction or faith that we can be, do or have something we desire opens us up to the inner wisdoms under discussion. Such faith may or may not be linked to our life purposes, or to archetypal images with which we personally resonate, although each of these serves as an "intelligence" of sorts. Knowing what we want to do with our lives helps us choose from among options and even sustains us during hardship, but belief in ourselves seems deeper still. It is affirmation of being, a fidelity to life, that claims a right to life whether or not we fulfill ourselves as achievers, as members of a specific social community or as individuals. To be faithful to what we are, and to life itself, seems of higher value than to be successful in specific life endeavors.

Only when we possess a passionate belief in our ability to bring our desires to pass and to express our life's potential—or the passionate belief in the value of trying to bring it into being— do we lay the foundation for the set of synergistic skills I have discussed. Hansel appears to have had this sort of passionate belief. In several versions of the tale, Hansel tells himself and Gretel, "God will provide." He reassures Gretel at various points along the way, with his approach to problems and his "Have no fear" philosophy. Hansel's faith sustains him—gives him staying power. His belief or conviction and his desire for life keep him going.

Creative adaptors, whatever their age, reveal an unrelenting, abiding conviction that they are capable, that their answers will be forthcoming, or—in the worst case—that at least their struggle is meaningful. Even if events turn against them such persons exude dignity and respect for their lives by trying to turn the tide in their favor. Their faith inspires, whether it be faith in their inner strength, God, fate or some other unseen force.

Our tiniest acts and frailest attitudes will display our self-affirming beliefs. Catherine's case offers an example of self-affirmation: her stubborn refusal to forgo her dream of living in a remote, rural location—despite the fact that she doesn't know yet how she will manage financially—is a form of conviction; she believes she can work things out. Her own belief empowers her. Yet another person's identical conviction will take an entirely different form. A writer who suffered a grave illness says that if there is one word to explain the power that furthered his remarkable physical healing it is "faith":

> Not many years ago, I developed an abiding faith in a loving God (as opposed to a punishing God that I emotionally and spiritually grasped back in my parochial school days). I believe that God loves us. Period. Thus I endure with a faith that things will work out.

The trick for all of us, it would seem, is to learn to cultivate the conviction that things will work out. Then we must act in accordance with our faith.

This conviction—that things will somehow work out if we stay and conquer the hard challenge facing us—I view as passionate, affirmative belief in what is possible. Creative adaptation does not require that we know what we will do or how to do it. It merely asks that we, in faith, take whatever prudent, active step is possible today—here and now—toward what we want. It is as if our choices become ends in themselves for the time being. However tentatively we move, these faithful steps align us with our positive beliefs and move us incrementally toward what is possible.

Our primary problem is not to find the energy, the confidence or the plan for our next steps. It is simply to change our mind for the better, to make up our minds—create an inner decision, an intention—to begin a hero's journey. In time, as we come to know that hero or heroine in ourselves, specific steps, energy and confidence present themselves.

We have seen that to create ourselves and to live our solutions in this way requires that we discard outworn ideas and activities (and even people) if these undermine our revised productive viewpoint or our efforts on its behalf. This means boldly facing loss, transitions, rejections while concurrently creating evidence for ourselves that what we wish and need to be true *is* true.

Earlier I suggested that restructuring personal reality involves metanoia—that complete and total regeneration of mind, heart and spirit by and through which we experience a rebirth or a conversion of thinking. This rebirth of mind transfigures our world view (and self-view) so thoroughly that we can evade, or transcend, the world's idea of what can and cannot be done. Our reoriented way of being creates the very escape hatch we are looking for, since our mind created the no-escape clause in the first place.

A person who has suffered a stroke must be convinced that he will be all right in time. He must convince himself that effort each day to retrain brain and limbs to cooperate will pay off, that the achievement he has in mind is possible. He must keep this best-case possibility in his mind's eye as real even while his senses present evidence that contradicts this image.

I have admitted this is risky business, highly individualized and completely without guarantee. Our "re-creation project" can involve goals of improved health, or an unconventional life, or finding sufficient psychological strength to fight an emotional war. Here too, building faith in what is possible lets us somehow reconceptualize our present state and then draw forth those answers that empower our tangible construction of the now nonexistent ideal. I have attempted to describe how this manifestation process occurs, by considering at length the requisite merging of conscious and nonconscious processes from which invention flows.

Metanoia

Hansel and Gretel's metanoic work seems to have entailed their helping each other sustain the belief that they would return home again. This belief kept them going when all else seemed to fail. No doubt our work is different. The real achievement is not so much that we enter an improved reality, as it is that we learn to use our own mind, imagination and internal resources productively to get us "there." People have been deemed insane for attempting to do just this.

No amount of self-affirmation, or faith, is going to transform us into Napoleon or St. Joan, even though it is possible to embody some of their characteristics. Instead, we start reconstructing our life from a base of sheer lucidity, knowing that insanity or faulty delusional grasp of reality represents the very demonic force we would escape.*

Healthy, autonomous or self-actualizing adults have a superior perception of reality. This same clear-mindedness or objective perception must be our first goal, our primary order of business. Even with a superior grasp of reality, we can still expect that others will criticize us or even think we're "crazy" when we begin to move in uncharted, untried directions.

No one can guarantee that things will go our way. When we choose against convention, when we change our minds about who we are, those who know us in one way may be loath to watch us change into someone else with whom they share little in common or who challenges their comforts, habits and values. We can easily find ourselves feeling isolated, misunderstood or unhappy in their company as well. In these transitions, we are alone. If we cling too tenaciously to the approval of friends, or if we need the support of family more than we need our healthiest ideas or behaviors, then we risk trading in our lives in order to stay acceptable. We should know, in advance, that our metanoic process will probably not take hold.

At the very least, we must selectively screen in what helps us stay healthy and screen out what would destroy us. This is an attitude and an attention of a disciplined mind. Such a mind is not developed through any one specific technique, nor is it ex-

---

* In the film *Dream Team*, an escaped mental patient believes he is Jesus. In one droll scene, he blesses a bedridden man whom he sees in a hospital hallway, advising, "Rise, my son, and walk." The patient obediently gets up, only to fall flat on his face. This is delusion—on whatever side of the story line we happen to find ourselves. We can do ourselves a favor and stay away from such contaminated thinking, unless of course we want to fall on our face or be incarcerated.

pressed through any one social convention. Changing our personal realities, our self-views, our health or our lives means fixing our attention on what we want, seeing that as possible for us. This is what I mean by self-affirming, passionate conviction. First we build belief. Then we experience belief as reality. Our disciplined attention is central to this process, as previous chapters have already indicated, since this allows us to avoid excessive preoccupation with data, worldly wisdom or conversational evidence that contradicts what we want to believe. Here again, there is no single way, no formula. Four different "forms"—from a self-styled method to an ancient one—may be helpful to review, if we keep in mind that although the techniques differ the pattern is the same: each way manages attention skillfully, repeatedly and creatively and produces, in time, a specific way to be.

A man named Carl described his efforts to reconstruct his life. He wanted to become a more effective, independent person. Early on, while still in college, Carl saw that his life was a mess. He felt out of control. He wasn't getting what he wanted. At the time he was reading Eastern philosophies about detachment and personal autonomy, and he decided he needed to be in a group that put those ideas into practice.

Carl learned that one of his professors was directing a group according to the principles of Georges Gurdjieff, an extraordinary mystic philosopher. Gurdjieff's teachings and writings have students question everything they know, to understand their life's purpose and objectives, to discover what forces control them. Carl observes:

> The director of our group videoed us playing basketball and volleyball. The playback sessions helped us observe ourselves, especially our body movements. I was shocked when I first saw myself. I had to confront my illusions about myself and the fact that I didn't have the control I wanted. A key to this visual feedback was trying to be neutral in our observations—nonjudgmental about ourselves and about others in the group.

The director of the group tried to instill autonomy in each member. Initially, Carl remembers the other members let him control their life and their minds:

> This is dangerous. Less ethical, more control-hungry types will gladly take over your whole life. But he [the director] made us

aware of our weaknesses and encouraged us to strengthen ourselves at the point of our weaknesses.

He used what is called situational learning—put us into the exact situations that we avoided. I'd be avoiding responsibility, so he made me the head of the gardening service. This was a take-charge experience for me and I had to exert my will and my leadership.

Today Carl publishes his own thriving magazine. He retains much of the detachment and philosophical flexibility that he sought in joining the cloistered group. He still tries to see both sides of an issue, understand his biases and build nonjudgmental attitudes. Carl admits that the level of autonomy he seeks is hard to attain. One reason for this, he believes, is that it is hard to be responsible:

> Certain books have helped me understand how and why we avoid responsibility. *Listen Little Man,* by Wilhelm Reich, for instance, shows how we cling to outer supports of all kinds, how we don't want freedom, how we hate being responsible. *The Murder of Christ* is also wonderful in this respect and describes how we murder that part of ourselves that is autonomous, that wants and seeks life. If we see ourselves striving for life, or if we see this in others, we try to kill it.

Joseph Chilton Pearce's autobiographical remarks shed light on how he approached the reconstruction of reality when his goal was his wife's physical healing. When his wife was dying of cancer, Pearce remembered a time in college when he entered a trancelike state wherein he could hold lighted cigarettes against his hands and face without being burned. He writes that he attempted to reconstruct his altered reality in, and for, his wife, hoping to activate her body's healing mechanisms. For five and six days at a time she fasted while he subjected her to total "brainwashings."

> Through all her waking hours I read her literature related to healing, and while she slept I endlessly repeated suggestions of hope and strength. I had no thought of how the restructuring would take place, but in a few hours, some three weeks later, she was suddenly healed and quite well. (Pearce, 1971, p. 6)

Sadly, some time later, his wife's cancer returned and she died. In part at least, Pearce attributes the reversal of her cure to their reentering the reality construct of traditional medicine. Doctors reintroduced Pearce's wife to their conventional belief that her kind of cancer always kills. Sad ending aside, his experiment still gives us an intriguing look at one way to reconstruct belief.

Admittedly, it is still difficult to locate competent professionals who can help us reconstruct our personal reality. However, there is growing interest in the subject and we can expect a host of seminars, books, magazines and experts to help us along. The young journal *Critique*, whose purpose is to "expose consensus reality," devotes whole issues to these themes. There already are tapes, videos and workshops that rely on positive role models and classic brainwashing techniques for their retraining objectives. One of the most novel, "Medical Brainwashing," a weight-reduction seminar designed by psychiatrist Dr. William Nagler, a Harvard Fellow among his other substantial academic achievements, promises to "create a biochemical shift in your brain and to plant a new thin belief system in your mind." "Medical Brainwashing" assures its graduates that they will experience a loss of cravings, cessation of bingeing and compulsive eating. Apparently, over the last six years, thousands of people have made the shift successfully from an overeater's belief system to that of a slim person as a result of Nagler's techniques. Most of these methodologies remain in the hands of the professionals who run the show. It is one thing (and not too hard a task at that) to have our brains washed for us, and quite another to find ways to wash our brains—and keep them clean—on our own.*

Lynette's example seems a prudent way for those who wish to combine therapy and a self-directed improvement program.

Lynette endured more than a decade of abuse as a battered wife. She speaks, in familiar terms, about how to regain positive self-esteem and grow a passionate belief in her life's potential. Lynette demonstrates that it is possible to alter personal reality

---

* A simultaneously whimsical and quite serious overview of how the brain can be modeled by a computer is found in Robert Anton Wilson's *Prometheus Rising*. Wilson's treatment of various neurological circuits that receive imprinting is rich and informative, and provides an amusingly thorough exploration of the adage, "Whatever our thinker thinks, our prover proves."

by enlisting the help of others. In her case, she leaned initially on a psychotherapist who knows something about learning and reinforcement methods. Not every psychotherapist does. Lynette's therapist augmented her individual therapy sessions with group sessions. During these sessions, Lynette received affirmations to repeat and note cards to read that bore self-bolstering ideas. She had a safe forum in which to discuss her new thinking and behaviors. Over time, her self-view improved, and with it so did the strength of her autonomy and the quality of her life. Today Lynette is a poet, has had one book of poetry published and continues to grow as a creative, independent person.

Clearly this sort of growth is not simply psychological but spiritual as well. Anytime we align ourselves with a force that spurs our highest, most satisfying and life-supportive drives we are developing spiritual (as well as emotional) health. The Cistercian monk and now renowned author Thomas Merton wrote that all people struggle to regain the "spontaneous and vital awareness of their spirituality." Our intellect and rational mind fight this notion. Yet without wholesome spiritual growth, our creative adaptive skills lack depth. Without cultivating our spiritual dimension, we move along shadowy, unreal and hollow, even dangerous, lines. The person who rigidly follows textbook self-help formulas or who leans on cult leaders to get him what he wants exemplifies this potential danger.

By contrast, we know we are approaching our happiest days when we think, choose and behave along the lines of what St. Thomas called our own dynamic tendency. This dynamism draws us to our highest wisdom and joy.

The techniques for discovering inner peace and our dynamic tendencies are not new. The classic text *The Way of the Pilgrim* describes an ancient metanoic technique. Written in eastern Russia between 1853 and 1861, the book describes how a simple, unschooled and crippled pilgrim induced his own dynamic tendencies by obeying St. Paul's injunction, "Pray without ceasing." In his straightforward narrative (which some believe is merely an adult folktale, not a true story) the pilgrim describes how he locates a spiritual teacher in order to learn how to pray unceasingly. After lengthy wanderings through central Russia without food, money or shelter, the pilgrim finds an elder mystic who teaches him the secret Jesus Prayer. He is instructed to repeat this one-line prayer day and night so that eventually it will continue in his heart spontaneously. This automated action purifies his life, his entire perspective, and the pilgrim enters what Hindu mystics might call "bliss consciousness." Although the pilgrim has a spiritual teacher, the teacher's role is to lead the student back to himself. By this, the pilgrim's own dynamic tendency is developed.

Lest we think that this story too is only dimly helpful to our discussion, or that we—being modern and advanced—can gain little from either fairy tales or an old Russian technique (and a religious one at that), J. D. Salinger's luminous contemporary treatment of this tale in his short story "Franny" may shed brighter light on the profound and lasting benefits hidden in this ancient teaching.

The specifics of Franny's life are less critical to this discussion than is her application of the method in question. When we meet Franny, she is falling apart. Disoriented by problems that seem overwhelming, Franny drinks too much, smokes too much and appears to be getting sick. In short, like many young people today, she is becoming unglued. However, Franny has found and feels helped by *The Way of the Pilgrim.* In one scene she is trying to describe its supernatural healing logic to her friend, Lane:

> "The thing is, the marvellous thing is, when you first start doing it, you don't even have to have *faith* in what you're doing. . . . Nobody asks you to believe a single thing when you first start out. . . . All you have to have in the beginning is quantity. Then, later on, it becomes quality by itself. On its own power or some-thing. . . .
>
> "In the Nembutsu sects of Buddhism, people keep saying 'Namu Amida Butsu' over and over again—which means 'praises to the Buddha' or something like that—and the *same thing* hap-pens. . . . I just think it's a terribly peculiar coincidence . . . that you keep running into that kind of advice—I mean all these really advanced and absolutely unbogus religious persons that keep tell-ing you if you repeat the name of God incessantly, something *happens.*" (Salinger, 1961, pp. 37–39)

Indeed. *Something happens.* However we prefer to interpret or structure this eventuality, help is available. Whether we travel back hundreds of years to find our help, or step back only a few decades, or remain firmly, squarely in the present; whether we consult mythical, psychological or theological traditions, or seek assistance from classical Eastern or Western thinking, the advice we get is pretty much the same: A long-term developmental course, involving a mix of self-knowledge, active learning and a disciplined, perhaps reoriented mind, is required for individual fulfillment, however we each define that phrase. Even the notions of fulfillment, or what is usually called happiness, remain universally constant. These blend a harmonious, individuated, creatively effective existence with a healthy, loving, relational life.

For most, psychoanalysis and other therapies will be the reeducational tools of choice for personal growth. These work surprisingly well, provided of course the therapists have empathy for, direct experience with and knowledge of the creative adaptive process. In other words, we can and probably should ask our therapist how he or she feels about these mysterious subjects. The therapist whose speciality is pathology, who reduces every discomfort to neuroticism, or—worst yet—whose vocabulary and manner stem from a bleak, hindering or intimidating spirit, may be a therapist to avoid. There are growing numbers of actualizing, innovative practitioners who themselves live by, and understand, the natural human drive for autonomy. Their methods can help us draw out rich creative responses from ourselves. These practitioners can help us develop our own dynamic tendencies.

The four methods I have described share this precept: Attention is power. The Hindu mystic and meditation guru Maharishi Mahesh Yogi puts it this way: "Whatever you put your attention on grows stronger in your life." Jesus taught that if our eye be single, light would fill our bodies. I interpret this mysterious statement to mean that if our attention is focused on a single possibility, we will be illumined. Single-mindedness bears the fruit of its own idea—self-verifyingly producing in the external world the likeness of its own seed that we ourselves have planted. However we want to phrase this notion, however we prefer to think about it, the fact remains that a mind fixed on a new possibility and closed to the old is essential to the creative adaptive response. We can use this methodology to enhance our own lives, but must do so cautiously—with professional guidance—especially when the stakes are high.

Love for Self and Others

Creative adaptation is a life process—not just an occasional episode of Sunday painting or a one-time good idea. If we are creatively adaptive, our solutions expand us as individuals. We are increasingly adept at using the mind's various functions and intelligences. We grow in self-awareness. We realize somewhere along the path of our lives that when we respect ourselves, when we are disciplined or secure learners, we can acquire—and apply—more complex understandings. We become progressively responsible; our choices reveal our values and true selves and we develop real strength—a strength that has the power to care and to contribute to others.

> Creative work . . . may be seen to have a dual role: at the same time as it enlarges the universe by adding or uncovering new dimensions, it also enriches and expands man, who will be able to experience these new dimensions inwardly. (Arieti, 1976, p. 4)

The world around us benefits from our having attempted the creative act. A woman who reflected on a long custody case—a battle she unwillingly entered—said she felt overwhelmed. She reported that if someone had told her she would have to spend three years in court, she would have said, "My God, I cannot deal with it." As she faced each day's difficulty, as she turned toward each moment's demand instead of away from it, she managed to endure those years and—ultimately—enriched her own life and that of her family. Figure 3 illustrates how positive emotions, primarily love, motivate the actualizing person. Reviewing Maslow's Hierarchy of Needs we see that the creative adaptive response develops as we grow into autonomous functioning. Whereas in our previous state fear may have been our most dominant emotion, as we grow whole, mature love is the most powerful force in our life. While we may have experienced the crippling effects of fear, we now realize—as Erich Fromm has written—that our deepest unconscious fear may be that of loving. This mature love is "the highest expression of potency" by which we tap our strength, our wealth, our power (Fromm, 1956, p. 23).

The sense that she "had to do it" was a constant for the

FIGURE 3
Subjective Motivations

Positive Subjective States
 (e.g., love, relatedness, inner balance, transcendence, autonomy)

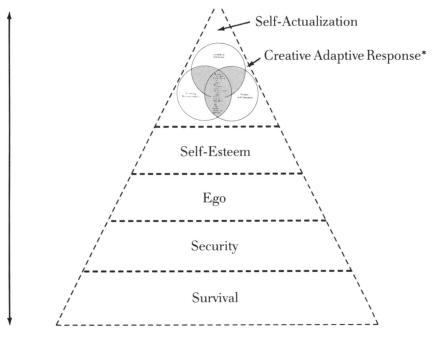

Negative Subjective States
 (e.g., fear, dependencies, self-involvement, unrelatedness)

*The creative adaptive response seems a natural, integrative phenomenon, occurring along with healthy, full-functioning growth and development. Figure 3 puts this response into the context of Maslow's well-known Hierarchy of Needs, to illustrate that as self-actualization increases, so does creative adaptation. It must be understood that creative adaptation does not magically appear in us as adults, but rather these skills develop as we develop into full persons.

woman who fought for custody of her children despite three years of almost uninterrupted anxiety. Love for her family—as well as strong feelings of self-respect—enabled her to stay on her course. As a result, she gained new self-respect and trust in her own strengths and power. She now feels, that no matter what comes her way, she can handle it: "Although the bottom may fall out again, it is as if my inner muscles have strengthened. Each little workout builds you up on the inside until you know that you can handle life."

Developed and used effectively, our productive side also gives life meaning. As we cultivate our autonomy and become expressive in a contributive sense, we gain valuable traits that can be shared with others. From our mature development we gain wisdoms, perhaps even material wealth, so that we become sources—not drainers—of energy for our communities. When Hansel and Gretel were finally able to return home, they brought with them the jewels the witch had hoarded. Similarly, we grow more able to give substantively to those we love when we find our own treasure: namely, we find our maturing, responsible selves from whom gifts of real value are given.

Bettelheim suggests that contribution to others is the entry price we—and the children—pay to live happily ever after:

> Rather than expecting everything good to come from the parents, the older child needs to be able to make some contribution to the emotional well-being of himself and his family. . . . All has changed because inner attitudes have changed. No more will the children feel pushed out . . . and lost in the darkness of the forest . . . since they have proved to themselves that through their combined effort they can be victorious. (Bettelheim, 1977, p. 165)

If we can recall times when we gave something to others from *our* emotional, spiritual or material reserves, or when we found the strength to rise to a high moral, ethical or caring standard, then we can relive our own responsible behavior. This behavior is love. And with love lies our true power to "live happily ever after," since one of love's faces is the passionate belief in life's potential in general, and in our lives in particular.

Martin Buber wrote that when we cultivate an active love and turn it toward our own existence our lives will be full of meaning. Without active love—which at the core is responsibility turned inward—existence becomes shallow and meaningless. Erik Erikson's theory of generativity supports this point. His study of fully functioning adults in their later years reveals that those who turn their efforts toward future generations recover, or sustain, a deeply meaningful life. Individuals whose lives are merely self-serving, whose projects or problems center only on their immediate needs or materialistic concerns feel, in age, that life lacks purpose and meaning.

Process, Not Form, Is a Key

Heeding both internal and external realities, we avail ourselves of two important types of information: our own nonconscious wisdom and the feedback from the world at large. These blend into a "magic synthesis" of creativity. Hansel and Gretel received guidance and cooperation from one another. So can we receive support from each other. Or we can be guided primarily from within ourselves. Since our goal, in large part, is to be and live happily in the real world (and not simply to live out a fiction in our minds), we must link ourselves contributively, responsibly, to others by merging several sources of feedback and information. Some people rely on others to help them stay balanced; others seek their own counsel for this.

Hansel and Gretel leaned on supernatural help. So can we. By attending to our subjective world as I suggested, we have access to a boundless storehouse of mystery and direction. Many people, believing in God—and I am one—pray for guidance, support and help. Others prefer to go it alone. There is also a wide range of reality-based information in the world, concretely and readily available. Books, classes, counseling can coexist as allies to our unconscious directives or communiqués. At times, if we integrate these two primary feedback sources—internal and external—we gain insight that neither source alone can provide. We can use our dreams, diary notations and various cultural symbols of the nonconscious (art, music, dance, poetry, myths) to remind us of answers our nonconscious already has prepared for us. These cues and patterns guide us to greater competence and deeper understanding of what we need, want or must do. This is input from timeless and universally relevant sources of mystery. When acknowledged and interpreted effectively, when lived out skillfully, such input can help us reach our fullest humanity.

There is yet another way to think about this integration, or mix, of inner and outer feedback. Gregory Bateson acknowledged this mix when he described his own thinking. He tried to discipline himself to use what he called a "loose-strict" mode of thought. Whenever he followed a too strictly scientific line of thought, he believed he lost something valuable; yet when he rebelled against disciplined thinking, he also lost something valuable. Bateson wrote that he was happy he possessed a mystical viewpoint which allowed him a "double habit of mind" and let him respect his wild hunches while disciplining them with more formal thinking:

> As I see it, the advance in scientific thought come from *a com-bination of loose and strict thinking, and this combination is the most precious tool of science. . . .*
> [My preferred way of thinking encourages] looseness of thought and then immediately . . . that looseness [is] measured up against a rigid concreteness. The point is that the first hunch from analogy [might be wild] and then, the moment I begin to work out the analogy, I am brought up against the *rigid formu-lations* which have been devised in the field from which I borrow the analogy. (Bateson, 1972, p. 75)

To embrace this subjective and "objective" mix of thought, we must stop relying *too* heavily on what others do or recommend.

I recently heard a minister tell this old cleric's story: Two ancient hermits lived in isolation on a remote island. One day a church official who was rowing his boat out at sea happened upon the island and discovered the hermits. He was untroubled by their primitive way of life until he inquired what prayers they said. The hermits didn't know exactly what form they were using. "We just pray," they told the official. On hearing this disturbing news, he admonished them: "You must say *this* prayer," and proceeded to teach them his church's required prayer.

The two aging hermits sincerely tried to cooperate but had enormous trouble memorizing the formal prayer. They had to be coached repeatedly by the official, who went over the words again and again. Still, they couldn't concentrate. They kept forgetting exactly what to say. Finally, after much diligent effort and time, they learned the prayer. Satisfied with his instruction, the church official felt he had done his duty and was free to return to the mainland. After rowing halfway to shore, while in the middle of the ocean, he heard his name being called and looked out to sea. To his amazement, there out on the depths—walking on the shimmering water—he saw the two old hermits following him: "Wait! Wait! Come back! We forgot the words to that prayer you wanted us to say. What comes after 'Give us our daily bread'?"

The tale of these hermits, the story of Hansel and Gretel, the case examples of real people in this book reveal that truth always transcends any particular form of instruction. Not everyone should do the same thing. Who is to say precisely how we will discover our answers? Who is to tell us exactly how to gain self-knowledge or return home? Life's specific answers cannot be fathomed in advance—part of the fun is figuring things out. To wish to be told our answers before needing them is to wish to deny ourselves heroic adventure. This wish denies us life itself.

As fables and fairy tales demonstrate, instructions on how to live life or master its hard tasks vary widely. From ancient, primitive teachings to contemporary success stories, we see that while deep truths stay the same, styles and forms of instruction change. However, patterns of truth, universalities of lessons do remain constant. These can point the way while still allowing us room to experiment and find our own unique route.

Hansel and Gretel reassure us. They embody and display patterns of skill, belief and behavior that let them meet life heroically. Yet they are not really heroes. They are merely little children, with natural childlike weaknesses. This too sends a message, for, shortcomings and all, they survive their ordeal, surmounting both psychological and physical struggle. This means that despite our limitations we too can be victorious. They believe, and show us, anything is possible. They enter good-naturedly and fully into the realistic demands of their adventure, lovingly cooperating with each other. Yet they also learn to stand alone, to use their wits and think independently. They expend as much time and trouble for their own life as they do for one another's. They overcome fear and anxiety with productive, effective action. They gain autonomy, emotional strength and sufficient material reserves to contribute support to those who need them—despite the fact that these others, through passivity or overt hostility, abandon and endanger them. Finally, young as they are, Hansel and Gretel forgive. In other words, emotionally they grow up. So can we.

Even in adulthood, we can build these same generous, life-enhancing attitudes and skills—for these are old necessities, not new. To live happily ever after means to accept the unique summons of our personal journey—no matter how harsh, strange or even ordinary it is. We can face each task along our way heroically, knowing ourselves all the while to be full of flaws. We can learn to forgive, serve and complete one another. We can grow to realize that what others lack, we have. What we lack, others have. We can develop our ability and goodness, just as Hansel and Gretel developed theirs. Regardless of chronological age, gender or cultural heritage, these universal principles, competencies and virtues exist within us now—if only in a latent state— as part of our shared human heritage. These release our power for living resourcefully and give us faith in the worth and value of life itself. These help us "return home," where indeed we can live happily ever after (although perhaps not in the exact manner we pictured necessary for joy).

Here, at the heart of our own dynamic tendency, a formless, energizing spirit mysteriously bonds us to what we need and want. Here we are free to move beyond the world's strict logic and instructions for happiness. Here we know these recipes for what they are—just inventions and re-creations of the mind, however venerated, helpful or inspired.

Here, at the center of our being, we find courage, trust and faith enough to create our own practical answers. And then, in time—tomorrow, maybe the day after, perhaps in a month or so—because we have found joy, we can quietly and surely forget former things, can release things of old. Even this.

List of References

Anon. *The Way of the Pilgrim*. ed. R. M. French. New York: Seabury, 1965.

Arasten, Reza A. *Final Integration in the Adult Personality*. New York: E. J. Brill, 1965.

Arieti, Silvano. *Creativity: The Magic Synthesis*. New York: Basic Books, 1976.

Atchity, Kenneth. *A Writer's Time*. New York: W. W. Norton, 1986.

Bandler, Richard, and John Grinder. *The Structure of Magic*. Palo Alto, CA: Science & Behavior Books, 1975.

Bandura, Albert. *Principles of Behavior Modification*. New York: Holt, Rinehart & Winston, 1969.

———. *Social Learning Theory*. Morristown, NJ: General Learning Press, 1971.

Bateson, Gregory. *Steps to an Ecology of Mind*. New York: Ballantine, 1972.

Bettelheim, Bruno. *Surviving and Other Essays*. New York: Alfred A. Knopf, 1952.

———. *The Uses of Enchantment*. New York: Vintage Books, 1976.

Bloomfield, Harrold. *Inner Joy*. New York: Love Books, 1980, 1982.

Bly, Robert. *A Little Book on the Human Shadow*. San Francisco: Harper & Row, 1988.

Bruner, Jerome. *In Search of Mind*. New York: Harper & Row, 1983.

———. "Models of Learner," *Educational Researcher,* 14, no. 6 (June–July 1985), pp. 5–8.

Buxbaum, Edith. "Remarks on Aggression," *Journal of Child Psychotherapy*, 7, no. 2 (1981), pp. 167–174.

Campbell, Anthony. *TM and the Nature of Enlightenment*. New York: Harper & Row, 1976.

Campbell, Joseph, with Bill Moyers. *The Power of Myth*. New York: Doubleday, 1988.

Caplan, Gerald. *Principles of Preventative Psychiatry*. New York: Basic Books, 1964.

Chesterton, G. K. *St. Francis of Assisi*. Garden City, NY: Image Books, 1957.

Clabby, John F., and Elaine J. Belz. "Psychological Barriers to Learning: An Approach to Using Group Treatment," *Small Group Behavior*, 16, no. 4 (November 1985), pp. 525–533.

Colerick, Elizabeth J. "Stamina in Later Life," *Social Science and Medicine*, 21, no. 9 (1985), pp. 997–1006.

Coopersmith, Stanley. *The Antecedents of Self-Esteem*. San Francisco: W. H. Freeman, 1967.

Cousins, Norman. *The Healing Heart*. New York: W. W. Norton, 1983.

Critique: Exposing Consensus Reality, P.O. Box 11368, Santa Rosa, CA 95406

de Bono, Edward. *Tactics*. Boston: Little, Brown, 1984.

de Ropp, Robert S. *Warrior's Way*. New York: Merloyd Lawrence, 1979.

Eikerenkotter, Frederick. *Science of Living Study Guide*. Brookline, MA.

Erikson, Erik. *Insight and Responsibility*. W. W. Norton, 1964.

"Exposing Consensus Reality," *Critique*. Santa Rosa, CA.

Fromm, Erich. *The Art of Loving*. New York: Harper/Colophon, 1956.

———. *The Autonomy of Human Destructiveness*. New York: Holt, Rinehart & Winston, 1973.

———. *Escape from Freedom*. New York: Avon, 1965.

Geldof, Bob. *Is That It?* New York: Ballantine, 1986.

Gendler, Ruth. *The Book of Qualities*. New York: Harper & Row, 1984.

Glasser, William. *Positive Addiction*. New York: Harper & Row, 1976.

Glatzer, Nahum. *Martin Buber: The Way of Response*. New York: Schocken Books, 1952.

Goertzel, Victor, and Mildred G. Goertzel. *Cradles of Eminence.* Canada: Little, Brown, 1962.

Goldberg, Herb. *The Hazards of Being Male.* New York: New American Library/Signet, 1976.

Grimm, Wilhelm and Jakob. *The Complete Grimm's Fairy Tales,* commentary by Joseph Campbell. New York: Pantheon, 1944. Reprinted 1972.

——. *Hansel and Gretel.* New York: Delacorte, 1971.

Gruen, Arno. *The Betrayal of the Self.* New York: Grove Press, 1986.

Guiness, Alec. *Blessings in Disguise.* New York: Alfred A. Knopf, 1985.

James, William. *The Principles of Psychology.* New York: Dover, 1950. (Originally published in 1890.)

——. *The Will to Believe.* New York: Dover, 1956.

John-Steiner, Vera. *Notebooks of the Mind.* New York: Harper & Row, 1987.

Jong, Erica. *How to Save Your Own Life.* New York: New American Library/Signet, 1977.

Jourard, Sidney. *The Transparent Self.* New York: Van Nostrand Reinhold, 1971.

Jung, Carl G. *Man and His Symbols.* New York: Dell, 1964.

——. *Psychological Reflections,* ed. Jolandi Jacobi and R. F. C. Hull (Bollingen Series XXXI). Princeton, NJ: Princeton University Press, 1953.

——. *The Undiscovered Self.* Boston: Little, Brown, 1957.

Kaha, C. W. "The Creative Mind: Form and Process," *Journal of Creative Behavior,* 17, no. 2 (1983), pp. 84–94.

Kazantzakis, Nikos. *The Saviors of God.* New York: Simon and Schuster/Touchstone, 1960.

Kerr, Michael. "Chronic Anxiety and Defining a Self," *The Atlantic,* 262, no. 3 (September 1988), pp. 35–58.

Kiley, John Cantwell. *Equilibrium.* Los Angeles: Guild of Tutors Press, 1980.

——. *Self Rescue.* New York: Fawcett Crest, 1977.

Kropf, Richard. *Evil and Evolution.* London: Associated University Press, 1984.

——. *Faith, Security and Risk* (work in progress).

Laing, R. D. *The Politics of Experience.* New York: Ballantine, 1967.

Lampl, A. W., and G. W. Oliver, "Vision Without Sight,"

Journal of Analytical Psychology, 30, no. 3 (1985), pp. 297–309.

Levinson, Harry. "Criteria for Choosing Chief Executives," *Harvard Business Review*, 58, no. 4 (July/August 1980), pp. 113–120.

Lily, John. *The Center of the Cyclone*. New York: Bantam, 1972.

Lindner, Robert. *Prescription for Rebellion*. New York: Grove Press, 1952.

Loehr, James E. *Mental Toughness Training*. Lexington, MA: Stephen Greene, 1982.

MacKinnon, Donald W. "The Nature and Nurture of Creativity," *Creativity Week*, 1979.

Maddi, Salvatore, and Suzanne Kobasa. *The Hardy Executive*. Chicago: Dorsey/Dow Jones–Irwin, 1984.

Maslow, Abraham. *Toward a Psychology of Being.*. Princeton, NJ: Van Nostrand, 1962.

May, Rollo. *The Courage to Create*. New York: Bantam, 1975.

Merton, Thomas. *The New Man*. New York: Farrar, Straus & Giroux, 1961.

———. *The Way of Chuang Tzu*. New York: 1965.

Miller, D. Patrick. "Altered States," *The Sun*, no. 148 (March 1988), pp. 2–9.

———. "Reflections on a Course of Miracles," *The Sun*, no. 153 (August 1988), pp. 2–8.

Monte, Christopher. *Beneath the Mask*. New York: Praeger, 1977.

Moos, Rudolf. *Human Adaptation*. New York: D. C. Heath, 1976.

Morse, John, ed. *Ben Shahn*. New York: Praeger, 1972.

Murphy, Michael. *Golf in Inner Kingdom*. New York: Dell, 1972.

Naisbett, John. *Trend Letter* (Washington, DC), March, April, May, 1988.

Naranjo, Claudio, and Robert E. Ornstein. *On the Psychology of Meditation*. New York: Penguin, 1971.

Neihan, D. C., and D. H. George. "Personality Traits That Correlate with Success in Distance Running," *Journal of Sports Medicine and Physical Fitness*, 27, no. 3 (September 1987), pp. 345–356.

Nisbet, John, and Janet Shucksmith. "The Seventh Sense," *Scottish Education Review*, 16, no. 2 (November 1984), pp. 75–87.

Norem, Julie K., and Nancy Cantor. "Anticipatory and Post Hoc Cushioning Strategies: Optimism and Defensive Pessimism in 'Risky' Situations," *Cognitive Therapy and Research,* 10, no. 3, pp. 347–362.

Ornstein, Robert E. *The Psychology of Consciousness.* New York: Pelican, 1972.

Parker, Dorothy. *The Portable Dorothy Parker.* New York: Penguin, 1973.

Pearce, Joseph Chilton. *The Crack in the Cosmic Egg.* New York: Washington Square Press, 1971.

Pearson, Carol. *The Hero Within.* New York: Harper & Row, 1986.

Pilon, Grace. *Peace of Mind at an Early Age.* New York: Vintage, 1978.

Pines, Maya. "Psychological Hardiness," *Psychology Today,* 14, no. 7 (1980), pp. 34–36, 39–40, 43–44, 98.

———. "Resilient Children," *American Educator,* 8, no. 3 (Fall 1984), pp. 34–37.

Robbins, Anthony. *Unlimited Power.* New York: Fawcett Columbine, 1987.

Roberts, Jane. *The Nature of Personal Reality.* Englewood Cliffs, NJ: Prentice-Hall, 1974.

Rogers, Carl. *On Becoming a Person.* New York: Houghton Mifflin, 1961.

Roethke, Theodore. "The Dying Man," in Robert J. Lifton and Eric Olson, *Living and Dying.* New York: Bantam, 1976.

Salinger, J. D. *Franny and Zooey.* New York: Bantam, 1961.

Sarnoff, David P., and Henry P. Cole. "Creativity and Personal Growth," *Journal of Creative Behavior,* 17, no. 2 (1983), pp. 95–102.

Schlain, L. "Cancer Is Not a Four-Letter Word," in C. Garfield, ed., *Stress and Survival.* St Louis: C. V. Mosby, 1979.

Schumacher, Ernst F. *A Guide for the Perplexed.* New York: Harper & Row, 1977.

Selye, Hans. *Stress Without Distress.* New York: New American Library, 1974.

Shainess, Natalie. *Sweet Suffering (Woman as Victim).* New York: Pocket Books, 1985.

Siegel, Bernie. *Love, Medicine & Miracles.* New York: Harper & Row, 1987.

Siegel, Eli. *Self and World.* New York: Definition Press, 1981.

Sinetar, Marsha. *Elegant Choices, Healing Choices*. Mahwah, NJ: Paulist Press, 1988.

———. "Entrepreneurs, Chaos and Creativity," *Sloan's Management Review*, 26, no. 2 (Winter 1985), pp. 57–62.

———. *Ordinary People as Monks and Mystics*. Mahway, NJ: Paulist Press, 1986.

Singer, June. "The Use and Misuse of the Archetype," *Journal of Analytical Psychology*, 24, no. 1 (1979), pp. 3–17.

Stegner, Wallace. *Angle of Repose*. New York: Fawcett Crest, 1971.

Sternberg, Robert J. "Intelligence and Nonentrenchment," *Journal of Educational Psychology*, 73, no. 1, 1–16 (1981), p. 4.

———. "The Nature of Intelligence." *New York University Education Quarterly*, pp. 10–17.

———. "Teaching Critical Thinking," *Phi Delta Kappan*, February 1987, pp. 52–60.

Sulivan, Jean. *Morning Light*. Mahwah, NJ: Paulist Press, 1988.

Tiger, Lionel. *Optimism: The Biology of Hope*. New York: Simon & Schuster, 1979.

Training, 25, no. 10 (October 1988), pp. 41–44.

Trotter, Robert J. "Stop Blaming Yourself," *Psychology Today*, February 1987.

Ueland, Brenda. *If You Want to Write*. St. Paul, MN: Graywolf Press, 1987.

Untermeyer, Louis and Bryna. *Grimm's Fairy Tales*. New York: Heritage Press, 1962.

Villoldo, Alberto, and Stanley Krippner. *Healing States*. New York: Simon & Schuster/Fireside, 1986.

Viscott, David. *The Language of Feelings*. New York: Pocket Books, 1976.

Wagner, Richard K., and Robert J. Sternberg. "Practical Intelligence in Real-World Pursuits," *Journal of Personality and Social Psychology*, 49, no. 2 (1985), pp. 436–458.

Warner, Samuel. *Self-Realization and Self-Defeat*. New York: Grove Press, 1966.

White, Robert W. "Strategies of Adaptation," in Rudolf Moos, *Human Adaptation*. New York: D. C. Heath, 1976.

Wilson, Robert Anton, *Prometheus Rising*. Falcon Press, 1983.

Wood, Garth. *The Myth of Neurosis*. New York: Harper & Row, 1983.

Yamamoto, Kaoru. *The Child and His Image*. Boston: Houghton Mifflin, 1972.

Yamamota, Tsunetomo. *Hagakure, The Book of the Samurai*, trans. William Scott Wilson. Kodansha International, 1979.

Yeager, Jeana. *Current Biography Yearbook*, Charles Moritz, ed. New York: H. W. Wilson, 1987, pp. 620–623.

Zaleznik, Abraham. "Managers and Leaders," *Harvard Business Review*, 55, no. 3 (May/June 1977), pp. 67–78.

Zumalt, Elmo, Jr., and Elmo Zumalt III. *My Father, My Son*. New York: Macmillan, 1986.

About the Author

MARSHA SINETAR is an organizational psychologist, educator, and author and heads Sinetar & Associates, Inc., a human resource planning and development firm located in Santa Rosa, California, specializing in change management for corporations. She is the author of *Ordinary People as Monks and Mystics, Elegant Choices, Healing Choices,* and the best-seller *Do What You Love, The Money Will Follow.* Marsha Sinetar currently lives in Northern California.